DESEGREGATION

RESISTANCE AND READINESS

Desegregation

RESISTANCE AND READINESS

———◆———

BY MELVIN M. TUMIN

with the assistance of

WARREN EASON, PAUL BARTON, BERNIE BURRUS,

RAY COLLINS, ROBERT CUTLER,

RICHARD DWYER, WILLIAM MARSH, ROBERT ROTBERG,

FRANK SEIDNER, FRANK TYSSEN,

LEILA MATTSON

PRINCETON, NEW JERSEY
PRINCETON UNIVERSITY PRESS
1958

Printed in the United States of America
The Maple Press Company, York, Pa.

Publication of this book has been aided by
the Ford Foundation program to support publication, through university presses, of works in
the humanities and social sciences.

For Sylvia,
and
Jonathan and Zachary

PREFACE

THIS study was conceived as an educational venture: the training of graduate students in methods of research in the social sciences. The study ended, however, as a product of a scientific venture: a systematic analysis of attitudes toward Negroes and toward desegregation of the public schools.

From the perspective of both the conception and the end product, the emphasis upon science is central. Therefore it is proper that we also emphasize methods, concept-building, and instruments of inquiry and design. These in turn command the use of statistical methods of analysis wherever appropriate.

In this report, then, we do not attempt to paint a picture quite as broadly or as metaphorically as would a sensitive journalist interested in the same topic. We care, as we must, about the extent to which we can show with evidence that certain attitudes exist and that certain factors bear upon them in various ways. We care also that the persons about whose attitudes we inquire shall be selected from their respective communities in ways which minimize the likelihood of bias and distortion. Finally, we care strongly that any professional reader who is interested in the details of our analysis, and the steps in our procedure, from hypothesis to conclusion, shall be able to examine the evidence and judge for himself how sound we have been in these procedures and in the findings we have drawn from our evidence.

At the same time, the topic of which we write, school desegregation, is not something remote and oblique in its implications for life in our society today. It would be difficult to conceive of a topic more central to the well-being of all of us, or one in which more profound emotions are invested. For these reasons, we have tried in this volume to report our experiences and findings not only to a limited professional audience but to a larger audience of non-professional persons whose interest in the topic of school desegregation is quite evident.

It is unfortunately only too easy to fall between two stools when one tries to reach out to two such diverse audiences. Each of these audiences unavoidably takes its turn in dominating the focus of attention of the writer at different points in the report. At some of these points, the professional reader is likely to find himself most annoyed with what are for him either unnecessary explanations of procedure and method, or the uncalled-for allocation of statistical materials to the appendix. At other of these points, when concern for communication with professional colleagues was uppermost, the non-professional reader may find himself put off by what are for him unnecessary and unintelligible tables that provide the evidence on the basis of which discursive summaries are attempted. In turn, the writer runs the risk of incurring a plague from the houses of both sets of readers. But, at least, one can hope.

An over-all view of the book may help each set of readers to read selectively.

Chapter One provides a rather detailed background of the study. In it we consider such matters as the basic terms we use, the methods of sampling, the justification of the sample, the choice of the area, who the interviewers were and what were some of their experiences, how reliable we may consider the interview materials, what factors we initially selected to analyze, and how general is the significance of the findings of this study.

We turn in Chapter Two, to a rather detailed description of the basic instruments of investigation, and of the attitudes of our respondents, as these were measured by the instruments.

Chapter Three is given over to a consideration of some eleven factors whose influences upon attitudes toward Negroes and race relations in general have most frequently been cited in previous research literature and prior theorizing about race relations. We test the gross relationship between each of these factors and certain attitudes. Those tests enable us to select eight out of eleven factors for further analysis. Those tests also make it possible for us to justify very detailed attention to three of the variables, and less detailed attention to the remaining five. The three prime factors are formal education, occupational status, and exposure to the mass media. The five secondary factors are income, church attendance, number of children in the family, residence, and occupational mobility.

Chapter Four then examines the differences in the attitudes of members of different educational groups in the sample, without regard for other characteristics they manifest, such as income, age, or occupation.

In Chapter Five, however, the results of the analysis in Chapter Four are re-examined while each of the secondary factors, except occupational mobility, is held constant in turn.

Chapters Six and Seven repeat the procedures of Four and Five, but this time the focus is primarily upon the factor of exposure to the mass media.

Chapters Eight and Nine then go through this double analysis with the factor of occupational status. It is in these Chapters, too, that some aspects of occupational mobility are examined.

The materials reported in Chapter Ten stand somewhat apart from the rest of the book. Here, instead of dealing with a random sample of the adult White population, we turn to the attitudes of a carefully selected panel of the most prominent men in Guilford County, North Carolina, from whose population the rest of the sample was drawn. Here we try to relate the qualities and roles of these leaders to the over-all direction and quality of change in the county as a whole. Specifically, we are concerned with the direction and force of the influence which these leaders were exerting upon attitudes and actions among their constituents.

With the systematic canvas of the range of attitudes in hand, we try, in Chapter Eleven, to draw two social portraits, one of the kind of person who is most ready for desegregation and the other of those who are most resistant. The emphasis is placed primarily upon the latter portrait, but, at least by implication, the main features of those who are most ready are made to stand out.

Finally, in Chapter Twelve we ask what most general and

persistent findings are worthy of being highlighted. We report on ten such findings which, in our judgment, are both most certified by the data and most significant for the problem of readiness and resistance to desegregation.

The volume is ended with a series of appendices in which we present detailed statistical evidence which was summarized, and to which we referred, in the body of the text. In addition, there are supporting and ancillary materials not otherwise mentioned in the main report. Needless to add—at least needless to call to the attention of the professional reader—what is finally reported in this volume is only a small portion of some aspects of the data we collected during the course of the study.

Some of the present volume has already seen publication in articles in a variety of professional journals. The materials on education were reported, in part, in an article by Paul Barton, Bernie Burrus, and myself entitled, "Education, Prejudice, and Discrimination: A Study in Readiness for Desegregation." *American Sociological Review,* Vol. 23, No. 1, February 1958, pp. 41–49. A preliminary analysis of the materials on Mass Media appeared in *Public Opinion Quarterly,* Vol. XXI, No. 2, Summer 1957, pp. 237–251, under the title "Exposure to Mass Media and Readiness for Desegregation." A study of leadership, co-authored by Robert Rotberg and myself, appeared as "Leaders, the Led, and the Law: A Case Study in Social Change," *Public Opinion Quarterly,* Vol. XXI, No. 3, Fall 1957, pp. 355–370.

An analysis of the characteristics of the hard-core resistants appeared in *Social Forces,* March 1958.

An examination of the significance of occupational status and mobility will appear in a forthcoming issue of the *British Journal of Sociology,* in an article co-authored with Ray Collins.

An analysis of the significance of number of children, as a factor in attitudes, is due to appear in a proximate issue of *School and Society.*

We have deliberately refrained from engaging in elaborate cross references to the vast body of literature in the field of prejudice, discrimination, attitude formation, race relations, and the like. Instead, we have chosen to refer to other literature only at very selected points. There are numerous bibliographies covering the relevant literature. The interested reader can refer to any of the standard texts in the field for a sample of the kinds of materials available to one who desires to follow up in greater detail the topics we have raised in this volume. An example of these is the excellent volume by George E. Simpson and J. Milton Yinger, *Racial and Cultural Minorities*, New York, Harper and Bros., 1953.

A recent summary and digest of some of the best research literature of the last five years will be found in Melvin M. Tumin, *Segregation and Desegregation: A Digest of Recent Research*, New York, Anti-Defamation League, 1957.

A rather special and highly significant document that surveys selected portions of the field is Vol. IX, No. 4 (1953) of the *Journal of Social Issues*, entitled, "Desegregation: An Appraisal of the Evidence." Kenneth Clark is the issue editor.

Another valuable source with special reference to personality materials is Richard Christie and Peggy Cook, "A Guide to Published Literature Relating to the Authoritarian Personality Through 1956," *Journal of Psychology*, 45, 1958, pp. 171–199.

A very valuable earlier compilation is *Studies in the Reduction of Prejudice*, published by the American Council of Race Relations, Chicago, 1947.

See, also, the later compilation by Robin Williams, *The Reduction of Intergroup Tensions*, New York, Social Science Research Council, Bulletin 57, 1947.

A summary of research trends has been recently compiled by Herbert Blumer, "Research Trends in the Study of Race Relations" (UNESCO, forthcoming).

The classic standard work in the field is, of course, *An American Dilemma*, by Gunnar Myrdal, *et al*, New York, Harper and Bros., 1944.

Each of the volumes just cited contains bibliographical references to a wide variety of works in the areas of problems with which we deal in this volume.

ACKNOWLEDGEMENTS

THE persons who are listed as having provided assistance in the creation of this book include a faculty colleague, nine former graduate students of the Woodrow Wilson School of Public and International Affairs at Princeton, and a professional research assistant. Each of them has made a significant contribution. Their names on the title page indicate that. I do not propose to try to distinguish separately the type of contribution made by each. But since I am alone writing the preface, and signing the book as its major author, I eagerly take this opportunity to extend to them the appreciation I owe them.

Prof. Warren Eason, of the Department of Economics and Sociology at Princeton, shared with me the major burden of design of the study and the conduct of the field work. A heavy burden of prior academic committments prevented him from working with me on the analysis of the data and the drafting of manuscript.

Mrs. Leila Mattson, staff research assistant, helped shape the study, intellectually and physically, and is principally responsible for the great amount of statistical analysis which went into the volume. She was indispensable.

The nine graduate students are now scattered throughout the country, and abroad, at various schools and jobs. I have told them personally but I delight in telling them again that I value them highly as professional colleagues—for such they proved to be—as well as personal friends, for such we were. I shall refrain from listing their present addresses, since they are likely to be in very different places by the time this book appears in print. But I do once again formally extend my thanks to them, in alphabetical order, as follows: Paul Barton; Bernie Burrus; Ray Collins; Robert Cutler; Richard Dwyer; William Marsh; Robert Rotberg; Frank Seidner; Frank Tyssen.

At Princeton, a number of other people played significant

parts in the shaping of the project and the completion of the study.

Prof. Dana G. Munro, Director of the Woodrow Wilson School, provided the very best type of administrative support one could have wanted.

Prof. Stephen Kemp Bailey, then Director of the Graduate Program of the Woodrow Wilson School, inspired the study; excited the interest of the graduate students; saw to it that all material support required by the study was forthcoming; did yeoman public relations work on behalf of the project; developed and maintained liaison with people at North Carolina; and, altogether, gave us the kind of endorsement, guidance, and support that made the study possible.

Prof. Richard Quandt, of the Department of Economics and Sociology, taught me and the other authors how best to use and how least to abuse statistics. If the manuscript does not now show the influences of his superb command of the field, it is simply and purely because I have not learned well what he teaches so well.

Mrs. Doris Lake and Mrs. Elizabeth Sangston, secretaries at the Woodrow Wilson School, suffered cheerfully and with great patience the tribulations which our project imposed upon them.

Various members of the faculty, in whose courses our graduate students were registered during the period of the project, are owed, once again, a vote of thanks for making it possible for the students to re-arrange their academic obligations to conform with the requirements of field work in North Carolina.

In North Carolina, itself, a host of persons helped us in a variety of ways.

Prof. George Simpson, of the Institute for Social Research, was our major liaison in the field, and helped design our study, guide it during its field stages, prevented us from making gross errors, and saw to it that we were informed about the mores and modes of life in North Carolina.

Prof. John Monroe, of the Survey Operations Unit of the University of North Carolina, designed our sample, taught sampling to the students, and helped us over some of the greatest difficulties one encounters in doing field work in an unfamiliar culture.

Prof. Joseph Himes of the North Carolina State College at Durham gave us the rare kind of understanding of Negro-White relations which comes only from a man who combines deep wisdom with a sound command of the science of social behavior.

A number of faculty members of the Institute for Social Research at the University of North Carolina welcomed us, taught us about their state, and about social science. For their hospitality, their cordiality, and their professional assistance we thank Professors: Gordon Blackwell, John Gillin, Alexander Heard, Katherine Jocher, Guy Johnson, William Noland, Daniel Price, and Rupert Vance.

Mr. Oscar Cohen, Director of the Program Division of the Anti-Defamation League of B'Nai B'rith, has provided encouragement and material support throughout the study. He is principally responsible for the preparation and publication of an extended inventory of the research literature on desegregation, and on the basis of this our initial hypotheses and research design were constructed.

I have been helped considerably in the preparation of the manuscript by the fine work of Freda R. Milner.

Financial support for this study came primarily from a grant of the Carnegie Corporation, administered as part of a program of research training by the Graduate Program of the Woodrow Wilson School of Public and International Affairs.

A final note of appreciation must be extended to all those persons in the general sample and in the special sample of leaders who gave us generously and willingly of their time and of their feelings, opinions, and attitudes about segregation and desegregation.

MELVIN M. TUMIN
Princeton, N. J.
March 1958

CONTENTS

Preface   vii

Acknowledgments   xiii

Chapter I. Background of the Study   3

Chapter II. Attitudes Toward the Negro and
Desegregation   29

Chapter III. Eleven Factors Which Influence
Attitudes: A Selection   52

Chapter IV. Education and Attitudes Toward
Desegregation   83

Chapter V. Education and Attitudes, with other
Factors Held Constant   96

Chapter VI. Exposure to Mass Media and Attitudes
Toward Desegregation   105

Chapter VII. Exposure to Mass Media and Attitudes,
with other Factors Held Constant   116

Chapter VIII. Occupation, Mobility, and Attitudes
Toward Desegregation   127

Chapter IX. Occupation, Mobility, and Attitudes, with
other Factors Held Constant   142

Chapter X. The Quality and Role of Leaders in the
Process of Desegregation   149

Chapter XI. Two Collective Portraits: The Hard Core
and Those Who are Ready   171

Chapter XII. Ten Major Findings and Their
Implications   189

Appendices   205

DESEGREGATION

CHAPTER ONE

BACKGROUND OF THE STUDY

IN this book we report on attitudes toward desegregation expressed by 287 White males, 18 years or older, who are members of the labor force in Guilford County, North Carolina.[1]

From these attitudes, we try to answer the question, Who is ready and who is resistant to desegregation? Our chief concern is with the quality and quantity of readiness and resistance, and the reasons for whatever similarities and differences are found among the members of the sample of North Carolinians.

The assumption that some are more and some less ready for desegregation is not hard to defend. One sees the difference in the contrast between the violence at Little Rock and the relative peace and ease of social change at Louisville, St. Louis, Nashville, and Greensboro. These are variations on the theme given by the 1954 Supreme Court ruling that the schools of the nation should be desegregated with all deliberate speed.

Some states of the South chose to emphasize the deliberateness, and others the speed commended in the ruling. These differences in emphases could have come as a surprise only to those who conceived of the South as a homogeneous region, united in intransigent resistance to any change in the traditional pattern of segregation of the Negro.

When this study was first conceived in 1956, Little Rock had not yet become a focus of public attention. But some states had openly declared their intention to resist the Court ruling, and still others had equally firmly declared their intent to comply. Some states were saying "never," others were saying "wait a bit" and still others were saying "immediately."

This evident diversity of Southern reaction on a crucial

[1] A statistical description of some principal characteristics of the sample will be found in Appendix A. That appendix also contains a selective comparison of some of the characteristics of the sample population with those of the populations of Guilford County, North Carolina, and the United States.

3

issue attracted the attention of a number of us at Princeton University who had the task of designing a field study as part of training in research for graduate students in the Woodrow Wilson School of Public and International Affairs. In this varied reaction of Southerners, we saw an opportunity for a field study which, in addition to the chances for basic training it offered, could also yield some valuable information on a crucial problem of the day.

The question of who was ready and who resistant was posed by the students themselves. They perceived how variably the South was responding to the Court's ruling, and they wanted to become familiar at firsthand with the attitudes on the different sides of the issue.

Their interest in acquiring such firsthand familiarity came from a number of sources. Some of the students looked forward to careers in foreign service and realized they would probably be called upon frequently to account for America's behavior in Negro-White relations. Other students were vitally concerned with the implications of the current state of race relations for the internal stability and productivity of the United States. Still others responded primarily from the passions of citizenship and what they felt to be the obligations of such citizenship. Whatever the source of the interest, all were agreed on the importance of firsthand knowledge to be gotten only through personal contact with Southerners. Field work in some Southern state thus became a *sine qua non*.

We chose North Carolina for a number of reasons. Perhaps most important was the fact that North Carolina seemed at that time intermediate between hard core and so-called border states of the South in its attitude toward desegregation. Certain more intransigent Southern voices now insist on calling North Carolina a border state because there has been desegregation of public schools in three large cities. But this insistence reflects only the shifting definition of what constitutes the "true South," rather than any sound sociological estimate of the resemblances and differences between North Carolina and other states of the South.

Another consideration was the relative nearness of North Carolina to Princeton. Our budget was small and a good portion of it had to be given over to transporting the staff to and from North Carolina several times during the semester. The transportation bill was not small in any event. But it would naturally have been larger had we gone to a state deeper in the South.

Finally, a number of us had good friends at the University of North Carolina on whom we could rely for aid.

These three reasons were most important in our choice of North Carolina.

Our next task was to choose one county within the state. To help us make this choice, several graduate students were sent on a preliminary reconnaissance of a number of counties. On the basis of their reports, and with the aid of census and other materials, we selected Guilford County as the unit of study.

Perhaps the single most important reason was the fact that this county contains within its boundaries as wide a variety of conditions of life as are found anywhere in North Carolina, and perhaps anywhere in the South. On the one extreme stands the city of Greensboro which exemplifies some of the newest trends in urbanization, modernization, and industrialization in the South. On the other extreme are isolated farm dwellings, far removed from the amenities of modern urban life, and exemplifying certain of the most salient features of depressed agricultural areas.

It will be noticed that the initial emphasis in our selection was upon the contrast between urban industrialization and rural agriculture. Much of the research literature suggests that along these lines of division one is also likely to find important differences in social relations and intergroup attitudes.

We therefore assumed that we would find differences in readiness for desegregation falling along these axes.

This assumption gave us trouble from the very outset of the study. For when one applies these distinctions to Guilford County, one encounters great difficulty in locating distinct ways of life neatly contained in separate geographical units. Surely the city of Greensboro is a different place than a rural hamlet in Guilford County. But preliminary explorations had shown that it would be very dangerous to assume that mere residence within the city or within a rural hamlet would be correlated with differences in ways of life and in basic attitudes to desegregation.

Our original plan was to draw a sample in which there would be proportionate representation of respondents in terms of their different involvements in an "industrial complex." But in view of the difficulties encountered, the basis of sampling was shifted.

The final decision was to draw a sample of the general labor force. Specifically, the universe of respondents was defined as households in each of which there was at least one employed White male, 18 years or older. The sample was initially stratified by urban-rural residence in proper proportions. But within these strata, the households were drawn at random. (The details of our sampling procedure will be found in Appendices B and C.) The sample may therefore be defined as a random sample of the households containing White, adult male members of the labor force in the rural and urban areas of Guilford County.

Can Northerners, graduate students, with the wrong accents and the wrong credentials, possibly hope to get from a panel of Southerners frank responses to questions on which North and South have traditionally and bitterly been split? We have been asked this question many times. It is not easy to give a certain response. But some things can be said.

If one asks how a traditional Southerner is likely to respond to a "Yankee" questioning him on segregation, two mutually opposed possibilities spring immediately to mind. The first is that the Southerner will clam up and say only the polite things he thinks the Northerner wants to hear. The second is that the Southerner will take the opportunity to vent his feelings on the Northerners, or, at least, to try to make clear to him the attitudes toward segregation which, by some Southern lights, have not received a decent and sympathetic press in Northern papers and journals. A third possibility, one which negates both of the first two, is that he will slam the door in the face of the interviewer.

The third possibility must be ruled out. Some cases were lost through refusal, but not many—somewhat less than five per cent. A larger number of possible interviews were lost, but for other reasons, such as the person's not being at home time after time, or a mislisting of the name and address, or other such reasons not relevant to the question of having doors slammed in one's face.

The choice then narrows down to the possibility that the responses are "excessively" frank or "excessively" reticent. There is good reason to reject both of these possibilities.

First off, it must be said that a letter of introduction bearing the imprint of Princeton University is a rather helpful thing in many areas of the South. The reasons for this are complicated and have to do with various facts in the history of Princeton and the constituency of its alumni. The details need not be recited. But if one must come from a northern University on a field trip in the South, Princeton's tag is about as good as any one can wear by way of reducing initial suspicions and, on the positive side, by way of opening doors that might otherwise be closed. This is not to boast, but only to explain.

A second important fact is that the graduate students were reasonably well trained in interviewing by the time they got into the field. Extensive preparatory work had been done. The students were in command of the literature. Some of them came from the South and knew their way around. Above all, they knew how to conduct themselves. And, when needed, they knew how to spot evasions and withholdings, and to probe and press in the right way. To be sure, there are gaps and shortcomings in the final interviews. But they are surprisingly few in view of the fact that these men had not had any previous training in these matters before they started the course.

The credit for these achievements is all theirs. They learned exceedingly well the little which one can teach about such things in the classroom. With this formal background, they became inventive and imaginative interviewers, who knew when to flatter and when to scold a respondent, when to be still and when to push hard, when to relax and when to lay on. Finally, just in case they missed, as happened often enough, every interview was edited in the field by field supervisors. Questions were cleared up; houses revisited; and often enough, interviews which had been denied on a first visit were secured on a second. With few exceptions, the final interviews were close to professional in their quality.

Perhaps the best evidence that one can trust the interview data is the variation in the responses from the 287 North Carolinians. These responses range all over, from the intransigent resistance of some to the immediate readiness of others.[2]

Nor are the resisters all one kind and the ready ones another. There are enough internal variations within educational, occupational, and income categories so that it is evident that there is not an outlandish type of bias from the low status and an equal though contrasting bias from the high status persons in the sample. There are, to be sure, different average tendencies in these different groups. But these different averages make perfectly good sense on grounds which have nothing necessarily to do with the assumption that some Southerners would tend to deceive us one way and other Southerners in another way.

Still another check on misinformation—as any person who has had interviewing experience will recognize—is the fact that one quickly begins to spot the times and places when the respondent is being something less than frank. It was gratifying to see how quickly the interviewers picked up these cues and how skillfully they learned to deal with such situations. Again, since only abstract approximations at these skills can be taught in the seminar room, the credit for this learning is all the students'.

Another indicator that the materials are reliable is that there are preciously few surprises or novelties to be found in this report. There are some, and they are important. But by and large, the findings bear out what has most ordinarily been assumed about the central issues, and what the best theory— not common sense, but scientific theory—has suggested in the literature.

The biggest surprises have to do with the relative *unim-*

---

[2] See, for instance, the range of scores on the scale which measures readiness for desegregation of the schools reported in Chapter II.

portance of certain factors which ordinarily are thought to be important in shaping attitudes toward segregation. Frequency of church attendance is one. Rural residence is another. The fact that one works in a factory or on a farm proved, equally surprisingly, to be of little significance.

There are few surprise findings that can claim the importance of factors ordinarily considered to be unimportant. We did not—with the major exception of childlessness—discover new major factors which had previously been ignored in the literature.

When one finds his own study checking out in this way with the data and theory in a reasonably well-ploughed field of study, one develops some assurance that he is working with reliable information.

A final cue to the reliability of the findings is not as significant as it is interesting. It has to do with how infrequently the interviewers were taken by the respondents as nosy Yankees, compared with how frequently they were taken for such things as FBI agents, Revenue Agents, Tax Department investigators, and Security Clearance field men. None of these misidentifications was frequent enough to cause anything but amusement in the retelling. But neither was the open confrontation of one's Northern origins. In short, the interviewers were just as frequently met by suspicions having nothing to do with attitudes toward segregation, as by true judgments about origins which were relevant to these attitudes.

After all is said and done, and in spite of all the checks and rechecks which one makes, one ends up having to leave the final judgment to the reader. Our own assurance comes not only from the things just cited. Rather, when common sense yields two equally good but mutually exclusive possibilities,[3] one must resort to other bases such as those just offered, to make a sounder choice than can be made on the basis of common sense.

The single most important factors in securing reliable in-

[3] For a clever and illuminating discussion of the value of "common sense" see Paul Lazarasfeld, *"The American Soldier: An Expository Review," Public Opinion Quarterly,* Vol. XIII, No. 3, Fall 1949, pp. 377–404.

formation are the instrument of measurement and the methods of administering that instrument. The issues at stake here are whether one is asking questions which will yield the kind of data one needs and, are they asked in the right way?

We have already said some things on the question of how one asks. Some further remarks are in order about the instrument itself.

The instrument used in this study is known technically as an interview schedule. The schedule was first formulated in Princeton. It incorporated questions about issues in which we were interested, and whose significance had been strongly suggested in previous research. The interviewers tried out these questions numerous times on persons in the Princeton area. Frequent meetings were held to discuss how the questions were working, and to revise and modify the schedule accordingly. Finally, two students went to North Carolina a week ahead of the rest of the group and pre-tested the schedule on a number of residents of that state. Final revisions were made when the students arrived in North Carolina to take up residence and begin the actual field interviewing.

The value of these procedures, obviously, is to give some assurance that the questions aren't ridiculous or inappropriate, or phrased in the wrong language, or put in such an order that natural flows of conversation and interest are broken. One also discovers, in this way, how long an interview can go before fatigue sets in or interest begins to lag. One also gets a fair estimate of the range of likely responses to any given question. With this information, loosely structured questions can be tightened up, and the respondent presented with a series of alternatives from which to choose his answer, rather than being allowed to ramble on in his answer. An effort was made to close up as many questions as possible. Some questions, however, simply had to be left open-ended since we were unable or unwilling to standardize and close them up beforehand.

There is not much point in reciting these technical details at any greater length. We are reasonably satisfied with the schedule. Our satisfaction rests upon the fact that we were able to use the information from virtually every question without doubt about the meaning of the answers. We say "virtually" every question rather than all the questions because there are some places where we are not really very sure how best to interpret the data. But in the vast majority of cases there was no such trouble. In the actual report, those items whose meanings are unclear are left out, or, if included, the meaning assigned to them is stated explicitly.[4]

One naturally tries to synchronize his own research with previous researches, so that his own data can be used as evidence to support or create doubt about previous findings. The most important elements to synchronize are the basic terms and concepts. Wherever possible, one tries to define his terms in the same way as these terms have previously been defined, and to state his questions and hypotheses in the same terms.

Social science research is rather badly plagued by a large amount of research material which nominally but not actually deals with the same problems. The difficulties arise from inconsistencies in the use of terms and concepts. The body of research concerned with prejudice and discrimination is no exception. One can discern a common core of interest in most of the researches. But, there is also a great deal of variability in the ways in which terms are defined and used.

In this study an effort has been made to stick as close as possible to the central core of definitions and interests found in the research literature. But we were also deeply concerned with measuring prejudice and readiness and resistance to desegregation in rather special ways and as precisely as we could, rather than going by loose impressions garnered from incidental conversations. We therefore found ourselves forced to develop our own measures.

Some readers will naturally object that the way prejudice is here defined is something very different from what they have ordinarily taken the term to mean. The same objection may be raised to the way readiness and resistance are defined. The only answer to these objections is that definitions are

[4] See Appendix B, "Coding and Scaling Operations," for a discussion of the problems involved in making sure of the meanings of questions and answers.

11

explicit. One should have no difficulty in seeing clearly just what is meant by prejudice and just how it is measured. The same applies to readiness and resistance. If the content of these terms differs from the reader's own usages, there is nothing we can do. The reader may wish to give different labels to the contents of our various terms.

Our own feeling is that these terms have been assigned certain contents and meanings found in most of the previous researches. But we do not claim that every connotation these terms have born in the past has been included. To have tried to include everything would have led to working with variables which would simply be incapable of being clearly defined and measured. After all, the pig is not rightly called a pig because he is a dirty beast. He is called a pig because we agree to call him so.

In this book, then, the customary procedure has been followed of selecting a certain number of items and questions in which we were interested; finding out what others in the past have had to say about these matters; setting up our own instruments and measures, harmonizing as closely as possible with previous work; and finally reporting on the outcome in the terms as defined. Such selective attention and delimiting of the field of interest is unavoidable if one seeks after some degree of control and accuracy.

Finally, the materials are laid out in such explicit terms that anyone who desires can try out the same questions and measures on a different population to see whether what was found to be true for North Carolinians may be true for others. One loses a great deal of content when he operates this way. But one gains considerably in the amount of precision and in the replicability of his work.

Now we must speak for a while about measuring attitudes.[5] There is a vast body of literature which deals with the question of what it is one knows about a person when one has a measure of his attitudes. First, certain key questions keep ask-

[5] For an excellent set of essays and a valuable bibliography see M. Jahoda, M. Deutsch and S. W. Cook, *Research Methods in Social Relations, with Especial Reference to Prejudice,* Part One, New York, Dryden Press, 1951.

ing themselves: Can one predict actions from verbally expressed attitudes? Is it better to infer attitudes from action? Are there serious and disturbing differences between what people say they think and feel and what they finally do?

Without attempting to review the literature in the field, some answers may be suggested. When we phrase our question "Who is ready and who is resistant to desegregation?," it is thereby implied that we are willing to make some predictions about how the respondents will act on the basis of what they say, think, and feel.

For example, throughout the study, it is argued that the more education a man has, the more likely he is to be relatively moderate in what he will do to prevent desegregation. This estimate is based on the kinds of things such educated persons say they would be willing to do compared with the kinds of things that persons with less education say they would be willing to do. Whether, in fact, when the chips are down, these differences will really show, one cannot say with any certainty.

If we were to judge by what has happened in North Carolina so far, one would have to say that apparently everyone in the three major cities in which desegregation has taken place was ready for desegregation because, in fact, virtually nobody did anything actively to impede desegregation when it was finally ordered. Or, at least, nobody did anything like using force, or insisting on closing the schools, or pushing hard for a constitutional amendment. And these are the kinds of measures which different respondents either advocated or insisted they would not take.

But it is obvious that before desegregation as well as afterwards, there were very different feelings about mixing Negro and White students in the same schools; there were very different degrees of indignation and resentment; there were very different amounts of reluctance and acceptance.

Can one sensibly say that these differences are meaningless in view of the fact that no one really done anything serious to prevent the desegregation once it got underway? The best answer to this question is given by the events at Little Rock, Arkansas.

Background of the Study

Observers of the Little Rock situation quite uniformly agree that there was considerable difference of opinion and feeling in Little Rock prior to the opening of school in the fall of 1957. Subsequent events seem to bear this out. Some of the people of Little Rock behaved as though the entrance of Negroes into the public school was the greatest moral outrage and threat to civilization since the Bolshevik Revolution. Others, on the opposite extreme, acted as if the security, health, welfare, and prosperity of our nation depended on the successful desegregation of Central High School.

The majority of people in Little Rock did so little by way of overt and observable action that one would have a most difficult time deciding what they thought and felt. One would have to go there and ask them how they were feeling, what they were thinking, and what they wanted.

In North Carolina, we studied desegregation before it took place. The sample was asked what they were feeling, thinking, and planning before they were faced with the necessity of acting. From their responses, we tried to predict what would probably happen *in general* in North Carolina when and if desegregation were finally tried. The prediction was based not alone on what was known about the feeling of the respondents, but on their statements of what they would do if confronted with the likelihood of desegregation.

Obviously, there was a range of different feelings and plans of action. The prediction about the behavior of the community, as a unit, was based on what was thought to be the balance of forces on various sides of the issue. The prediction, simply, was that if the forces at work at the time we studied kept enjoying the same relative strength, desegregation would occur relatively peacefully whenever it was tried.

This is not any boastworthy accomplishment. Anyone with the same data in hand could have reasonably made the same kind of prediction. Indeed, one could have made the same prediction without the data in hand. But he would be doing it on the basis of different information and different understandings. We felt that we had reasonably good measures of the balance of forces on which one could base a prediction.

If others feel more sure in their predictions by using other kinds of information and insight, this is all to the good. The crucial difference lies in the fact that when one is explicit about the bases of prediction, one can probably spot the reasons why a prediction goes wrong, and in this way, one can probably correct our understanding of human behavior and social process more accurately. More of the variables are under the kind of intellectual control which is needed to make the required correction.

We come back to the point, then, that knowing how a given population is thinking and feeling can be valuable and useful for understanding why it behaves the way it does later on, and for correcting and revising wrong estimates in a more systematic fashion. All these judgments are, of course, matters of more and less, rather than of yes and no, and they are questions of probability rather than of certainty. Prediction of the probable course of events in a community is at best a hazardous procedure. But only when one runs these hazards in ways which help one detect where his analysis got off the track, can one reduce the risk of error and increase the margin of probable success.

Aware of these risks and hazards, we rely in this book on verbal statements by the respondents for our basic information. From those statements we derive certain measures of attitudes of various kinds. We then try to analyze the connections between these measures, that is, the correlations and contingencies among them.

What kind of statement do we hope to be able to make? Some words, first, about what is *not* intended.

We are not concerned with individual differences, e.g., what it is about the unique facts of Mr. A's life history that seem to have made him feel and think differently than Mr. B. about segregation and desegregation. Nor are we interested here in understanding the intimate facts and connections among facts of the individual life history of any individual, taken as a clinical exhibit. The data do not permit us to do more than to hazard very tentative guesses at some of the anxieties which may be effecting some types of respondents in the sample.[6] The data *never* permit any understanding in depth of the psychological makeup of any single respondent.

Nor are we concerned with giving a full-scale community description and analysis of Greensboro or Guilford County or North Carolina or the region called the South. The data have not been collected with any such objective in mind and so there is no intention to report in these terms.

What is implied by the question of who is ready and who is resistant, is that it will probably be found that certain types of attitudes toward Negroes and desegregation are more characteristic of certain types of persons than of others. "Types of persons" are defined in terms of a number of factors about their lives and their situations which have been suggested in previous work as probably important: age, occupation, church attendance, and so on.

The measures of attitudes used in this study have been computed so that a score can be assigned to each individual, and, from these individual scores, averages for groups of individuals can be calculated.[7] Since every one has a score (for example, on how inferior he thinks the Negro is compared to the White), an average score can be computed for all persons over 50 years of age, and this average can be compared to the average score for persons under fifty years of age. By contrasting these average scores, ideas are developed about the relationship of a factor such as age to attitudes toward segregation. In short, the emphasis throughout the book is upon the average tendencies of certain kinds of groups to think and feel in ways different from other groups.

Whether we recognize it or not, most of us very frequently think and talk in terms of average group tendencies. We do

---

[6] See, for instance, John Dollard *Caste and Class in a Southern Town,* New Haven, Yale University Press, 1937, for a treatment of race relations in which psychological anxieties are used as important explanatory factors. See also, Nathan Ackerman and Marie Jahoda, *Anti-Semitism and Emotional Disorders: A Psychoanalytic Interpretation,* New York, Harper & Bros., 1950. The classic work in this branch of the field is, T. W. Adorno, Else Frenkel-Brunswik, *et al, The Authoritarian Personality,* New York, Harper & Bros., 1950.

[7] The technique for scaling we employed is described by Robert N. Ford, "A Rapid Scoring Procedure for Scaling Attitude Questions," *Public Opinion Quarterly,* Vol. XIV, No. 3, Fall 1950, pp. 507–532.

this, for instance, when we discuss women, or children, or teenagers, or college professors as groups, with certain average characteristics. So, too, when we talk of the character of nations, or of what kind of a place San Francisco is compared to New York in terms of cordiality and hospitality, or when we speak of what doctors and lawyers are like compared to tradesmen and engineers. When we make such comparisons—and these are grist in the mill of ordinary conversations—we are assigning to these large collectivities of persons, each of whom is on one level a unique individual certain common or average tendencies which we think we have observed.

Most of the time we go further. We not only say what we think these people are like, or how they differ, but we also say what it is we think makes them so. When we do this, we usually utter generalizations over which most social scientists would hesitate long and hard.

For instance, it is fairly common to assign a certain average or standard character to Americans, and ascribe this character partly to the fact that the ancestors of some of us were faced with new frontiers. In making these statements, we are giving credence to an hypothesis which has long had favor with students of the American scene. But this hypothesis is so incredibly complex and the evidence on the issue so varied and unclear, that a trained social scientist would boggle at the ease with which the otherwise careful, intelligent layman or journalist passes off the generalizations as a matter of course.

So, too, when we talk of juvenile delinquents, of whom much talk has been heard of late. When one thinks of the delinquents, whom one knows only remotely through incomplete newspaper accounts, and unpleasantly for what is told about them, one often talks as though they were a homogenous group and as though one knew pretty surely what it is that makes them the way they are. We are not sure, really, of what way they are, nor precisely who they are. But this does not ordinarily hinder us from making rather strong assertions about what ought to be done in order to prevent more of "them" from emerging.

The man on the street who talks of his society and of its

various segments in these general terms is uttering complex sociological propositions, whether he knows it or not. He is not necessarily right. He is often wrong in his judgments both of the central tendencies and of the reasons. But he is being an amateur sociologist, nevertheless. Frequently, too, he will rather strongly defend his right to his "opinion."

But such questions as the character and etiology of delinquency are not matters of opinion. They are issues of facts, which need researching, and of theory, which needs careful and systematic construction.

The need for careful research and construction of theory is nowhere so plain and urgent as in the field of Negro-White relations. For here there is a widespread tendency to ascribe the characteristics of the Negro to certain inherited biological traits. Since the evidence indicates that this assumption of inherited traits is highly dubious, one must systematically mistrust the policy recommendations which take this assumption for granted.

When the question concerns the attitudes of Whites, as in this study, there are two major tasks. The first is to find out just what the Whites do think and feel about Negroes and about desegregation. Then one must try to find out, if he can, why various groups of respondents feel and think differently or alike.

We have already said something about trying to measure what it is the respondents think and feel; and we have noted some of the factors which might help account for differences and similarities in attitudes. Another word can now be added about these factors.

The research literature suggests the probable relevance, in varying degrees, of the following factors:

1. education, usually measured by number of years of school completed;
2. occupation, with the major distinction between blue- and white-collar.
3. income, usually put in annual terms;
4. residence, the major distinction being between rural and urban;

5. religiosity, as measured by frequency of church attendance;
6. age.

To these six the following other factors have been added as subjects of analysis:

7. occupational mobility, measured by the differences between the job of the respondent and that of his father;
8. church membership, indicated simply by the denomination, if any, with which the respondent is affiliated;
9. exposure to the industrial complex, measured by whether the individual earns wages or is salaried, is self-employed or works for others, works at a manufacturing or non-manufacturing job, and the size of the work force at his place of employment.
10. exposure to the mass media, measured by the frequency with which the respondent listens to radio news reports, watches TV news reports, reads the daily newspaper and issues of national weekly magazines.
11. Number of children in family.

A number of other factors have also commanded attention during the course of the work. But they are not treated at any length.

To report the intricacies of the analysis of each of these factors, as they bear upon attitudes toward segregation, would result in a monstrously large and tedious volume. We have chosen, instead, to devote one chapter to a brief report of the findings about the probable importance of each of these factors, and to a discussion of the grounds on which the decision was made to discard some and retain others for fuller analysis. Then the bulk of the volume is devoted to analyzing the types and degrees of relationship between the smaller number of selected characteristics of the respondents and their attitudes.

We can anticipate the findings of that chapter by noting here briefly that three factors were selected for detailed analysis: years of school completed, occupational status (blue-*vs.* white-collar), and exposure to the mass media. Preliminary analysis had shown these to be probably the strongest factors at work in producing similarities and differences in attitudes toward segregation.

A second level of importance is assigned to the factors of income, residence, religiosity, occupational mobility, and number of children. These are termed secondary or control factors. We mean thereby that instead of directly analyzing the relationship between these characteristics and attitudes, they are held constant or under control while an analysis is made of how education, occupation, and exposure to mass media bear upon attitudes. By holding them constant we mean, for instance, that once the analysis is made of gross differences in attitudes of different education groups, a more refined comparison is then made of different education groups all in the same income bracket. For example, the attitudes of college educated respondents are compared to those of high school educated respondents, all of whom are in the "over $5000 a year" income bracket. By comparing only those who are in the same income bracket the possible effects of differences in income are held constant. This procedure is followed because analysis showed that such differences in income could produce differences in attitudes. Naturally, the major factors of education, occupation, and exposure to the mass media are also used as controls upon each other.

The factors to which virtually no attention is paid are: exposure to the industrial complex, age, and church membership. Preliminary analysis showed that there was no good reason to pursue the possible significance of these any further. In Chapter Three the reader will find the basic data which justifies the discard of these factors, and the assignment of primary and secondary significance to the other factors or variables listed above.

What does it mean, in fact, to assign primary or secondary or inconsequential importance to one or another factor, so far as their bearing on attitudes is concerned? When one says that "years of school completed" is of primary importance, what precisely does this mean?

Here is a question we can answer only by saying how we proceeded.

Background of the Study

The basis on which importance or relevance is assigned as a variable is two-fold. Take the case of schooling for an illustration. First, sociological theory suggests certain good reasons why exposure to school ought to do something to a person's attitudes toward segregation. Since considerable time is spent on this in the volume, this does not have to be explained in detail now. But it can be said that the reasons consist of assumptions about the impact of schooling which we must make if we want to give orderly sense to a lot of findings from other studies in which education has been found to be significant. The same general types of impact discovered in other studies make good sense in our text as well.

Our findings thus become consonant with existing fact and with the larger body of generalizations, called theory, which are needed in order to make organized sense out of our findings.

The supporting studies will be cited in the chapter on education. It is enough now to say that this consonance of our findings with previous research is one of the major grounds for our confidence in this factor.

Most impressive is the fact that if we did not make certain assumptions about how education works, we could not tie together large bodies of very different research findings. These assumptions simply try to state what it is about exposure to school which could produce the observed similarities and differences in attitudes.

The second meaning of the statement that education is of primary importance is a statistical meaning. We find, in statistical analysis, that the connections between educational achievement and attitude scores are such that it is highly unlikely they could have occurred by chance alone.

When relationships can be shown to be statistically significant, that is, beyond chance, and when there are good theoretical grounds for assuming a genuine connection among the factors, then one is permitted to claim importance for the factors at work.

As social science advances, it may become possible to test the truth of one's judgments as to what things about educational exposure seem to make such a difference. For the moment, at this stage in the development of sociological science, one is limited mostly to assumptions about what internal factors are at work. Perhaps if later we can distill out of the essential elements in the educational process which make the difference, we may be able to think of other places and conditions under which these elements can be found at work, aside from the educational process itself. But again, for the moment, we cannot do this.

Our factual statements then come down to statements of relationship among factors, grossly measured, and attitudes. A good deal of time is spent speculating about the possible essential elements at work. But the reader will always know when we are reporting facts and when we are speculating.

Many of the foregoing remarks are by way of an affirmation of basic premises underlying a sociological study of attitudes toward desegregation. For here we ask: Under what differing conditions of life will different attitudes toward desegregation emerge? Put this way, the question suggests that what men are prepared to do by way of acceptance or rejection of desegregation depends as much if not more upon the conditions under which they live and what actions are possible, as upon the feelings regarding Negroes and desegregation which they acquired in their earliest years.

It is true that many persons in the South do not seem to feel very different about Negroes and Negro rights than did their ancestors two and three generations ago. It is equally true that many of them behave very differently in these matters than did their ancestors. In short, social action has been modified and cultural patterns have been revised without any *commensurate* and corresponding modification and revision of the basic feelings involved.

This should occasion little surprise if one realizes that major social changes often occur without one-to-one changes in the feelings which men bring to their social relationships. Every social form, every modality of relationship among humans, represents a complex network of feelings, values, and goals. It is characteristically man's damnation and salvation that he is somewhat more than a creature of impulse and something other than a creature only of his social group.

Background of the Study

It is possible, then, and sensible to talk about *average* tendencies of groups and collectivities to behave in certain ways which differ from other groups. If well done, these averages yield us a kind of social portraiture of types of persons—collective portraits, really, of social groups. Necessarily, the distinctiveness of the individual members of any such group is blurred in order to permit the collective image to stand out. The ingredients or elements which go into such a portrait consist of such factors as age, occupation, residence, income, education, religion, and marital status.

Characteristics such as these define the nature of the different social positions which men occupy. By virtue of these positions, the training in the attendant rights and responsibilities, and the resources and rewards received for fulfilling the attached roles, men come to exhibit rather distinctive life modalities. It is the collective impress of these modalities whose importance and relevance for attitudes toward desegregation we seek here to explore.

If we can draw such social portraits, and understand the process by which distinctive types of feeling, thinking, and acting are generated, we shall have made a significant first step toward systematic generalization.

Much of the value of this study, as of any other study, from the scientific point of view, depends upon the general lessons one can learn from the particular case. But no general implications can reasonably be drawn from particular studies unless attention is paid carefully at the outset to problems of sampling and to problems of theory.

Sampling involves drawing from a larger universe of people a certain selected number who can be said, within known limits of error, to stand for the larger group—to be representative of them. The sample of 287 persons who are the respondents in this study were drawn from a larger group in such a way as to be as representative as possible, considering the limitations of time and money.

These persons are, as we stated earlier, 287 White, male adult members of the work force of Guilford County, North Carolina. In certain essential characteristics—essential because they are, to the best of our knowledge, those which are most

23

likely to be related to attitudes toward desegregation—these 287 are a fairly good sample of the total group of White, male adult members of the work force of Guilford County. The sample was picked with precisely this end in mind, namely, that we should feel reasonably safe about generalizing from the findings to the total White, male adult work force.

In what sense can Guilford County be taken to be representative of the other counties of North Carolina?[8] And of other Southern counties in general? Here we must proceed much more cautiously. Guilford County was chosen partly because it exhibits as wide a spread of the attributes of counties in North Carolina as we could hope to find in any one county. But it was picked for other reasons as well. As mentioned earlier, we chose Guilford in part because it contains a leading industrial center, Greensboro, and Greensboro is in some senses an atypical city in North Carolina and in the South in general. We also chose Guilford partly because of its relative convenience to Chapel Hill, which was our working headquarters and our center of liaison with persons at the University of North Carolina. For the profits to be gained from these conveniences, we have to pay the price of being quite unsure, on any statistical basis, that Guilford County can be said to be representative of the universe of counties of North Carolina. And because we chose to work with a sample of North Carolina, rather than one drawn from the totality of Southern states, we have to pay the price of being quite unsure about generalizing to the total South from the results of our particular study. But we do know some of the essential ways in which our particular county and state differ from other counties and states, and we can and will specify the points at which generalizations are likely thereby to be distorted and in error.

Our findings have to be taken then in somewhat the following way. Our data are reasonably good evidence about the feelings, beliefs, and actions of the White, adult work force of Guilford County, North Carolina. They are probably much less adequate commentaries about North Carolina, and even less adequate about the South in general.

[8] Appendices A and B contain the information required to judge the representativeness of the sample.

But now we must advance certain positive claims. We can safely insist that because of the way in which questions were asked and data analyzed, the generalizations deserve to be taken seriously as hypotheses about social processes. And we can definitely prefer the hypotheses we develop about such associations to hypotheses drawn out of thin air, out of intuition, or out of journalistic surveys.

The reason for this claim is that we were careful throughout the study to work in terms of what was already known in fact and in theory about factors connected with attitudes toward desegregation. Our evidence is therefore cumulative. At the same time, once again, we call attention to the tentative quality of our generalizations. There is always the chance that what we have found out about the dynamics of human behavior in Guilford County is highly particular to that county. It is a slim chance, but it is a chance. The greater likelihood is that the dynamic processes apply fairly widely throughout the South and perhaps throughout the nation. Where we are likely to be most wrong in such an assumption is in the extent to which we have failed to grasp certain complexities and variations on the general themes. Such failures are most often due to lack of imagination in the design of one's research and inadequacies of sampling. To some extent, every study fails on both these scores. We are certainly not free from either of these shortcomings.

One example will help make this more concrete. A basic finding of our study is that the more years of formal education, i.e., the more years of school completed, the more ready is the person for desegregation. The immediate qualification is "all other things being equal." But all other things are never equal. And where we can go very wrong is in failing to consider the kind of unequal things which may be present in other counties and in other states, and which we cannot possibly have taken into account because our sample was not designed to do so.[9]

[9] One can raise serious questions about the legitimacy of generalizing from our study of Guilford County when and if we attempt to predict the particular course of action likely to be followed in other places. The dynamic equilibrium of factors in Guilford County is likely to be different than in any other place, so far as the predictable proximate outcome is concerned. However, we avoid this problem by confining

For instance, Guilford County is in the Piedmont area of North Carolina. Typically, North Carolinians make a distinction between the Piedmont and the Plantation areas, and between both of them and the Mountain areas. One would expect, on the basis of what is generally assumed about the Plantation Belt, that differences in education would not be as closely related to differences in attitudes among Plantation Belt people as among those who reside in the Piedmont. This implicitly asserts that there are certain other features about the history and the lives of those in the Plantation Area which reduce the influences of formal education, as these are exhibited by Piedmont residents.

In general, for example, persons in the Piedmont area do not seem to be nearly so dependent upon the maintenance of certain traditional forms of Negro deference and subordination in their basic economic life. The Piedmont can and has devised ways to make a living which do not depend as critically (either objectively or by the subjective perception of the White residents) upon some form of insured Negro subordinacy.[10] The Piedmont area seems also to be generally freer from worry about the political and social consequences of equal rights for Negroes.

Because of such differences, one would expect the vision of a social system in which Negroes are more equal to be even less appealing to the Plantation Belt than to the Piedmont

---

ourselves to statements of the form, "if *x*, then *y*," rather than prophetic statements of the form, "In 18 months there will be, etc., etc."

[10] It is sociologically axiomatic that what men define as real is real in its consequences. The most problematic translation of this axiom takes place when Whites who believe that Negroes are inferior accord them second class opportunities for development and thus insure that Negroes will exhibit inferior performance. This performance is then taken as verification of the original assumption or "definition of the situation." By contrast, one of the principal effects of the Supreme Court Ruling and of earlier injunctions such as Fair Employment Acts has been to get Negroes into schools and positions of comparable qualities with those previously enjoyed mostly by Whites. This, in turn, has led to the improvement in Negro school and job performance, which thereby helps to destroy the original assumption of Negro inferiority. Considerable social conflict is to be expected during that period when Negroes, or any group, are first breaking through the barriers of second-rate opportunities and are beginning to move into first-class citizenship.

residents. Commensurately, one must expect that such factors as formal education, which help produce a somewhat more favorable climate of opinion in the Piedmont, would be less influential in the Plantation Belt. The reduction in the influence of formal education is likely to come about from two sources: the liberalizing impact of educational contact *per se* may be reduced; and the unfavorable factors which education has to overcome are greater in number and intensity in the Plantation Belt than in the Piedmont.

To balance this probable set of occurrences, there is the fact that the *ways* in which formal education can come to make a difference are probably much the same in all the areas. The truth of this statement, of course, depends on the kind of generalizations made about formal education. But here one can control for the major source of possible error and see to it that statements about the modes of influence of education are formulated so that they can be of general value and not simply limited to and particular to Guilford County.

We must then reasonably expect to find variations in the extent to which formal education makes a difference in attitudes toward desegregation. But these variations should be explainable as consequences of the particular type of sociocultural area in which this exposure to formal education comes into play. One can then begin to state the conditions under which one type and amount of effect will be expected as against others.

The limiting case on the one extreme is that situation in which the cards are so completely stacked against any possible effects of education that in this regard there might as well be no schools. On the other extreme, the situation is one in which *only* formal education has an influence. Obviously any actual case, in the South or anywhere else, falls between these two extremes.

The analysis here makes it possible to state in general terms the conditions under which, within our own sample, formal education does make one or another kind of difference. For example, we know that when a person has some college education and is also a white-collar worker, he is more inclined to accept desegregation than if he is a college man in a blue-collar job. Similarly, we know that, on the average, if a man has a blue-collar job and a college education, he is more desegregationist than a blue-collar worker with less than a college education.

If we distill out what are the essential qualities at work here, one would talk perhaps of the combined effects of *perspective* (via formal education) and *status* (via occupation). Put in these terms, one has the kind of generalization that can be advanced as working hypotheses of *general* usefulness.

This type of generalization about the conditions in the area we studied will have to be modified when one tries to fit it into other areas, if there are relevant differences between the areas. A relevant difference, simply, is one that influences the ways and degrees to which formal education is related to attitudes toward desegregation.

Such possible influences are of many types. They can include the most general features of the area, such as its topography and resources. The political history of the area may be relevant. But no attempt is made here to control such factors, nor even to specify them. Rather, out of the range of all such possibly relevant factors a certain set has been selected which is likely to be most related to the outcomes we are measuring.

CHAPTER TWO

ATTITUDES TOWARD THE NEGRO AND DESEGREGATION

TO be ready for desegregation of the schools is to be unwilling to resist the Supreme Court order to desegregate. That is how readiness is defined in this report. By contrast, to be resistant to desegregation is to be willing to do any one or several things to prevent desegregation, ranging from amending the United States Constitution to the use of force, if necessary.[1]

Clearly, there must be a number of other attitudes which precede and accompany these inclinations or disinclinations to impede the Court order. Such approval or disapproval of segregationist proposals is only one aspect—though it may be the most important—of the total attitude which the respondents have toward the Negro and the issue of desegregation. If these preceding and accompanying attitudes can be sorted out and understood, the inclinations to action of the respondents will in turn be more deeply understood.

What, then, are these other dimensions of White attitudes toward Negroes? What other things go into the final choice whether to impede the Court order?

We think in terms of five components or dimensions, as follows:

I. THE IMAGE. The term "Image" refers to the mental picture or conception which the White has of Negro characteristics compared to White characteristics. What does the White think the Negro is like as a human being? What are the Negro's moral standards? How about his intelligence? Is he responsible? Does he display as much ambition as the White?

II. THE IDEOLOGY. Given the Image which the White has of the Negro, what type of social relations would the White prefer to have with Negroes? What do the respondents say

[1] See here Appendix C in which we describe at length the operational definition we have given to our basic terms, the ways in which we construct our measures, and the types of responses which were coded as segregationist and desegregationist in their implications.

when they are asked how they would set up eating arrangements, and bus facilities, and job opportunities and relationships, and other things like that, if they could set these up any way they wanted? This vision of the desired set of social relationships held by the White is here termed "Ideology."

III. SENTIMENT STRUCTURE. How would the respondents *feel* if a Negro sat down next to them on a bus? In a restaurant? Suppose they found themselves at the same dinner party with Negroes? How would they *feel*? These questions about hypothetical situations (some of which the respondents have encountered or actually live through, day by day) and the *feelings* the respondent says he would have, are keys to "Sentiment Structure."

IV. GENERAL ACTION SET. Suppose the White was on a bus and a Negro sat down next to him? What would the respondent *do*? What would he *do* at the dinner party where the Negro came in as a guest? Or in a restaurant? The emphasis here is upon action as the respondent reports his probable behavior. The general or average tendency to act in a number of situations of hypothetical contact with Negroes is labeled "General Action Set."

V. SPECIFIC ACTION SET. Here attention is focussed directly and specifically on the public schools. Respondents were asked to approve or disapprove of various ways to prevent the desegregation of the public schools. From the range of their approvals and disapprovals, scores are calculated. These scores then stand for their "Specific Action Set," and, ultimately provide a measure of their readiness for or resistance to desegregation.

In a sense, these five dimensions can be separated into two groups: Image, Ideology, and Sentiment in one, and General and Specific Action in the other. The primary difference is one of private versus public matters. What we *think* about others, what we would do by way of relationships with them *if we could,* and how we *feel* when we are in a relationship with them: these are rather private matters. We do not ordinarily divulge these fully, except to those who share and sympathize with our points of view. By contrast, the kinds of things we say we would be willing to *do* in such relationships, and the kinds of measures we would be willing publicly to advocate, tend to be more tempered by consideration of the public world in which these proposals must be advocated and implemented.,

The distinction then is between the private world of feeling, believing, and desiring, and the more public world of acting, proposed or in fact. Between these two worlds there are gaps—for most of us most of the time. Only rarely can our private visions be translated into full public actuality. Most of the time we are probably secretly glad to be restrained from acting out in public the full-fleshed impulses which arise out of our private desires and fantasies.

Whether we are glad or not, however, it is imperative that we be restrained from total and spontaneous expression of all our private visions if we are to be able to live together over any period of time. What we surrender for the privilege of living together is matched by those things which our continuing group life makes possible.

The word "matched" is ambiguous, if not deceptive. Actually, many of the difficulties which a group or community encounters arise from the fact that the ratio between what is given up and what is gained is unequally attractive to different members of the group.

Put the matter in terms of responsibilities (what is given up) and rewards (what is gained). Then a rather important and far-reaching generalization can be made, as follows:

A member of a group will conform to its rules and identify himself with its collective goals in proportion to the extent to which he feels that the rewards are adequate compensation for the responsibilities.[2]

It is especially important to include in this generalization the person's own view of the matter. That is, the same reward may commend itself very differently to different individuals. X may find the reward perfectly satisfactory, or at least satisfactory enough to go along with the rules of the group and its

---

[2] For a discussion of the significance of the ratio between reward and responsibility as a factor in social identification and conscientious performance, see Melvin Tumin, "Rewards and Task Orientations," *American Sociological Review*, XX, No. 4, August 1955, pp. 419–423.

collective aspirations. By contrast, Y, who gets the same rewards for about the same amount of responsibilities, may find the rewards totally unsatisfactory. As a result, he may feel much less obliged to conform to the group rules and to participate in the activities required for the achievement of the group goals.

Many different reasons can account for why X and Y differ in their response to the "same" ratio of responsibility and reward. When it is truly a case of one individual differing from another, though both have the same "objective" situation in life, then we may be dealing with hidden individual differences, and biographical facts then become relevant. It may also be the case, however, that we have not scanned their social situations adequately and have missed certain differences in their positions in life which could be most relevant. For instance, we may have failed to equate the two individuals on age. Or, we may find that X's father and family enjoy higher prestige than do the father and family of Y, and that this counts heavily in X's view of life. In any event, before we engage in parlor psychoanalysis of the reasons for differences in the response of X and Y, we ought to check to be sure that we have taken account of the relevant aspects of their social situations.

Now we can offer a deduction from the first generalization, as follows:

Differences in obedience to rules and identity with group goals will arise when there are differences in the amount of responsibilities assumed, even though rewards are the same; or when, though the responsibilities are the same, the amount of rewards are different.

The relevance of these generalizations for our study here can be seen in the following issues.

First, will members of the sample differ in their willingness to assume the responsibilities which are implied in acceptance of the Supreme Court order? Taking the Supreme Court order as a guide to the behavior required for community welfare and the maintenance of peace and order in the community, who will accept the order fully this way, who will reject it totally, and who is mixed in his reactions to the order?

Second, assuming there are differences in these reactions to the Court order, how alike or different are the private visions and images held by these persons? Do they start from about the same kinds of private desires? Can the order therefore be seen as imposing an equal amount of compromise upon each of them? Or, do they have different private visions, so that the disparity between the private desires and public requirements is greater for some than others?

Third, if the disparities between the private desires and the public requirements are greater for some than for others, how can we account for this fact? Why is it that what is publicly required turns out to demand more compromise from some than from others?

Fourth, if the private worlds are about the same, but the acceptance of the order of the Court is different, how can we account for this? Why should some be more willing to compromise than others? Can we find out anything about differences in their life situations which will help us account for these disparities in the willingness to compromise?

Put in terms of prejudice and desegregation, where we equate prejudice with the private world and desegregation with the required public compromise, we are asking:

Are the respondents equally or unequally prejudiced against the Negro?

Do the respondents differ in their willingness to desegregate the schools?

Are there respondents who, though equal in prejudice, are different in their willingness to desegregate? If so, how can we account for this disparity?[3]

Are there respondents who, though unequal in their prejudice, are nevertheless equal in their willingness to desegregate? If so, why?

---

[3] The obvious four-fold classification has been spelled out by Robert Merton in his "Discrimination and the American Creed," Chapter XI in *Discrimination and National Welfare,* R. M. MacIver, ed. New York, Harper & Bros., 1949. Merton's names for the four types are: (1) the all-weather liberal (unprejudiced non-discriminator), (2) the fair-weather liberal (unprejudiced discriminator), (3) the fair-weather illiberal (prejudiced non-discriminator), (4) the all-weather illiberal (prejudiced discriminator).

Answers to these questions require measures of the content of the private worlds and of the willingness to meet the public requirements as implied in the court order.

We have developed such measures and applied them to the sample. A brief description of these measures can now be given. The full details, which may be of interest to the professional reader, will be found in Appendix C.

I. *Image*

Four current opinions about Negroes are frequently offered as justification by Whites for keeping social distance from the Negro and for keeping the Negro from effective participation in the total society. These opinions allege that the Negro has lower intellectual capacity, less ambition, inferior morality, and a less well developed sense of responsibility.

A series of tests showed that there was a rank order of credibility in these allegations; that is, some of these were said to be true by a larger percentage of the respondents, while smaller percentages affirmed others of these allegations.

Of the 287 persons asked, the Negro was alleged to be inferior to the White,

in Responsibility by	209	or 72.8%
in Morality by	198	or 69.0%
in Ambition by	191	or 66.5%
in Intelligence by	170	or 59.2%

Further testing showed that there was a pattern in these answers. Some respondents held the Negro inferior on all four counts, some on only three, some on only two, some on one, and some on none.

Moreover, the pattern was such that if a respondent picked only one trait in which he considered the Negro inferior, in more than 90 per cent of the cases he picked responsibility. If two traits were picked out, more than nine times out of ten these were responsibility and morality. If three were picked out, in better than 90 per cent of the cases these were responsibility, morality, and ambition. Finally, in nine out of ten cases, the Negro was held to be inferior in intelligence only if at the same time the respondent said the Negro was inferior on the other three counts as well.

When this kind of pattern of responses occurs, there exists what is technically known as a scale. The importance of this for us here is that we can assign to each pattern of response a score which will tell us not only in how many traits the respondent considered the Negro inferior, but in which ones, and we will be right more than nine out of ten times in interpreting the score in this fashion. Thus, we give a score of 4 to the persons who say the Negro is inferior on all four counts; a score of 3 for those who allege three inferiorities, a score of 2 for those who pick out only two inferiorities, a score of 1 for those who single out one trait, and a score of 0 for those who find the Negro not inferior to the White on any count. On the basis of the scaling factor just described, we can tell which inferiorities are meant with 90 per cent accuracy or better.

The value of these scores is that every individual can now be compared with every other individual on his Image (knowing what the score stands for), and one group of respondents can be compared with another in terms of the average score for the members of each of the groups. For example, we can compare the average or mean score on Image of those over fifty years of age with the average of those under fifty years of age. When we discover what differences there are between the means, we can estimate the significance of the difference and then begin to make some meaningful statements about the probable relationship of Age to Image.

Table 1 below is an example of how the use of scale scores enables one to give a condensed but intelligible and meaningful picture of the attitudes of a large number of people. In this table we list the number and per cent of 286 respondents (one interview was unusable) who scored in each of the possible ways. Remembering that a score of 4 stands for a belief that the Negro is inferior in four characteristics, and that a score of 0 stands for a belief that the Negro is not inferior in any regard, we can now see how the total sample felt about these matters.

TABLE 1

Distribution of Scale Scores on Image
(Beliefs about Negro Inferiority)

Scale Score	Number	Per Cent
4	143	50.00
3	43	15.03
2	36	12.59
1	17	5.94
0	47	16.44
TOTAL	286	100.00

Half of our respondents, it will be noticed, believe the Negro inferior in all four regards. Slightly over 16 per cent believe the Negro not to be inferior at all. The remaining numbers are distributed among those who think the Negro inferior in some ways but not others.

II. Ideology

What kind of a relationship would the White North Carolinians in the sample like to have with Negroes, if they could have any kind they desired? This is what is meant by Ideology.

We asked this question as the final one in a series of questions which had inquired into the respondents' contacts with Negroes and their various experiences in these contacts. The sequence of questions can be seen in Appendix C. In this appendix we also specify the ways in which we condensed and grouped answers so that we could assign some to the category of segregationist and some to the category of desegregationist.

We asked about desired relationships in eight different situations. These were: (1) eating in restaurants, (2) going to schools, (3) attending church, (4) having a Negro for a supervisor on the job, (5) riding on busses, (6) working side by side with a Negro in the same plant or office, (7) attending a dinner party, (8) living on the same block.

For a number of technical reasons the answers to questions about dinner parties and residing on the same block had to be dropped out of the calculations.[4] Every respondent was thus

[4] Primary among these reasons was the fact that situations of dinner parties and common residence do not fall with the 80-20 split ordinarily

36

scored for whether he would be willing to share facilities with Negroes or keep distance from them in each of the remaining six situations. Once again there emerged a rank order of willingness and resistance to mix with Negroes, depending on the situation. Thus, of the 287 respondents, separate facilities or relationships were preferred by:

235 or 81.87% in restaurants
217 or 75.61% in schools
211 or 73.51% in churches
203 or 70.72% in regard to having a Negro supervisor
181 or 63.06% on busses
114 or 39.72% in regard to working side by side with a Negro

In other terms, the largest per cent of the respondents rejected social relationships with Negroes in restaurants and the smallest per cent expressed this reluctance to have Negroes working side by side with them.

As in the case of the responses to Image, we tested whether there was a further pattern to these responses. Could we devise a set of scores which would tell us not only in how many of these situations separation was preferred, but in which ones? The answer is yes, and this time the scores are reliable indicators more than 92 times out of a 100.

---

required by scaling conventions. It should also be noted, however, that one other convention is sometimes violated in the scales we use. This is the rule that scale items should be at least 5% apart in the per cent of positive responses given to them. These conventions are, of course, not without significance and one violates them at some risk. Still, they are conventions and so long as one knows and makes explicit how his own procedures have deviated from conventions, and so long as one takes into account the weakness in his instruments which is thereby induced, one can proceed. Perhaps the best instance of this is the convention which states that Guttman-type scales may not be said to exist unless the coefficient of reproducibility is at least .90. The selection of the .90 cut-off point, is, of course, arbitrary. All that is implied thereby is that one doesn't wish to run the risk of being wrong more than 10 times out of 100. In general, it seems the better part of wisdom to follow these rules. When, however, certain complex data come close to forming a scale pattern, it doesn't seem to make much sense to surrender a series of items with .89 reproducibility.

Attitudes Toward the Negro and Desegregation

The scores range from 0 for those who accept the Negro in all the six situations, to 6 for those who reject the Negro in all. Again, if the respondent rejects only one situation, in 92 per cent of cases it is the restaurant. The one he almost never rejects except when he rejects all others is co-working.

Once again, then, we can calculate how many and what per cent of the respondents totally or partly reject the Negro and how many of them accept the Negro. These numbers and percentages are shown in Table 2.

TABLE 2
Ideology
(Avoidance or rejection of Negro in various situations)

Scale Score	Number	Per Cent
6	93	32.51
5	67	23.43
4	34	11.88
3	24	8.40
2	22	7.69
1	19	6.64
0	27	9.44

This table shows, among other things, that more than 55 per cent (32.51 + 23.43) of the respondents reject the idea of any relationships with Negroes except, perhaps, as co-workers, and that just over 16 per cent (6.64 + 9.44) are willing to accept the Negro as a social partner of sorts, except for sitting down at a table next to him in a restaurant.

Here we have a rank order of resistance to sharing of relationships with Negroes,[5] or what Gunnar Myrdal has called

[5] If we view these percentage distributions as expressing "rank orders of discrimination" we can then compare our results with the well known Myrdal hypothesis, and some subsequent retests of this hypothesis. Generally, our own results here tally with those of Myrdal, but vary from those of Edmunds (Edwin R. Edmunds, "The Myrdalian Thesis: Rank Order of Discrimination," *Phylon*, Vol. 15, 1954, pp. 297–303). It is impossible to state to what extent our findings conform or disagree with those of Banks (W. S. M. Banks, II, "Rank Order of Sensitivity to Discrimination," *American Sociological Review*, Vol. XV, 1950, pp. 529–534), since he interviewed only Negroes and we interviewed only Whites.

a "rank order of discrimination." Different situations appear to have different meanings for the Whites. It seems to them considerably worse to eat side by side with a Negro than to work side by side with him. But they would rather sit on the same seat of a bus than worship at a church beside a Negro. At least this is what the respondents say they would prefer if they could have their preferences.

One might have expected the respondents to reject the Negro uniformly and without exception. In fact, they did not. As we shall later see, there are probably good reasons for this. By way of preview, the acceptance of the Negro—such as it is, and as it is shown by these scores—is probably due to the fact that some of the respondents simply don't dream in pure cost-free and consequence-free terms. When they express a preference they are already taking account of costs and consequences. Their preferences contain these cost-estimates as intrinsic and organic parts.

In any event, we have here a fair summary picture of how the Whites would construct the world of social relations with the Negroes if they could, with all the ambiguity that is carried in the phrase "if they could." This is certainly one dimension of their attitudes toward Negroes. It is different from their Image. And it differs, too, from what actions they would be willing to take about these relationships.

III. Sentiment Structure

The next dimension of attitude concerns feelings. The six situations examined for Ideology were submitted to an analysis of their content of probable feelings. Instead of asking what the respondent would like, we now asked him to imagine how he would feel if in fact a Negro did sit down next to him on a bus; or in a pew at church; or in a restaurant. The answers were then classified into either segregationist feelings (e.g., wouldn't like it at all; would hate it, etc.) or desegregationist feelings (e.g., wouldn't mind it; it would be all right with me, etc.).

Again the responses were analyzed for statistical patterns, and again a rank order of segregationist sentiment was discovered.

39

Attitudes Toward the Negro and Desegregation

Of the 287 respondents, segregationist feelings were expressed by:

205 or 71.77% about mixed Negro-White schools
193 or 67.59% about having a Negro supervisor
177 or 62.02% about attending Church with Negroes
170 or 59.58% about eating in a restaurant with Negroes
163 or 57.15% about riding on a bus with Negroes
128 or 44.95% about working with Negroes

Clearly, some changes have taken place. Now that the question has shifted from an Ideological preference to a matter of feeling, different situations seem most difficult for the respondents to accept with equanimity. The schools become the most troublesome; co-work remains easiest to go along with.

But now the actual per cent of the total group who reject the Negro is smaller in all but one instance. Schools drop from over 75 per cent to over 71 per cent; the church situation becomes less obnoxious, so that where 73.51 per cent rejected the church relationship ideologically, only 62.02 per cent reject it in terms of how they would feel.

The only situation which increases in segregationist responses is co-work. Here, approximately 5 per cent more of the population wouldn't like it if they found themselves in a co-work situation.

It is difficult to explain the differences in the rank order of resistance when this is measured first by Ideology and then by Sentiment. Why should the Negro supervisor be fourth on the former and second on the latter? One can only suggest that these situations vary in their meanings, relative to each other, depending on whether it is an abstract preference one is expressing or a feeling one thinks he probably would experience.

It seems clear that when the respondents have to imagine the feelings they might experience if they found themselves in contact with Negroes, they tend to be more moderate than when they are expressing abstract preferences. The probable *feeling* is a more concrete and hedged type of response than is the Ideology. This is due perhaps to the fact that many of the respondents have actually had such contacts with Negroes and are reporting to us how they remembered they felt at those times and how they think they might feel the next time such contacts occur. The feelings are thus more tied to reality than the Ideologies. This greater closeness to reality tends to express itself in lower percentages of rejection of the Negro.[6]

The only situation in which this is not true is co-work. Of all the situations, co-work is the one in which our respondents have had most actual contact with Negroes. But we do not know if those who have had this actual contact are those who reject the Negro more on feeling-tone than in terms of ideological preferences. We cannot say, therefore, that actual contact leads to greater rejection. It may be true, but we do not know.

---

[6] Two alternative but compatible explanations may be offered here, provisionally, to account for these differences on the various scales. On the one hand, we are probably dealing with the well known "crystallization" effect which results from making issues concrete and specific. Familiar landmarks are provided by the concrete issue, to which, then, interviewees can and often do respond more particularly in conformity with their own special inclinations.

Alternatively, we can view these scales as tapping different "memberships." That is, the most general question regarding cognitive stereotypes and idealized versions of social systems evoke those responses appropriate to the person's membership in the largest cultural system, the South. The more specific and concrete questions begin to force the respondents into their differentiated subcultures within the larger culture. Another way of saying this is to consider the larger and smaller cultures as different reference groups to which the respondents become oriented by the quality of the question.

It is clear that the two kinds of explanations jibe with each other. The reference group-subculture explanation may constitute an initial description of the dynamics of the "crystallization" process.

Both of these explanations are consonant with the findings of Olive W. Quinn, "The Transmission of Racial Attitudes Among White Southerners," *Social Forces,* Vol. 33, 1954, pp. 41–47. The ordinary distinction among different aspects of an orientation to another individual involves distinguishing between cognitive, affective, and behavioral components of the relationship, i.e., knowledge or belief, feeling and action. These dimensions can be further sub-classified by such cross-sections as have been suggested by Chein, e.g., the degree of certainty, intensity, overtness, consistency, salience, consciousness, and tenacity. See, I. Chein, "Notes on a Framework for the Measurement of Discrimination and Prejudice," Appendix C in M. Jahoda, M. Deutsch, and S. W. Cook, *Research Methods in Social Relations,* Part One, New York, Dryden Press, 1951, pp. 386–390.

Be that as it may, the respondents do have ranked preferences for various types of contact, in so far as their feelings about these contacts with Negroes are concerned. And this rank order of preference again forms a scale, permitting the assignment of scale scores with 91 per cent reliability.

Table 3 shows the number and per cent of the respondents who score in each of the six scoring categories. Once again the score of 6 stands for complete rejection of the Negro, i.e., the respondent expressed segregationist-type sentiments regarding contact in all six of the situations. By contrast, a score of 0 stands for acceptance of the Negro as a participant in each of the six situations. The intervening scores represent intermediate degrees of acceptance and rejection, in the order earlier specified.

TABLE 3

Sentiment Structure

(How Whites would feel if they found themselves face to face with a Negro in each of six different situations)

Scale Score	Number	Per Cent
6	93	32.51
5	44	15.38
4	25	8.74
3	23	8.04
2	33	11.54
1	19	6.64
0	49	17.14
TOTAL	286	100.00

From Table 3 it can be seen that about one-third of the Whites reject the Negro totally. But some definite shifts have taken place from the pattern of scale scores on Ideology. Nearly twice as many respondents now indicate a willingness to accept the Negro in all six situations (17.14 per cent *vs.* 9.44 per cent on Ideology). Also, more than one-third of the sample (35.32 per cent) are now distributed through the three lowest scores, i.e., 0, 1, and 2. This compares with the less than one-fourth of the sample (23.77 per cent) who are in these scoring boxes on Ideology. Apparently, a core of total rejecters remains constant, while the less hardened resisters now become more moderate.

IV. General Action

What would the respondents *do* if a Negro sat down next to them in a restaurant? Or on a bus? Or if the Whites found themselves under the supervision of a Negro at their place of work?

The emphasis here is on doing and acting, not just feeling. All six situations were once again probed for this dimension of attitudes. Answers were once again coded to distinguish acceptance and rejection. For instance, if a person said he would get up and leave if a Negro came and sat down next to him in a restaurant, this is clearly a rejection of the Negro. If he said, however, that he wouldn't do anything, but would just keep eating his meal, we scored this as an acceptance. This is not to imply that he would necessarily like it. But it is to say that as he imagines or recalls his behavior under these circumstances, he would do the kind of thing that would make it possible for both Negro and White to share the same facility. Or, at least, he would not do the kind of thing, such as raising a fuss or getting up and leaving, which would make it difficult or impossible for the Negro to enter the restaurant again.

The number and per cent who indicated they would take segregationist-type actions if they came in contact with a Negro in the six situations were as follows:

193 or 67.59% reject Negro as *supervisor*
159 or 55.74% reject Negro children in *schools*
148 or 51.91% would take action against Negroes in *restaurants*
146 or 51.21% would be unwilling to have Negroes in same *church*
128 or 44.94% would react unfavorably to Negroes on *busses*
113 or 39.71% would take action against Negroes as *co-workers*

Once again some shifts—this time only minor ones—have taken place in the rank order of resistance of the Whites to relationship with the Negro. The idea of a Negro supervisor is now most severely rejected. The most frequent type of response to the question of "What would you do if a Negro was named supervisor over you at your place of work?" was "I would quit."

Another significant change is the drop in the per cent who expressed segregationist sentiments. Apparently the requirement to state a course of action produces even greater moderation.

The total pattern of responses to "What would you do" questions once again forms a scale, with 90.07 per cent reliability. A score of six stands for rejection of Negro in all six situations; a score of 0 indicates acceptance in all six.

Table 4 lists the number and per cent in each of the scale score categories.

TABLE 4

General Action

(What Whites would do if face to face with Negro in six different situations)

Scale Score	Number	Per Cent
6	72	25.17
5	35	12.24
4	25	8.74
3	27	9.44
2	32	11.19
1	35	12.24
0	60	20.98
TOTAL	286	100.00

The shifts in the pattern of scale scores is much more impressive this time. The one-third of the sample who score 6 on Ideology and Image now drops to just over 25 per cent. The number who accept the Negro in all six rises to over 20 per cent. Over 45 per cent score in the three most accepting categories (2, 1, and 0). A general moderation in response seems to have guided the whole sample. On the average, the White respondents are not nearly as segregationist in their action proposals as in the sentiments they bear in their hearts or in their ideological visions of a desired social system.

V. Specific Action

The fifth and final dimension focusses specifically on Negro-White relations in the public schools. Respondents were asked to approve or disapprove of a series of four proposed ways to deal with the "threat" of desegregation. Each of these proposals had enjoyed some currency and popularity prior to the time of the interview. Each was prefaced by comments indicating that the measure had previously been advocated.

Briefly put, the four proposals were:

1. Amend the Constitution.
2. Withhold state funds from school districts which desegregated.
3. Close the public schools if necessary.
4. Use force if necessary.

The respondents were asked to approve or disapprove these ways to prevent desegregation.

The number and per cent approving each of the measures was as follows:

Amend the Constitution	221	or 77.30%
Withhold state fund	159	or 55.55%
Close the public schools	124	or 43.46%
Use force if necessary	71	or 24.82%

The responses once again form a scale pattern, with 95.65 per cent reliability. Scores range from 4 for those who approve of all four measures to 0 for those who approve of none.

The number and per cent in each of the five scoring groups are given in Table 5.

Several salient facts emerge from these tabulations:

1. Almost 25 per cent of the sample were willing to use force if necessary;

2. More than 77 per cent were willing to try to get through a constitutional amendment to prevent desegregation;

3. Only 18.88 per cent of the total sample approved of all four ways to prevent desegregation. About one-fourth of those who said they would be willing to use force balked at approving other methods. (We do not know whether this is because the other methods are seen as too mild, or whether this is a case of sheer inconsistency.)

TABLE 5

Specific Action

(Which proposals to prevent desegregation the White accepts or rejects)

Scale Score	Number	Per Cent
4	54	18.88
3	71	24.82
2	53	18.53
1	58	20.28
0	50	17.49
TOTAL	286	100.00

4. Most of the sample (81.12 per cent) rejected at least one of the four measures, and, most frequently, this was the use of force.

5. Almost 18 per cent of the sample disapproved of all four techniques. This 18 per cent includes those who would also take positive measures to implement desegregation.

One takes comfort or is dismayed by these statistics depending on what he would like to see and on what he thinks a sample such as ours ought to be like in its average tendencies. The most striking impression is that there is considerable heterogeneity in the group of Whites. They differ from one another; and many of them vary in their own reactions from one dimension of attitudes to another. Finally, within dimensions II, III and IV, different situations evoke different responses from the same persons. In short, we do not have a solid South and we do not have solid Southerners.

Some sense can be made out of the diversity of response by thinking in terms of prejudice and discrimination. Prejudice literally means prejudgment. But it has come to stand for a set of unfavorable *beliefs* about and desires for distance from certain types of persons.

More often than not, unfavorable qualities are ascribed to whole groups of persons on the basis of limited experience with a few members of that group. It is equally often the case that these unfavorable qualities are assumed to be inborn and incapable of being altered.

By contrast, discrimination refers to types of *actions* taken to keep distance from the disfavored group and/or to prevent that group from having access to certain facilities, such as schools, jobs, and voting. Most simply, discrimination involves denying to others the rights which one claims for himself.

For some time now it has been fashionable to contend that there is an automatic connection between prejudice and discrimination. This implies that the prejudiced person naturally tends to practice discrimination. As a corollary, it is held that discrimination cannot be eliminated except as one first removes the prejudicial feelings which underlie the tendency to discriminate.[7]

More recent research and theory, however, have been very persuasive in demonstrating that there exists a gap between the thing we call prejudice and that which we call discrimination. In this gap a variety of factors can be interposed which will either facilitate the acting out of the prejudice or inhibit the prejudiced person from discriminating. Moreover, it has also become evident that there are significant numbers of people who practice discrimination even though they do not carry in them nearly the amount of prejudice which one

[7] For a thorough review of the major viewpoints, see G. W. Allport, *The Nature of Prejudice,* Cambridge, Addison-Wesley, 1954. For more specialized surveys of related problems, see J. S. Brunner and R. Tagiuri, "The Perception of People" in Gardner Lindzey, ed., *Handbook of Social Psychology,* Vol. II, pp. 634–654 Cambridge, Addison-Wesley, 1954; and J. Harding, B. Kutner, H. Proshansky and I. Chein, "Prejudice and Ethnic Relations," *ibid.,* pp. 1021–1061.

For analysis of the "vicious circle" and the effectiveness of interpositions at various points, see, for example, R. K. Merton, "The Self-Fulfilling Prophecy," Chapter VII, in his *Social Theory and Social Structure,* Glencoe, Illinois, The Free Press, 1949; and R. M. MacIver's *The More Perfect Union,* New York, Macmillan, 1948.

would expect on the basis of their discriminatory acts. What these findings suggest then is that prejudice and discrimination are independently variable. That is, there are no necessary connections between the amount of prejudice which a person expresses and the amount of discrimination which he actually practices. The discrepancies can work two ways. The prejudice can be more than the discrimination suggests, or the discrimination can be more than the prejudice implies.

Here we are dealing simply with a special version of what is most generally true about human beings in all cases of human action and interaction. That is, there almost always is a disparity between the private world of belief and feeling and the public world of action. Only under the most exceptional circumstances is one able to act out in public the fullness of his own private images and desires.

The relevance of this distinction here concerns the nature of the five scales which we are using to measure readiness. When we call them scales which measure readiness for desegregation, we imply thereby a type of action for which the person is more or less ready. We are trying to judge the readiness for this type of action, or for this pattern of co-existence with the Negro, on the basis of the answers given to the questions. We suggest that the questions which get at the man's Image and Social Ideology come closer to reflecting prejudice, while the questions which define General Action Set and Specific Action Set come closer to defining readiness to discriminate. This is not to say that one set of questions is a better index of what the man is really like than is another set. But there are different aspects or facets to any individual's orientation to the Negro, and one must make a distinction between the more private facets of that orientation and the more public ones.

The distinction can be seen in operation if we look at Table 6. There we see the five scales as we have previously described them, and next to each is the per cent of all the responses which were pro-segregationist.

From this table we see that on Scale I, the Negro Image, of the 1148 possible responses given by 287 respondents to each of four items some 67.77 per cent were pro-segregationist. As one reads down the column of per cent figures, he will see that as we go from the Image and the Ideology, on the one extreme, to the General and Specific Action Sets, on the other, the per cent of pro-segregationist responses declines noticeably. It will be further noticed that the scores on Scales I and II are virtually identical, at the one extreme, as are the

TABLE 6
Per Cent Pro-Segregationist Responses on Five Scales

Scale	Per Cent Pro-Segregationist
I. Image of the Negro	67.77
II. Social Ideology	67.41
III. Sentiment Structure	60.51
IV. General Action Set	51.85
V. Specific Action Set	50.28

TABLE 7
Mean Scores for Total Sample on Each of Five Scales

Scale No.	Mean	Limits	Means Expressed as Fractions of Their Ranges
I.	2.75	0–4	55.04
II.	4.07	0–6	58.13
III.	3.60	0–6	51.40
IV.	3.09	0–6	44.20
V.	2.06	0–4	41.26

scores on Scales IV and V, on the other, while the scores on Scale III, Sentiment Structure, are intermediary between these two extremes.

A second illustration of the point we were making about the difference between what the scales seem to be measuring is to be seen in Table 7, where we take each of the scales and list the mean score achieved by all of the respondents.

Because the ranges on the different scales are different, as will be seen in the column marked "limits," we convert the means into fractions of the total range. When we do this we get the results as shown in the last column, and we note there roughly the same results as were just cited. The scores on Image and Ideology are about the same, on the one extreme, as are those on General Action and Specific Action, on the other. Now we can suggest that since the means on Image and Ideology are closer to the segregationist extreme, and the means on General Action and Specific Action are closer to the desegregationist pole, Scales I and II are probably measuring more of the private world of prejudice, and Scales IV and V are measuring attitudes which are more likely to receive open and public expression.

We are making a rough equation here, to the effect that the more private the expression the more segregationist it is likely to be. The Image and Ideology scores are more segregationist because, being more private, they do not ordinarily get tested in public action, as much as do the things measured by Scales IV and V. Implicit here is the notion that the attitude toward the Negro tends to become more favorable as the respondent feels the need to consider the consequences of his actions. In his expression of his Image of what the Negro is like and his Ideology of preferred social relations, the White respondent does not have to take consequences into account. But this reckoning of consequences seems to be more forced upon the respondent when he is being asked to state what he would probably *do,* both in general and specifically, than when faced with a hypothetical situation.

In actual or hypothetical situations the respondent has to consider the presence and the rights and powers of other persons. He is aware that there will be reactions to his own actions, and that his actions will produce unfavorable consequences along with whatever he will gain. In short, when we focus upon action, and thus clearly imply consequences, we seem to force the respondent to reckon with these. Such reckoning seems to produce a more moderate response.

We cannot state unequivocally that the Image Score is consistently more segregationist than the Ideology score or that the Specific Action responses are consistently more desegregationist than the General Action responses. But we can say that for the sample as a whole the average tendencies are consistently toward relatively high segregationism on Image and Ideology and toward relatively low segregationism, on General and Specific Action Sets.

The consistency of these trends for the sample as a whole provides us with a most interesting set of questions: If awareness of consequences is responsible for the difference in the average score on the scales, then what factors are responsible for producing this awareness, other than the nature of the questions themselves? Does amount of education matter, and, if so, in what way? At what point in the attitude-set of persons with different educational achievement will the awareness of consequences manifest itself? If we can definitely show an influence of education, what is the nature of this influence; that is, how does formal education come to produce a greater awareness of consequences? Will age matter? Will residence matter? Will occupational position make a difference? Will some of these factors make more of a difference than others?

We are hypothesizing that *the major factors responsible for differences in attitudes toward desegregation are the degree of awareness of consequences and the degree of concern for them.* This now sets us the problem to which the rest of our analysis can be turned: *Who shows more and who less of this awareness and this concern, and who, therefore, is more and who is less ready for desegregation?*

CHAPTER THREE

ELEVEN FACTORS WHICH INFLUENCE
ATTITUDES: A SELECTION

A SALIENT fact about Southern attitudes in general has now been confirmed for the particular sample of North Carolinians, namely that there are significant differences in White Southern attitudes toward the Negroes.

What causes these differences? Or, more conservatively, what factors are related to these differences in attitude?

In the Introduction, eleven factors were cited as probably important. These were: Age, Education, Occupation, Income, Residence, Religiosity, Occupational Mobility, Church Membership, Exposure to the Mass Media, Exposure to Industrial Complex, and Number of Children in the Family. These eleven were chosen partly on the basis of what previous research had shown to be important, partly also on some hunches.

Since it is unlikely that all eleven factors will be equally important, a further selection must be made among them. This choice ought to be made on the basis of good evidence, rather than guesses, and the evidence ought to speak *specifically* about the North Carolina sample, more than about the South in general. Once the list has been culled, a more thorough analysis can be made of the smaller number remaining.

There is a simple but effective technique for choosing. The factor of education will serve as an example. First, the sample is divided into three different educational groups: all those with grammar school (8 years) or less, all those with 9–12 years of education, and all those with some college training. Then the average scores for these three groups on each of the five scales is calculated. The pattern of difference or similarity in scores is observed. The differences are then tested statistically to see how likely it is that they could have occurred by chance alone. A significant difference, by standard convention, is one which could have turned up by chance alone less than five times out of a hundred.

Eleven Factors Which Influence Attitudes

The decision whether to submit a factor to more detailed analysis is made in terms of both the number of significant differences and the patterning, that is, between which groups and on what scales do these differences occur. The only exceptions to this procedure occur in the cases of religious denomination and exposure to the industrial complex. The mean scores of various subgroups are shown for each of these factors. But no tests were made of the significance of the differences, because there is no discernible pattern in the scoring which would enable us to follow up with more detailed analysis.

This general procedure can be followed for each factor, dividing the sample anew each time, so that on one round the age clusters are the major focus, on another the income groupings, and so on.

In the following pages, the results of testing the probable importance of each of the factors is presented. For each factor (with the two exceptions) two tables will be offered: (1) the mean scores on the five scales for the various groups involved; (2) results of testing the significance of the differences between scores. The non-professional reader can skip these tables and grasp the findings from the discursive summaries.

Eleven Factors Which Influence Attitudes

I. Education

TABLE 8

Mean Scores and Standard Deviations of Three Educational Groups on
Five Attitude Scales

Scale	Scale Limits	Education Group		
		(I) 1–8 Years	(II) 9–12 Years	(III) 13 or More Years
I. Image of Negro	0–4	$\overline{X} = 2.82$ $\sigma = 1.56$	$\overline{X} = 2.79$ $\sigma = 1.53$	$\overline{X} = 2.57$ $\sigma = 1.61$
II. Ideology	0–6	$\overline{X} = 4.73$ $\sigma = 1.56$	$\overline{X} = 4.17$ $\sigma = 1.85$	$\overline{X} = 3.01$ $\sigma = 2.38$
III. Sentiment	0–6	$\overline{X} = 4.09$ $\sigma = 2.07$	$\overline{X} = 3.69$ $\sigma = 2.26$	$\overline{X} = 2.78$ $\sigma = 1.83$
IV. General Action	0–6	$\overline{X} = 3.50$ $\sigma = 2.22$	$\overline{X} = 3.04$ $\sigma = 2.49$	$\overline{X} = 2.45$ $\sigma = 2.23$
V. Specific Action	0–4	$\overline{X} = 2.39$ $\sigma = 2.40$	$\overline{X} = 2.08$ $\sigma = 1.33$	$\overline{X} = 1.75$ $\sigma = 1.28$

NOTE: In this and the following tables, $\overline{X}$ is used to denote the Mean and σ is used to denote the Standard Deviation.

TABLE 9

Tests of Differences Between Mean Scores of Educational Groups

Scale	*Groups Compared*	*dm*[a]	*t*[b]	*p <*[c]
I. Image (0–4)	1 , 2	0.03	—	n.s.[d]
	1 , 3	0.25	—	n.s.
	2 , 3	0.22	—	n.s.
II. Ideology (0–6)	1 , 2	0.56	2.40	.01
	1 , 3	1.72	5.10	.001
	2 , 3	1.16	3.41	.001
III. Sentiment (0–6)	1 , 2	0.40	1.31	n.s.
	1 , 3	1.31	4.28	.001
	2 , 3	0.91	2.83	.01
IV. General Action (0–6)	1 , 2	0.46	1.42	n.s.
	1 , 3	1.05	3.00	.01
	2 , 3	0.59	1.60	n.s.
V. Specific Action (0–4)	1 , 2	0.31	1.14	n.s.
	1 , 3	0.77	2.23	.05
	2 , 3	0.46	2.28	.05

[a] *dm* = difference between means
[b] *t* = t value
[c] *p <* = probability value of the *t*
[d] n.s. = not significant

The following results (Tables 8 and 9) stand out:

1. The grammar and high school groups are virtually identical in their scores on Image. The college group has a slightly more favorable Image than either of the others. Education seems therefore not to matter much when it is a question of the Image of the Negro.

2. By contrast, on the other four scales, differences in education seem to matter all the way through. The general finding is that the higher the education, the more favorable the attitude toward the Negro.

3. Out of fifteen sets of differences, eight proved statistically significant. These include all three differences on Ideology scores, two on Sentiment Structure, one on General Action, and two on Specific Action. None of the differences on Image scores is statistically significant.

4. In seven of the eight significant differences, the college group is involved.

Differences in education thus seem to be selectively but significantly related to differences in attitudes toward Negroes. There is good reason to look into this relationship in greater detail.

II. Age

TABLE 10
Mean Scale Scores of Different Age Groups

Age Group		I Image (0–4)	II Ideology (0–6)	III Sentiment (0–6)	IV General Action (0–6)	V Specific Action (0–4)
(1) 18–24	$\overline{X} =$	2.40	4.45	4.10	3.50	2.35
	$\sigma =$	1.66	0.87	2.29	2.46	1.45
(2) 25–34	$\overline{X} =$	2.78	4.05	3.84	3.29	2.11
	$\sigma =$	1.65	2.18	2.44	2.43	1.42
(3) 35–44	$\overline{X} =$	2.80	3.80	3.21	2.81	1.96
	$\sigma =$	1.63	1.92	2.15	2.22	1.37
(4) 45–54	$\overline{X} =$	2.72	4.06	3.40	2.87	1.93
	$\sigma =$	1.58	2.10	2.35	2.37	1.38
(5) 55–64	$\overline{X} =$	2.69	4.48	3.81	3.21	2.12
	$\sigma =$	3.04	1.80	2.05	2.13	1.34
(6) 65 and over	$\overline{X} =$	3.30	4.25	4.0	3.76	2.61
	$\sigma =$	1.22	1.48	2.16	2.17	1.0

Eleven Factors Which Influence Attitudes

TABLE 11
Tests of Differences Between Mean Scores of Age Groups

Scale	Groups Compared	dm	t	p <
I. Image (0–4)	1 , 2	0.38	—	n.s.
	1 , 3	0.40	.98	n.s.
	1 , 4	0.32	—	n.s.
	1 , 5	0.29	—	n.s.
	1 , 6	0.90	1.80	.1
	2 , 3	0.02	—	n.s.
	2 , 4	0.06	—	n.s.
	2 , 5	0.09	—	n.s.
	2 , 6	0.52	—	n.s.
	3 , 4	0.08	—	n.s.
	3 , 5	0.11	—	n.s.
	3 , 6	0.50	—	n.s.
	4 , 5	0.03	—	n.s.
	4 , 6	0.58	—	n.s.
	5 , 6	0.61	.97	n.s.
II. Ideology (0–6)	1 , 2	0.40	1.53	n.s.
	1 , 3	0.65	2.74	.01
	1 , 4	0.39	1.41	n.s.
	1 , 5	0.03	—	n.s.
	1 , 6	0.20	—	n.s.
	2 , 3	0.25	—	n.s.
	2 , 4	0.01	—	n.s.
	2 , 5	0.43	1.08	n.s.
	2 , 6	0.20	—	n.s.
	3 , 4	0.26	—	n.s.
	3 , 5	0.68	1.78	.1
	3 , 6	0.45	.94	n.s.
	4 , 5	0.42	1.03	n.s.
	4 , 6	0.19	—	n.s.
	5 , 6	0.23	—	n.s.
III. Sentiment (0–6)	1 , 2	0.26	—	n.s.
	1 , 3	0.89	1.57	n.s.
	1 , 4	0.70	1.16	n.s.
	1 , 5	0.29	—	n.s.
	1 , 6	0.10	—	n.s.
	2 , 3	0.63	1.72	.1
	2 , 4	0.44	1.10	n.s.

Eleven Factors Which Influence Attitudes

TABLE 11, continued

Scale	Groups Compared	dm	t	p <
	2 , 5	0.03	—	n.s.
	2 , 6	0.16	—	n.s.
	3 , 4	0.19	—	n.s.
	3 , 5	0.60	1.38	n.s.
	3 , 6	0.79	1.22	n.s.
	4 , 5	0.41	—	n.s.
	4 , 6	0.60	.90	n.s.
	5 , 6	0.19	—	n.s.
IV. General Action (0–6)	1 , 2	0.21	—	n.s.
	1 , 3	0.69	1.14	n.s.
	1 , 4	0.63	1.01	n.s.
	1 , 5	0.29	—	n.s.
	1 , 6	0.26	—	n.s.
	2 , 3	0.48	1.29	n.s.
	2 , 4	0.42	—	n.s.
	2 , 5	0.08	—	n.s.
	2 , 6	0.47	—	n.s.
	3 , 4	0.06	—	n.s.
	3 , 5	0.40	—	n.s.
	3 , 6	0.95	1.49	n.s.
	4 , 5	0.34	—	n.s.
	4 , 6	0.89	1.33	n.s.
	5 , 6	0.55	0.78	n.s.
V. Specific Action (0–4)	1 , 2	0.24	—	n.s.
	1 , 3	0.39	1.08	n.s.
	1 , 4	0.42	1.15	n.s.
	1 , 5	0.23	—	n.s.
	1 , 6	0.26	0.61	n.s.
	2 , 3	0.15	—	n.s.
	2 , 4	0.18	—	n.s.
	2 , 5	0.01	—	n.s.
	2 , 6	0.50	1.56	n.s.
	3 , 4	0.03	—	n.s.
	3 , 5	0.16	—	n.s.
	3 , 6	0.66	2.08	.01
	4 , 5	0.19	—	n.s.
	4 , 6	0.68	2.09	.01
	5 , 6	0.49	1.35	n.s.

Eleven Factors Which Influence Attitudes

The following are the salient findings from Tables 10 and 11.

1. While there are differences in mean scores, these are not patterned in any regular way. It is not possible to say either that the younger the group the more favorable the attitude, or that the older the group the more favorable the attitude. Only the over-65 group seems to have a consistently unfavorable attitude.

2. The size of the differences is usually small. Testing shows that out of ninety sets of differences only three are statistically significant. This is a smaller number than would be expected by chance alone out of a group of ninety.

Age seems to be relatively inconsequential as a factor in attitudes toward Negroes—at least in this sample—and the decision is therefore made not to investigate age any further.

III. Exposure to the Mass Media

TABLE 12
Mean Scale Scores of Different Exposure Groups

Exposure Group		I Image (0–4)	II Ideology (0–6)	III Sentiment (0–6)	IV General Action (0–6)	V Specific Action (0–4)
0[a]	$\overline{X} =$	2.77	5.60	5.33	4.33	2.55
1	$\overline{X} =$	2.84	5.0	4.78	4.15	2.73
	$\sigma =$	1.48	1.35	1.75	2.18	1.15
2	$\overline{X} =$	2.80	4.01	3.64	3.08	2.23
	$\sigma =$	1.45	2.00	2.19	2.31	1.43
3	$\overline{X} =$	2.74	3.94	3.28	2.81	1.81
	$\sigma =$	1.58	2.01	1.76	2.27	1.30
4	$\overline{X} =$	2.58	3.34	2.87	2.53	1.65
	$\sigma =$	1.59	2.27	2.42	2.21	1.23

[a] The mean for the 0-group is reported here only *pro forma*. The small $N = 9$ forbids any use of this group in subsequent analysis.

Eleven Factors Which Influence Attitudes

TABLE 13

Tests of Differences Between Mean Scores of Exposure Groups

Scale	Groups Compared	dm	t	p <
I. Image (0–4)	1 , 2	0.04	—	n.s.
	1 , 3	0.10	0.36	n.s.
	1 , 4	0.26	2.39	.02
	2 , 3	0.06	—	n.s.
	2 , 4	0.22	0.75	n.s.
	3 , 4	0.16	—	n.s.
II. Ideology (0–6)	1 , 2	0.99	3.05	.01
	1 , 3	1.06	3.60	.001
	1 , 4	1.66	3.96	.001
	2 , 3	0.07	—	n.s.
	2 , 4	0.35	0.84	n.s.
	3 , 4	0.60	1.59	n.s.
III. Sentiment (0–6)	1 , 2	1.14	3.11	.01
	1 , 3	1.50	4.17	.001
	1 , 4	1.91	4.04	.001
	2 , 3	0.36	—	n.s.
	2 , 4	0.77	1.74	.1
	3 , 4	0.41	0.87	n.s.
IV. General Action (0–6)	1 , 2	1.07	2.49	.02
	1 , 3	1.34	3.23	.01
	1 , 4	1.62	3.28	.01
	2 , 3	0.27	—	n.s.
	2 , 4	0.55	0.65	n.s.
	3 , 4	0.28	—	n.s.
V. Specific Action (0–4)	1 , 2	0.50	2.07	.05
	1 , 3	0.92	4.08	.001
	1 , 4	1.08	4.41	.001
	2 , 3	0.42	—	n.s.
	2 , 4	0.58	2.37	.02
	3 , 4	0.16	—	n.s.

Tables 12 and 13 tell us the following:

1. In general, the greater the exposure to the Mass Media the more favorable the attitude to the Negro. This includes Images as well, though on this scale the differences seem smaller than is true elsewhere.

2. Out of thirty sets of differences, fourteen prove statistically significant. These are distributed rather regularly through all the dimensions except Image. Only the "most exposed" and "least exposed" groups differ significantly in their Images of the Negro. The close correspondence between these findings and those on Education strongly suggest further analysis of the impact of exposure to the Mass Media.

IV. Income

TABLE 14
Mean Scale Scores of Different Income Groups

Income Group		I Image (0–4)	II Ideology (0–6)	III Sentiment (0–6)	IV General Action (0–6)	V Specific Action (0–4)
(1) $1–$2999	$\overline{X}$ =	2.90	4.71	4.08	3.77	2.47
	σ =	0.78	1.65	1.47	1.73	1.36
(2) $3000–$4999	$\overline{X}$ =	2.73	4.32	3.82	3.10	2.29
	σ =	1.50	1.03	1.71	1.64	1.36
(3) $5000–$6999	$\overline{X}$ =	2.68	3.95	3.68	3.05	1.68
	σ =	1.54	2.13	1.50	2.39	1.25
(4) $7000 or over	$\overline{X}$ =	2.75	2.88	2.46	2.36	1.50
	σ =	1.64	2.40	1.50	2.25	1.22

61

Eleven Factors Which Influence Attitudes

TABLE 15
Tests of Differences Between Mean Scores of Income Groups

Scale	Groups Compared	dm	t	p <
I. Image (0–4)	1 , 2	0.17	—	n.s.
	1 , 3	0.22	—	n.s.
	1 , 4	0.15	—	n.s.
	2 , 3	0.04	—	n.s.
	2 , 4	0.02	—	n.s.
	3 , 4	0.04	—	n.s.
II. Ideology (0–6)	1 , 2	0.39	1.69	.1
	1 , 3	0.76	3.22	.01
	1 , 4	1.83	4.84	.001
	2 , 3	0.36	2.53	.01
	2 , 4	1.43	4.37	.001
	3 , 4	1.06	3.20	.01
III. Sentiment (0–6)	1 , 2	0.25	—	n.s.
	1 , 3	0.39	1.29	n.s.
	1 , 4	1.62	6.00	.001
	2 , 3	0.14	—	n.s.
	2 , 4	1.36	5.44	.001
	3 , 4	1.23	3.96	.001
IV. General Action (0–6)	1 , 2	0.67	2.48	.02
	1 , 3	0.72	1.62	n.s.
	1 , 4	1.41	3.90	.001
	2 , 3	0.05	—	n.s.
	2 , 4	0.74	2.32	.05
	3 , 4	0.69	1.44	n.s.
V. Specific Action (0–4)	1 , 2	0.17	—	n.s.
	1 , 3	0.78	2.96	.01
	1 , 4	0.96	4.13	.001
	2 , 3	0.60	2.53	.02
	2 , 4	0.78	3.84	.001
	3 , 4	0.18	—	n.s.

Tables 14 and 15 give the results of comparing the scores of different income groups on five scales.

The most persuasive findings are as follows:

1. In general, income groups tend to differ from each other at about the same places and to about the same extent as did the educational and mass media groups.

Eleven Factors Which Influence Attitudes

2. With certain reservations about Image scores, it can be said that the higher the income, the more favorable the attitude toward the Negro.

3. Out of thirty possible differences, sixteen are significant beyond chance. None of these sixteen occur on the Image scores.

The findings justify giving special consideration to the factor of income.

V. Religious Affiliation

TABLE 16
Mean Scale Scores for Different Religious Denominations

Religious Membership	I Image (0–4)	II Ideology (0–6)	III Sentiment (0–6)	IV General Action (0–6)	V Specific Action (0–4)
(1) Catholic[a]	3.00	4.33	3.00	3.40	2.30
(2) Jewish[b]	4.00	1.00	0.00	0.00	1.00
(3) Other[a]	1.30	4.33	2.30	2.70	1.70
(4) None	2.87	4.34	3.39	3.52	2.48
(5) Baptist	2.81	4.51	4.04	3.41	2.24
(6) Methodist	2.77	3.74	3.35	2.83	1.90
(7) Episcopalian	2.40	3.20	2.80	2.80	1.60
(8) Quaker[a]	3.70	4.00	3.70	3.00	1.70
(9) Presbyterian	2.50	3.25	2.70	2.15	1.50
(10) Other Protestant	2.61	4.10	3.84	3.28	2.18

[a] $N = 3$
[b] $N = 1$

In Table 16 are seen the scores on five scales for the members of different denominations. The Catholic, Jewish, Quaker, and "Other" groups are included. But because they contain few people, their scores are not to be given much weight. The general drift of the findings is as follows:

1. Presbyterians tend sometimes to have more favorable attitudes than members of other denominations, but not strikingly so. They are followed in order by Episcopalians, Methodists, Baptists, and "non-affiliated."

2. This pattern does not persist throughout the five scales. The various denominations change their rank order positions on different scales.

3. The size of the differences is clearly insignificant in most of the cases. No further analysis seems called for.

VI. Religiosity

TABLE 17
Mean Scale Scores for Different Religiosity Groups

Church Attendance	I *Image* (0–4)	II *Ideology* (0–6)	III *Sentiment* (0–6)	IV *General Action* (0–6)	V *Specific Action* (0–4)
(1) Never	2.81	4.05	3.36	3.0	2.22
(2) Less than once a month	2.92	4.41	3.85	3.48	2.02
(3) More than once a month, less than once a week	2.91	4.25	3.85	3.34	2.09
(4) Once a week or more	2.52	3.77	3.39	2.77	2.00

Eleven Factors Which Influence Attitudes

TABLE 18
Tests of Differences Between Mean Scores of Religiosity Groups

Scale	Groups Compared	dm	t	p <
I. Image (0–4)	1 , 2	0.11	—	n.s.
	1 , 3	0.10	—	n.s.
	1 , 4	0.29	—	n.s.
	2 , 3	0.01	—	n.s.
	2 , 4	0.40	1.62	n.s.
	3 , 4	0.39	—	n.s.
II. Ideology (0–6)	1 , 2	0.36	—	n.s.
	1 , 3	0.20	—	n.s.
	1 , 4	0.28	—	n.s.
	2 , 3	0.16	—	n.s.
	2 , 4	0.64	2.17	.02
	3 , 4	0.48	1.51	n.s.
III. Sentiment (0–6)	1 , 2	0.49	—	n.s.
	1 , 3	0.49	1.05	n.s.
	1 , 4	0.03	—	n.s.
	2 , 3	0.00	—	n.s.
	2 , 4	0.46	—	n.s.
	3 , 4	0.46	—	n.s.
IV. General Action (0–6)	1 , 2	0.48	—	n.s.
	1 , 3	0.34	—	n.s.
	1 , 4	0.23	—	n.s.
	2 , 3	0.14	—	n.s.
	2 , 4	0.71	1.96	.05
	3 , 4	0.57	1.59	n.s.
V. Specific Action (0–4)	1 , 2	0.20	—	n.s.
	1 , 3	0.13	—	n.s.
	1 , 4	0.22	.75	n.s.
	2 , 3	0.07	—	n.s.
	2 , 4	0.02	—	n.s.
	3 , 4	0.09	—	n.s.

Eleven Factors Which Influence Attitudes

The primary concern here was with frequency of attendance at church. This may not satisfy a fuller conception of religiosity, but it is at least a minimal indicator.

Tables 17 and 18 give us the results, as follows:

1. The only persisting fact in the pattern of scoring is the generally more favorable attitude of the group which goes to church once a week or more. Otherwise, church attendance seems to matter little. For instance, the score on School Desegregation of the group which goes to church less than once a month is virtually identical with that of the group which goes once a week or more. Those who go to church more than once a month but less than once a week are more unfavorable in their attitudes than either of these two groups.

2. On all but the School Desegregation scale, those who never attend church and those who most frequently attend have the most favorable attitudes.

3. Out of thirty sets of differences, only two prove statistically significant. This is less than chance expectation.

There is perfectly good ground for rejecting the factor of church attendance. But here we shall deviate from our normal pattern. For there is such widespread belief that church attendance is an important factor in the shaping of attitudes in intergroup relations that we are inclined to include this factor for at least some further examination. It is possible that there are some differences which will show up when we examine the impact of church attendance in combination with other factors.

Eleven Factors Which Influence Attitudes

VII. Occupation

TABLE 19
Mean Scale Scores for Different Occupational Groups

Occupation		I Image (0–4)	II Ideology (0–6)	III Senti- ment (0–6)	IV General Action (0–6)	V Specific Action (0–4)
(1) Professional, tech- nical, etc.	$\overline{X} =$ $\sigma =$	2.15 1.80	2.62 2.15	1.81 2.05	1.63 2.27	1.18 1.23
(2) Managers, officials proprietors, etc.	$\overline{X} =$ $\sigma =$	2.63 1.57	3.28 2.30	3.14 2.16	2.78 2.14	1.84 1.32
(3) Clerical, sales, etc.	$\overline{X} =$ $\sigma =$	2.69 2.93	3.66 2.04	3.09 2.57	2.11 2.31	1.91 1.03
(4) Craftsmen, fore- men, etc.	$\overline{X} =$ $\sigma =$	2.93 1.35	4.43 1.75	3.88 2.16	3.51 2.16	2.14 1.33
(5) Farmers	$\overline{X} =$ $\sigma =$	3.27 1.36	4.77 1.48	4.41 1.94	3.95 2.28	2.86 1.13
(6) Operatives, farm laborers, service workers, laborers, etc.	$\overline{X} =$ $\sigma =$	2.76 1.49	4.66 1.66	4.15 2.02	3.51 2.34	2.30 1.41

Eleven Factors Which Influence Attitudes

TABLE 20
Tests of Differences Between Mean Scores of Occupational Groups

Scale	Groups Compared	dm	t	p <
I. Image (0–4)	1 , 2	0.48	—	n.s.
	1 , 3	0.54	—	n.s.
	1 , 4	0.78	2.01	.05
	1 , 5	1.12	2.48	.02
	1 , 6	0.61	—	n.s.
	2 , 3	0.06	—	n.s.
	2 , 4	0.30	—	n.s.
	2 , 5	0.64	1.77	.1
	2 , 6	0.13	—	n.s.
	3 , 4	0.24	—	n.s.
	3 , 5	0.58	—	n.s.
	3 , 6	0.07	—	n.s.
	4 , 5	0.34	—	n.s.
	4 , 6	0.17	—	n.s.
	5 , 6	0.52	—	n.s.
II. Ideology (0–6)	1 , 2	0.66	—	n.s.
	1 , 3	1.04	1.89	.1
	1 , 4	1.81	3.83	.001
	1 , 5	2.15	4.14	.001
	1 , 6	2.04	4.58	.001
	2 , 3	0.38	—	n.s.
	2 , 4	1.15	2.88	.01
	2 , 5	1.49	3.28	.01
	2 , 6	1.34	3.76	.001
	3 , 4	0.77	1.80	.1
	3 , 5	1.11	2.32	.05
	3 , 6	1.01	2.52	.02
	4 , 5	0.34	—	n.s.
	4 , 6	0.23	—	n.s.
	5 , 6	0.11	—	n.s.
III. Sentiment (0–6)	1 , 2	1.32	2.66	.01
	1 , 3	1.28	2.12	.05
	1 , 4	2.06	4.22	.001
	1 , 5	2.69	4.71	.001
	1 , 6	2.33	5.21	.01
	2 , 3	0.04	—	n.s.
	2 , 4	0.74	1.77	.1

TABLE 20, continued

Scale	Groups Compared	dm	t	p <
	2 , 5	1.27	2.48	.02
	2 , 6	1.01	2.75	.01
	3 , 4	0.78	—	n.s.
	3 , 5	1.32	2.14	.05
	3 , 6	1.05	2.10	.05
	4 , 5	0.63	—	n.s.
	4 , 6	0.27	—	n.s.
	5 , 6	0.26	—	n.s.
IV. General Action (0–6)	1 , 2	1.16	2.18	.05
	1 , 3	0.48	—	n.s.
	1 , 4	1.88	3.60	.001
	1 , 5	2.32	3.56	.001
	1 , 6	1.87	3.77	.001
	2 , 3	0.67	—	n.s.
	2 , 4	0.72	1.75	.1
	2 , 5	1.17	2.05	.05
	2 , 6	0.72	1.83	.1
	3 , 4	1.39	2.80	.01
	3 , 5	1.84	2.91	.01
	3 , 6	1.39	2.95	.01
	4 , 5	0.45	—	n.s.
	4 , 6	0.00	—	n.s.
	5 , 6	0.45	—	n.s.
V. Specific Action (0–4)	1 , 2	0.66	2.19	.05
	1 , 3	0.72	2.41	.02
	1 , 4	0.97	3.28	.01
	1 , 5	1.68	4.97	.001
	1 , 6	0.12	—	n.s.
	2 , 3	0.06	—	n.s.
	2 , 4	0.29	—	n.s.
	2 , 5	1.02	3.36	.01
	2 , 6	0.46	1.96	.05
	3 , 4	0.23	—	n.s.
	3 , 5	0.86	2.83	.01
	3 , 6	0.39	—	n.s.
	4 , 5	0.72	2.42	.02
	4 , 6	0.08	—	n.s.
	5 , 6	0.56	1.98	.05

Eleven Factors Which Influence Attitudes

Data on occupational groups was originally analyzed in terms of eleven occupations (see Appendix Table A-4). For purposes of convenience, these eleven groups are now condensed into six, as seen in Table 19. These six categories are arranged in an order which is assumed to represent an order of prestige. This assumption is justified to the extent that the skill requirements and the average income of these categories also fall into about this order.

The findings given us by Tables 19 and 20 are as follows:

1. With the exception of Group 5, Farmers, the higher the occupational category, the more favorable the attitude toward the Negro.

2. Out of ninety differences, thirty-eight are significant. The majority of these significant differences occur between some white-collar or high-status group (categories 1, 2, and 3) and some blue-collar or low-status group (categories 4, 5, and 6). Almost never do two white-collar groups or two blue-collar groups differ significantly from each other. This suggests the feasibility of condensing the occupational ladder even further, so that we compare all white-collar or high-status occupations, taken together, with all blue-collar or low-status occupations considered as a unit.

TABLE 21
Mean Scale Scores for Different Status Groups

Group	I Image (0–4)	II Ideology (0–6)	III Sentiment (0–6)	IV General Action (0–6)	V Specific Action (0–4)
High Status	2.66	3.62	3.12	2.70	1.68
Low Status	2.88	4.71	4.24	3.59	2.44

TABLE 22
Tests of Differences Between Mean Scores of Status Groups

Group		I Image	II Ideology	III Sentiment	IV General Action	V Specific Action
High Status *vs.* Low Status	$p =$	n.s.	.001	.001	.001	.001

Eleven Factors Which Influence Attitudes

The comparison of scores between high and low status occupations is shown in Tables 21 and 22. These comparisons tell us:

1. The high-status group has a consistently more favorable attitude toward the Negro.

2. All the differences, except those on the Image scale, are statistically significant.

Occupational status emerges clearly as an important factor, deserving further analysis.

VIII. Occupational Mobility

TABLE 23
Mean Scale Scores for Different Mobility Groups

Mobility Group	I Image (0–4)	II Ideology (0–6)	III Sentiment (0–6)	IV General Action (0–6)	V Specific Action (0–4)
High Stationary	2.55	3.41	2.95	2.66	1.65
Upward Mobile	2.80	3.88	3.31	2.75	1.98
Low Stationary	2.95	4.82	4.19	3.69	2.45
Downward Mobile	2.64	4.35	4.39	3.28	2.39

TABLE 24
Tests of Differences Between Mean Scores of Mobility Groups

Mobility Group	I Image	II Ideology	III Sentiment	IV General Action	V Specific Action
High Stationaries vs. Upward Mobiles	n.s.	n.s.	n.s.	n.s.	n.s.
High Stationaries vs. Low Stationaries	n.s.	.001	.001	.01	.01
High Stationaries vs. Downward Mobiles	n.s.	.05	.01	n.s.	.02
Upward Mobiles vs. Low Stationaries	n.s.	.001	.02	.01	.05
Upward Mobiles vs. Downward Mobiles	n.s.	n.s.	.05	n.s.	n.s.
Low Stationaries vs. Downward Mobiles	n.s.	n.s.	n.s.	n.s.	n.s.

Mobility is defined simply here as changed in occupational position from father to son. The following four groups were constructed:

(1) Blue-collar respondents of white-collar fathers = Downward Mobiles

(2) Blue-collar respondents of blue-collar fathers = Low Stationaries

(3) White-collar respondents of white-collar fathers = High Stationaries

(4) White-collar respondents of blue-collar fathers = Upward Mobiles

Once the sample was divided in this fashion, mean scores on five scales were calculated for these four groups. Tables 23 and 24 show those scores and the results of tests of significance of difference among them.

The major findings are as follows:

1. No pattern of differences is sufficiently consistent and clear to permit a firm distinction between mobility and stability as factors related to attitudes.

2. However, a large number of the differences are significant.

3. All of the significant differences occur in comparisons of white-collar group, whether mobile or stable, with a blue-collar group, whether mobile or stable. For instance, four of the five differences between High and Low Stationaries are significant. So are three out of five differences between High Stationaries and Downward Mobiles, and four out of five between Upward Mobiles and Low Stationaries.

In short, all significant differences appear between groups on different status levels, whether mobile or not. This suggests the predominance of status over mobility.

To test out this notion, we combine Upward and Downward Mobiles into a group called the Mobiles, and then combine High and Low Stationaries into another group called Stationaries. Average scores are then calculated for these two groups. These scores are shown in Table 25.

Eleven Factors Which Influence Attitudes

TABLE 25
Mean Scale Scores for Mobiles and Stationaries

Mobility Group	I Image (0–4)	II Ideology (0–6)	III Sentiment (0–6)	IV General Action (0–6)	V Specific Action (0–4)
Mobile group	2.76	4.02	3.62	2.90	2.10
Stationary group	2.75	4.09	3.56	3.16	2.04

The findings from these comparisons are:

1. There are no noteworthy directions or sizes of difference.

2. None of the differences even approaches statistical significance.

From these findings we can conclude that we can dispense with the factor of occupational mobility and concentrate upon occupational status for more information about the significance of occupation.

Here again, however, we will follow a guide other than our own analysis. For, as with religiosity, mobility is a very frequent object of research in studies of attitudes. We shall therefore spend some time looking further into this factor.

IX. Residence

TABLE 26
Mean Scale Scores for Different Residence Groups

Residence Group		I Image (0–4)	II Ideology (0–6)	III Sentiment (0–6)	IV General Action (0–6)	V Specific Action (0–4)
(1) Rural, less	$\overline{X} =$	2.09	4.27	3.54	3.81	2.63
than 5 years	$\sigma =$	1.78	2.15	2.69	2.75	1.07
(2) Rural, more	$\overline{X} =$	2.80	4.45	3.89	3.34	2.33
than 5 years	$\sigma =$	1.61	1.82	2.18	2.66	1.35
(3) Urban, less	$\overline{X} =$	2.33	3.84	3.48	2.82	1.94
than 5 years	$\sigma =$	1.59	2.22	2.52	2.40	1.42
(4) Urban, more	$\overline{X} =$	2.86	3.86	3.44	2.95	1.89
than 5 years	$\sigma =$	1.44	2.03	2.24	2.24	1.38

Eleven Factors Which Influence Attitudes

TABLE 27
Tests of Differences Between Scores of Residence Groups

Scale	Groups Compared	dm	t	p <
I. Image (0–4)	1 , 2	0.71	—	n.s.
	1 , 3	0.24	—	n.s.
	1 , 4	0.77	1.40	n.s.
	2 , 3	0.47	1.55	n.s.
	2 , 4	0.06	—	n.s.
	3 , 4	0.53	1.89	.1
II. Ideology (0–6)	1 , 2	0.18	—	n.s.
	1 , 3	0.43	—	n.s.
	1 , 4	0.41	—	n.s.
	2 , 3	0.61	1.52	n.s.
	2 , 4	0.59	2.33	.02
	3 , 4	0.02	—	n.s.
III. Sentiment (0–6)	1 , 2	0.35	—	n.s.
	1 , 3	0.06	—	n.s.
	1 , 4	0.10	—	n.s.
	2 , 3	0.41	0.88	n.s.
	2 , 4	0.45	1.54	n.s.
	3 , 4	0.04	—	n.s.
IV. General Action (0–6)	1 , 2	0.47	0.54	n.s.
	1 , 3	0.99	1.08	n.s.
	1 , 4	0.86	1.00	n.s.
	2 , 3	0.52	1.09	n.s.
	2 , 4	0.39	1.22	n.s.
	3 , 4	0.13	—	n.s.
V. Specific Action (0–4)	1 , 2	0.30	—	n.s.
	1 , 3	0.69	1.74	.1
	1 , 4	0.74	2.26	.01
	2 , 3	0.39	1.50	n.s.
	2 , 4	0.44	2.50	.02
	3 , 4	0.05	—	n.s.

Eleven Factors Which Influence Attitudes

In analyzing the possible significance of residence, two questions are being asked: (1) Does the fact of *present* residence in a rural or urban area matter insofar as attitudes toward Negroes are concerned? (2) Does the *length* of residence in either of these areas matter?

If rural and urban residence are significant, they should be significant proportionate to the amount of time the person has lived in an area. For the longer the term of residence, the greater the likelihood that a person will show the influence of sharing the patterns of thought and life of his area.

With these considerations in mind, the sample was divided into four groups, as follows:

(1) Rural-recent:—resident in rural area less than five years
(2) Rural-stable:—resident in rural area five years or more
(3) Urban-recent:—resident in urban area less than five years
(4) Urban-stable:—resident in urban area five years or more

The comparisons of scores and tests of differences for these four groups are shown in Tables 26 and 27.

The results are:

1. The groups are very variable in their attitudes. The Urban Stable has the most unfavorable Image of the Negro but the greatest readiness for desegregation of the schools. By contrast, the Rural Recent has the most favorable Image but the greatest resistance to school desegregation.

2. Out of thirty tests of difference, only five prove significant.

3. If stability or recency of residence is ignored, and the fact of urban or rural location alone is focussed upon, some patterns emerge. The rural group, taken collectively, is consistently more unfavorable in its attitudes toward Negroes.

It seems clear, then, that the fact of residence ought to be taken into account for possible further implications.

X. *Industrial Exposure*

TABLE 28
Mean Scale Scores of Different Industrial Exposure Groups

Industrial Exposure Group	I Image (0–4)	II Ideology (0–6)	III Senti- ment (0–6)	IV General Action (0–6)	V Specific Action (0–4)
(1) Wages & salaries 51 or more employees manufacturing	2.61	4.22	3.46	2.98	1.95
(2) Wages & salaries 51 or more employees non-manufacturing	3.15	3.90	3.53	2.81	1.90
(3) Wages & salaries 31–50 employees Manufacturing	2.50	4.33	4.00	3.16	1.86
(4) Wages & salaries 31–50 employees Non-manufacturing	2.50	4.00	3.20	3.10	1.90
(5) Wages & salaries 1–30 employees Manufacturing	2.73	4.00	3.46	3.33	2.20
(6) Wages & salaries 1–30 employees Non-manufacturing	2.83	3.82	3.65	3.02	2.04
(7) Self-employed[a] 51 or more employees Manufacturing	4.00	4.00	4.66	2.33	2.66
(8) Self-employed 51 or more employees Non-manufacturing	2.25	2.75	3.25	2.00	1.75
(9) Self-employed 31–50 employees Manufacturing	—	—	—	—	—

TABLE 28, continued

Industrial Exposure Group	I Image (0–4)	II Ideology (0–6)	III Senti- ment (0–6)	IV General Action (0–6)	V Specific Action (0–4)
(10) Self-employed[b] 31–50 employees Non-manufacturing	2.00	5.00	2.00	0.50	1.00
(11) Self-employed 1–30 employees Manufacturing	1.77	4.66	4.66	3.66	1.88
(12) Self-employed 1–30 employees Non-manufacturing	2.84	3.89	3.61	3.15	2.20

[a] $N = 3$
[b] $N = 2$

In the original conception of the study, it was considered highly likely that exposure to the urban industrial environment would be significantly related to attitudes toward Negroes and desegregation. In an effort to distill out major components of the exposure to an urban industrial environment, the following three distinctions seemed valuable:

(a) self-employed *vs.* working for salaries or wages
(b) employed in large plant (50 or more employees) *vs.* small plant
(c) employed in manufacturing *vs.* non-manufacturing plant or office

There are twelve possible combinations of these three elements, and these then give us twelve groups, for whom we calculate average scores. The results are shown in Table 28. This table tells us:

1. There is not a single consistent trend in either the size of differences or the groups between whom differences exist.

2. The only groups between whom differences seem significant have too few people to give credibility to an "average" for the group.

3. The groups with enough members to justify calculating

and comparing average scores are 1, 2, 4, 6, and 12. None of the differences between the mean scores of these groups is significant.

It may be concluded that there is little point in examining the factor of industrial exposure any further.

XI. *Number of Children*

TABLE 29
Mean Scores on Scale V For Different "Children" Groups

Number of Children	Scale V Specific Action (0–4)
0	2.31
1	2.17
2	1.89
3	1.67
4 or more	2.54

TABLE 30
Tests of Differences Between Scores of "Children" Groups

Scale	Groups Compared	dm	t	p <
V. Specific Action (0–4)	0 , 1	0.14	—	n.s.
	0 , 2	0.42	1.81	.1
	0 , 3	0.64	2.33	.02
	0 , 4	0.23	0.77	n.s.
	1 , 2	0.28	1.26	n.s.
	1 , 3	0.50	1.89	.1
	1 , 4	0.37	1.28	n.s.
	2 , 3	0.22	—	n.s.
	2 , 4	0.50	2.41	.02
	3 , 4	0.87	2.82	.01

Our attention was drawn to the possible importance of this factor on the common sense grounds that Southerners with children in schools ought to be far more worried about desegregation than those who do not have children in school. Originally we also thought that, by common traditional understanding, parents of girls ought to be more resistant to desegregation than parents of boys.

Analysis showed that neither the sex of the child nor the fact of being in or out of school mattered very much. What does seem to matter—at least on the scale of school de-segregation—is the sheer number of children. In Tables 29 and 30 are seen the means and tests of difference between mean scores on Scale V (School Desegregation) for groups of respondents set off from each other by their different numbers of children.

The results of these comparisons and tests are quite curious:

1. Those with no children and those with four or more are most resistant to desegregation.

2. Starting with no children and going up through three children, the finding is that the larger the number of children, the less the resistance to desegregation.

3. Five out of ten possible differences are statistically significant. Two of these involve the no children group, and two the group with four or more children.

Childlessness and large numbers of children (four or more) seem to be related positively to resistance to desegregation. Why?

The first assumption is that there are some significant differences in such things as education, occupation and income, which we now know make a difference. This is a good assumption, it turns out, for the four or more child group but a very bad one for the 0-child group.

The group with four or more children show the following characteristics:

(a) Their average education is significantly lower than any of the other children groups. Over 70 per cent have gone to school eight years or less; only three persons (9%) have had any college education.
In no other group are there more than 40 per cent who have only eight years of school or less. In no other group is the number of college educated less than 21 per cent.

(b) Low average income and a high percentage of blue-collar members also distinguish this group from the others.

But the group with no children cannot be set off from those with 1, 2, or 3 children in the same way. Quite to the contrary. Their average educational, income, and occupational characteristics compare favorably with those whose attitudes toward desegregation are considerably more favorable.

The clear indication is that we must control for number of children in one's family when we engage in more detailed analysis of our major factors. This can be accomplished by distinguishing three groups: (1) those with no children; (2) those with 1, 2, or 3 children taken collectively; and (3) those with four or more children.

Summary

We may now ask ourselves what guidance we have gotten from this brief look at a number of variables whose possible relevance for differences in attitudes toward Negroes and desegregation we have considered.

We can dismiss as of dubious significance the factors of age, mobility as measured by changes in occupational status, industrial exposure, residential stability and recency, most of the differences in frequency or infrequency in church attendance, and denominational affiliation.

The obviously most relevant variables are education, occupational status, exposure to the mass media, and income.

The two variables which were suggestive though not strongly so are, number of children and rural-urban residence.

We can now make some more reasonable decisions about the factors which we shall analyze further in detail. It is clear that we must consider at length: education, occupation, and exposure to the mass media. Income is also obviously a strong variable. But since we shall examine both education and occupation, with which income is so closely related, we can take income into account by using it only as a control variable. Similarly, we shall use as control variables the number of children in the family, the fact of rural or urban residence and the frequency of church attendance. Some attention will also be paid to mobility, for the reasons previously given.

This now gives us the bulk of the design of the rest of our book. In the next chapter we will look at education. This will be followed by an examination of the significance of exposure to the mass media. This in turn will be followed by an analysis of occupational status and mobility as they relate to attitudes toward the Negro.

For each of these three major treatments we will also use our control variables as ways of testing out the extent to which the differences we find in attitudes between educational, occupational, and mass-media-exposure groups may be modified by holding constant other factors which we have found to be of some relevance.[1]

In general, we can now say that the Image of the Negro becomes more favorable and the readiness for desegregation of the schools becomes relatively greater as the following factors are increased: (1) education (numbers of years of school completed); (2) occupational status (blue-collar *vs.* white-collar); and, (3) exposure to the mass media (exposure to only one or two media several times a week *vs.* exposure to three or four media several times a week).

We ought also now to expect the Image of the Negro to be somewhat more favorable and the readiness for desegregation to be more pronounced among urban as against rural residence. The data also suggest that at least among the highly religious group, those who go to church once a week or more, there will be a higher percentage of persons who have a favorable Image of the Negro and a greater readiness to desegregate the schools. Finally, the data suggest that the more children one has, up to and including three children, the more favorable the Image of the Negro and the greater the readiness for the desegregation of the schools.

These findings help us now to set our expectations with regard to the way in which each of these factors interacts with the others. For instance, if the more education one has, the greater is one's readiness for desegregation, and if, similarly, the more income the greater the readiness for desegregation, then, the differences between educational groups ought

[1] We have done partial analyses of the scoring patterns on each of these secondary variables with the others held constant, in turn. These will be found in Appendices G–L. Some of these analyses are more complete than others because of certain discrepancies in the data, especially on the tallies of those earning over $5000.00.

81

to be reduced when we hold income constant. The same general expectations will hold for any two variables which produce differences in the same direction. All our variables are scored in such a way that the more one has of them, the more favorable is the Image of the Negro, and the greater is the readiness for desegregation. Therefore, when we hold any one of them constant, we ought to expect a reduction of the differences which were observed when we examined each factor alone.

In turn the data permit the generalization that *there is an obvious strong supporting interaction of high education, high occupational status, and high exposure to the mass media. This combination of factors is found in those persons who hold a more favorable Image of the Negro and are more ready for desegregation of the schools.* This is the general hypothesis of which the rest of the book is based.

CHAPTER FOUR

EDUCATION AND ATTITUDES TOWARD DESEGREGATION

BETWEEN the private feelings and public actions of any individual there is almost always a noticeable disparity. This difference is produced by factors which shape the extent and ways in which the private feelings are publicly expressed. Almost never is the private feeling fully and immediately expressed. Almost always some force, such as law, custom, conscience, superego, or community norms, urges or forces the individual to compromise. As a result, what the individual finally does in public is almost always different than what he would have done had he been able to express his private feelings without interference from himself or others.

This process of compromise has long been recognized as an unavoidable fact of social life. Sometimes such compromise is seen as a necessary evil. Sometimes it is seen as a positive good. Almost universally it is recognized as the minimum price of continuous social existence in a community.

In spite of how widely accepted such a notion has been in matters of such needs as sex, hunger, sleep, and toilet, there has been a curious reluctance to apply the idea to the relations between groups. The reluctance is expressed in the contention that one can not eliminate discrimination without first eliminating prejudice. On this assumption, it is then further argued that laws against discrimination are equally useless or meaningless.

But there is a wealth of evidence to demonstrate that legal restraints upon discrimination have proved effective, sometimes remarkably so, without any commensurate or prior reduction in prejudice. The reduction of discrimination in employment under the impact of various fair employment practice codes is perhaps the best instance in point. The evidence is clear.[1] Discrimination can be reduced without equal reduc-

[1] Some of the relevant literature on the topic of law and discrimination is: Morroe Berger, *Equality By Statute,* New York, Columbia University

tion in prejudice. Laws against discrimination can be passed and made to work.

Indeed, the evidence is so persuasive that a great deal of enthusiasm has been developed for the use of legal restraints against discrimination. This enthusiasm has been tempered, in more sober appraisals, by the realization that no matter how temporarily effective legal restraints may prove, one can not hope to develop *continuous* and *stable* traditions of non-discrimination through legal instruments alone. What seems urgently required is some change in modes of life and in social institutions which, during the breathing spell provided by law, will persuade or induce the persons involved to develop a sense of the importance of *voluntary* restraint against translation of their prejudicial feelings into discriminatory action. What is it, then, which can be blended organically into the outlook of prejudiced persons and enable them to learn and desire to check themselves and prevent themselves from acting out their prejudices in public?

Very frequently one hears it suggested that a sound knowledge of the facts about racial and ethnic differences is the vital ingredient. But we know by now that no matter how important the public spread of this knowledge may be, there is no *necessary* connection between what men know to be true or false and what they feel impelled to do. Demonstrating that things believed in are false does not ordinarily do very much to reduce the feelings behind the beliefs.

Others have suggested that prejudiced people require emotional re-education, probably deep psychological therapy. But this notion is either false, in the sense that persons with prejudice are not demonstrably different in their mental health

Press, 1952; Louis Coleridge Kesselman, *The Social Politics of F.E.P.C.*, Chapel Hill, University of North Carolina Press, 1948; Gunnar Myrdal, *An American Dilemma,* New York, Harper and Bros., 1944; Louis Ruchames, *Race, Jobs, and Politics–The Story of F.E.P.C.*, New York, Columbia University Press, 1953; B. R. Brazeal, "The Present Status and Programs of Fair Employment Practices Commissions–Federal, State, and Municipal," *Journal of Negro Education,* 20, 378–397 (Summer 1951); New York State Commission Against Discrimination, *Article One,* 1955.

from those with less or no prejudice (if there be any such); or, the notion is unworkable as a basis for social policy. In the first place, prejudiced people could not be expected to submit voluntarily to psychotherapy. Secondly, the public budget will not bear the cost of such re-education and therapy. And the public temper and the national welfare cannot wait upon the realization of this long-term psychiatric dream. Nor may one reasonably expect patience and cooperation from the Negroes who suffer from the system of discrimination during this long-term emotional re-educational scheme.

We are therefore led to ask what other factors might be absorbed by prejudiced persons which would help counterbalance the prejudicial impulses toward discrimination. In this chapter, we look at one strong possibility.

The factor is that of formal education. We are led to this factor because the research literature of psychology, social psychology, and sociology is rich with the suggestion that a whole host of attitudes tend to shift under the impact of formal education.

The dynamics of this shift are not clearly understood. Nor is there any certain way of assuring oneself that these shifted emphases are stable. Nevertheless, there is considerable evidence that formal education does effectively help relate the private world of the individual to models of public behavior which a community can tolerate.

In the research literature are numerous studies which show that as formal education increases, there tend to occur noticeable shifts from:

(a) nationalism to internationalism, in political point of view;
(b) conservatism to liberalism, in general social philosophy;
(c) common sense to science, as acceptable evidence;
(d) punishment to reform, in penological theory;
(e) violence and direct action to law, as agents of policy;
(f) rigidity to permissiveness, in child rearing;
(g) patriarchy to democracy, in spouse relationships;
(h) anesthesia to creativity, in patterns of recreation.

Education and Attitudes

A common feature of all the changes just listed is that they imply the development of an awareness by the individual that there are: (a) other places than his own locality; (b) other times than the immediate present; (c) other persons besides himself and his immediate primary group; and (d) other values he himself cherishes.

In brief, the individual who goes through these changes has enlarged his perspective on *time, place, person,* and *values.* This enlargement, the literature suggests, occurs somehow as a result of prolonged exposure to formal education. In other terms, it is apparently through this process of enlargement of perspective that formal education produces the changes cited.

It seems likely, moreover, that these larger perspectives develop without any necessary or matching reduction in the emotional sets against which they are posed. In sum, these are *countervailing perspectives.*

How do they work?

We suggest that they serve to restrain the individual from acting upon blind and immediate impulse in search of immediate gratification for a limited number of values.

They urge upon him a certain greater caution and deliberateness, and the importance of keeping an eye on the long as well as the short run of events. The psychic bookkeeping of such an individual is thus rendered more complex and more balanced. A greater number and variety of alternative values are considered.

Under the guidance of these perspectives, the individual becomes oriented to the needs and wishes of others, and to the prevailing mores in communities other than his own. In turn, there is an increase in the range of reference groups which will be taken into account in his plans of action. In short, these countervailing perspectives, developed during the course of formal education, help produce an increasingly mature and socially responsible individual.

In this chapter we examine the extent to which formal education, through the mediation of countervailing perspectives, appears to restrain the translation of prejudice into discrimination by the members of our sample.

Education and Attitudes

To test these ideas, the sample of 287 was divided into three educational groups: (1) grammar school (1–8 years); (2) high school (9–12 years); and (3) college (13 or more years).

Table 31 shows the number of people in each of these groups, the per cent of the total sample which this number constitutes, and the mean number of years of school completed by each of the groups.

TABLE 31
Education

Years of School Completed	Number	Per Cent of Sample	Mean Years of School Completed	Standard Deviation
I. 1–8	103	35.88	6.22	1.66
II. 9–12	105	36.58	10.69	1.14
III. 13 or more	71	24.73	15.36	2.13

Table 32 lists the mean scores for each of the three groups on each of the five scales we used to measure attitudes toward Negroes and School Desegregation.

TABLE 32
Mean Scale Scores for Different Educational Groups

Education Group		I Image (0–4)	II Ideology (0–6)	III Sentiment (0–6)	IV General Action (0–6)	V Specific Action (0–4)
1–8 years	$\overline{X} =$	2.82	4.73	4.09	3.50	2.39
	$\sigma =$	1.56	1.56	2.07	2.22	2.40
9–12 years	$\overline{X} =$	2.79	4.17	3.69	3.04	2.08
	$\sigma =$	1.53	1.85	2.26	2.49	1.33
13 or more years	$\overline{X} =$	2.57	3.01	2.78	2.45	1.75
	$\sigma =$	1.61	2.38	1.83	2.23	1.28

Certain problems of interpretation are raised here by the fact that the scales differ in their total ranges. Scales I and V range from 0–4 and Scales II, III, and IV range from 0–6.

Education and Attitudes

One way to avoid these problems is to express the means in terms of the percentage point of the total range of each of the scales at which the means fall. In Table 33 the converted mean scores are presented.

TABLE 33

Means of Three Educational Groups on Five Scales
Expressed as Fractions of Their Ranges[a]

Education Group	I Image (0–4)	II Ideology (0–6)	III Sentiment (0–6)	IV General Action (0–6)	V Specific Action (0–4)
1–8 years	56.40	67.57	58.43	50.00	47.80
9–12 years	55.80	59.97	52.71	43.43	41.60
13 or more years	51.40	42.99	39.71	35.00	35.00

[a] E.g., the mean for the 1–8 group on Scale I is actually 2.82, which is 56.40 of the distance from 0–4, where this is counted as a 5-point range. The mean for the same group on Scale II is 4.73, which is 67.57 of the distance between 0 and 6, where this is counted as a 7-point range.

With these converted scores, it is now possible to see certain relationships more clearly.

The following findings stand out:

1. On all the scales, the mean scores decline as formal education increases. That is, the higher the formal education, the more favorable the attitude toward desegregation.

2. For all three educational groups, the mean scores tend to decline as one goes from Scales II through V. The sole exception is the college group, whose percentage score on Scale V is the same as its score on Scale IV.

3. The relative position of the score on the Image of the Negro is different in all three groups. For the grammar school group it is third most unfavorable among its five scores; for the high school group it is second; and for the college group it is first. But the same assertion must obviously also be made about the relative position of the scores on the other scales. Thus, we see the following rank orders expressed in terms of descending order of resistance to desegregation (Table 34).

Education and Attitudes

TABLE 34
Rank Order of Unfavorable Attitudes Toward Negroes for Three Educational Groups on Five Scales

Rank Order of Scale Scores	Education Group		
	(I) 1–8 *years*	(II) 9–12 *years*	(III) 13 *or more years*
1. (Unfavorable)	Ideology	Ideology	Image
2.	Sentiment	Image	Ideology
3.	Image	Sentiment	Sentiment
4.	General Action	General Action	General Action
5. (Favorable)	Specific Action	Specific Action	Specific Action

If these rank orders reflect the degrees of resistance to desegregation, *then the deepest resistances are located in different aspects for each of the three groups, but the greatest permissiveness occurs at the same places for each of the groups, i.e., on General and Specific Action.*

This interpretation must be enriched, if possible, by some notion regarding the logical sequence of these dimensions of attitudes of the White to the Negro.

The scales are numbered sequentially to express such a notion. That is, Image (Scale I) seems naturally to precede all other dimensions. Ideology of social relations (Scale II), which bases itself in part upon this Image, is next. Then, when respondents are asked to express their Sentiments (Scale III) in hypothetical situations of contact, this seems to evoke their prior Image of the Negro and their Ideology of social relationships as well, along with such other matters as may now enter into their calculations. The sequence then continues with the introduction of General Action Set (Scale IV), followed, finally, by the Specific Action Set (Scale V).

Only in terms of the relationship among the last two items are we seriously doubtful about this sequence. For the General Action Set may be as much an artifact of the procedure of analysis as something verifiable about the attitudes of the respondents. Yet in the administrative organization of the psyche, a *generalized* predisposition to action is probably prior to *specific* action tendencies.

On the assumption that the logical sequence is as postulated, our interpretation of the findings of Tables 33 and 34 would now state the following things:

1. The grammar school group does not have a substantially more unfavorable Image of the Negro than the other groups. But when deciding upon the type of social relations it would consider desirable, this group appears to add to its Image a host of other factors which reinforce the unfavorable Image, so that the idea of the Negro as a social partner is strenuously rejected. For this group the Ideology of social relations seems hardly influenced by any countervailing perspectives. Indeed, such new factors as enter deepen its resistance to desegregation.

2. The high school group expresses in its Ideology a milder version of the same process. This group, too, seems to invoke visions of unpleasant consequences of relations with Negroes. Hence, its score on Ideology also expresses a higher degree of resistance to desegregation than is apparent from its score on Image.

3. The college group stands in sharp contrast. For its rejection of the Negro declines, as we go from Image to Ideology, almost as sharply as did the scores for the grammar school group rise. This college group seems to take less account of its Image of the Negro when it considers the kinds of social relations it would ideally like to have.

In the college group, unlike the others, certain countervailing and balancing factors enter at this point (Scale II) to modify its unfavorable Image of the Negro. In its Ideology of social relations, this group seems to express an awareness of what is realistically possible, as well as what is ideally desirable. This awareness includes a consideration of the consequences and modifies the unfavorable images and ideal desires. In short, the college group does not feel as free as the others to be genuinely Ideological, that is, to indulge in some cost-free vision of an ideal situation. It is more cautious, more restrained, more aware of the actual context in which relations are had with Negroes.

Further light on these processes is shed by the information in Table 35 where we see the results of tests of significance of difference between scores of the different educational groups on the five scales.

TABLE 35

T-tests of Significance of Difference Between Mean Scores
of Three Educational Groups on Five Scales

Scale	Groups Compared	dm	t	p <
I. Image (0–4)	1 , 2	0.03	—	n.s.
	1 , 3	0.25	—	n.s.
	2 , 3	0.22	—	n.s.
II. Ideology (0–6)	1 , 2	0.56	2.40	.01
	1 , 3	1.72	5.10	.001
	2 , 3	1.16	3.41	.001
III. Sentiment (0–6)	1 , 2	0.40	1.31	n.s.
	1 , 3	1.31	4.28	.001
	2 , 3	0.91	2.83	.01
IV. General Action (0–6)	1 , 2	0.46	1.42	n.s.
	1 , 3	1.05	3.00	.01
	2 , 3	0.59	1.60	n.s.
V. Specific Action (0–4)	1 , 2	0.31	1.14	n.s.
	1 , 3	0.77	2.23	.05
	2 , 3	0.46	2.28	.05

We note first that the groups do not differ significantly from each other in their Images of the Negro. None of the differences even approaches significance. Compared to the differences between means on all the other scales, those for the scale of the Image are smallest. It is as though the entire sample were simply one relatively homogeneous group on its Image of the Negro. But on all other scales the groups show much more heterogeneity.

The greatest heterogeneity occurs on the scores for Ideology, where all three groups differ from each other significantly. Yet it will be recalled that on this scale, the 0–8 and the 9–12 groups express their greatest resistance, and the college group its second greatest degree of resistance to the Negro. In short, though, the differences among the groups are greatest, the level of scores is relatively high in unfavorableness.

In terms of the impact of education upon attitudes toward the Negro, it seemed as though advanced education is able to produce some absolute reduction of ideological resistance to desegregation, and thereby sets the groups off from each other by significant margins. This is the place at which education seems to make the greatest amount of *relative* difference.

The groups come to resemble each other most closely again in General Action Sets. Here the data show that only the grammar school and college groups differ from each other significantly. While the other differences are not totally inconsequential, they are less impressive than any comparable set of differences except for those on Scale I, the Image.

One may state then that education makes the least *relative* difference when the Image of the Negro is in question, and the second least difference when general patterns of action are called for.

In summary:

(a) The different education groups start out as relatively homogeneous in their unfavorable Images of the Negro.

(b) The scores then scatter, when Ideology is measured, so that while these groups remain generally unfavorable to Negroes, they differ significantly from each other in their degree of unfavorableness.

(c) The same trend of relatively high but differentiated scores persists through the measures of Sentiment.

(d) There is a rather sharp drop in unfavorableness for all the groups when General Action Sets are estimated. At this point, also, the scores of the groups become more like each other.

(e) Finally, the groups begin to differ distinctly, once again, when specific action plans are called for.

There is an important difference between the homogeneity on Scale I and that on Scale IV. In Scale I, the similarities occur at a relatively high level of unfavorable attitudes. In Scale V, by contrast, the similarities are at a relatively low level of resistance to desegregation. Moreover, the convergence of scores on IV is due to the movement down of the scores of the 0–8 and 9–12 groups to meet the low-level scores of the college group. For, while the college group undergoes considerable modification in its movement from Image to Ideology, it remains relatively constant from there on, as compared to the continuing drop in scores *throughout* the scales that is manifested by both the grammar and high school groups.

We may surmise then that the moderation which the college group expresses in the dimension of Ideology is not shown by the grammar and high school groups until plans of action are called for. At this point, these groups too seem to become aware of consequences and moderate their responses accordingly.

This is not to say that the college group is not also affected by the call for action. But this group seems able to *prevision* costs and consequences long before it is called upon to face them in its plan for action. *This is precisely what one ought to expect if countervailing perspectives work as we have earlier suggested.* These perspectives function as *anticipatory* modifiers of social behavior. They seem to be interposed between the prejudices expressed in Images and the other dimensions of attitudes toward the Negro, and thereby produce restraint early in the sequence of states which lead ultimately to action.

This last finding has the following major implication: The college group's ideological vision of a social system is a more reliable measure of its probable actions than the vision of the high school and grammar school groups. This is because the college group sticks to its model of a desired system more closely. *By contrast, one cannot reliably judge what lower-educated groups are likely to do by asking them how they feel about the Negro or what kind of social relations they would like.* In these aspects they seem relatively unconcerned with questions of what is concretely possible or what is likely to result from the translation of their private desires into public reality.

Countervailing perspectives thus seem to be the components of personal and social maturity. The person who is affected by them takes consequences into account in deciding upon his actions. He appears to be more rational and less impulsive than others. He takes consequences into account not only for the immediate values at stake, but also for other values he holds. He also considers other persons for whom he cares. In the most developed cases, he considers consequences for his local community and the total society with which he identifies.

Exposure to formal education thus seems to help transform a creature who acts immediately and directly upon impulse to one who tempers his actions in terms of anticipated consequences. This is the transformation from a self-centered creature to a balanced and mature citizen of a community.

We must confess ignorance of how the educational process achieves this transformation or what particular aspects of the educational content might have the most influence. But it seems that simple exposure to schooling in the South introduces balances and checks against impulsive action.

A crucial fact is that college education induces these restraints at the very earliest stages of the psychic set. Even in the college group's private vision of a desired social world, certain effective reality principles seem to be present.

This is not a case of disparate elements standing in opposition to each other, so much as a new blend of a variety of values which a person seems to feel and want. These impel the individual to consider the different private views of other members of the community. The final result is a more widely acceptable and realizable view of the world.

Another way to look at the impact of these countervailing perspectives is to think of them as giving to the persons affected by them a sense of a stake in the society. The better-educated people seem to act as if they had more at stake in the outcome of their actions. They appear to react to possible threats to the stakes they have in the system. As a consequence, they are moderate not only in the actions they are willing to take, but even in their images of an ideal system. Built into these ideological notions are a set of balanced stakes and claims upon the system.

If what we have just said is true, then we ought to find that the better-educated people differ from the others not only in their attitudes toward the Negro but in certain other manifestations of their stake in the system. They ought to be at a higher income level, and to have occupations which in general carry more prestige. This expectation is based on the most general and obvious grounds that occupation, income, and education form a kind of trinity in American social structure, so that from a knowledge of any one of them it is possible to make reasonably good predictions about the other two.

In Table 36 are two measures of the socio-economic characteristics of the three educational groups.

TABLE 36
Some Selected Characteristics of Three Educational Groups

Educational Group	Median Annual Income	Per Cent White-Collar
Grammar School (1–8 years)	$3200.00	8.6
High School (9–12 years)	4296.00	30.3
College (13 or more years)	7727.00	73.1

The table shows just what one would expect. The better educated group is more advantageously placed on the ladders of income and occupation. It enjoys a symbolically more prestigeful as well as materially more comfortable place in society. On these grounds alone, these people ought to feel more of a stake in the society, and a greater sense of responsibility to the institutions that maintain it. This sense of stake and responsibility seem to restrain these people from impulsively translating prejudiced feelings into discriminatory action, especially when the action would have those serious and deleterious consequences for the society which segregationist activities have been known to have in the past.

CHAPTER FIVE

EDUCATION AND ATTITUDES, WITH OTHER
FACTORS HELD CONSTANT

EACH of the educational groups whose attitudes were analyzed in the previous chapter obviously has other characteristics, such as an average income, and a certain per cent of blue-collar versus white-collar members. In Chapter Three eleven of these factors were analyzed in order to see which ones were most probably influential in shaping attitudes toward Negroes and desegregation, and six were selected for more detailed examination.

Now we turn to see how the different educational groups score on attitudes when we take these other influences into account. The small number of respondents in the sample forces us to analyze the interplay of education with only one of these factors at a time. First we shall examine the interaction of education and occupation; then education and income, and so on.

When we speak of the interplay of education and occupation, for example, we are really asking: Could it be that some of the differences in attitudes between educational groups are due to the influence of occupational differences? If, for instance, the college and high school groups differ significantly on their readiness for desegregation, how much of this difference can be attributed to the fact that the college group has a higher per cent of white-collar members? And how much of the difference can be ascribed to the influence of education alone?

The way we try to answer these questions is as follows:

1. Divide each of the three educational groups into two sub-groups; white-collar versus blue-collar. This gives six groups: college educated, white- and blue-collar; high school, white- and blue-collar; and grammar school, white- and blue-collar.

2. Calculate average scale scores for each of the six groups thus constituted.

3. Then compare scores of the three educational groups

within the white-collar segment, and within the blue-collar segment.

4. Match the results against those found when educational groups were compared without regard for their occupational characteristics. If the original differences between scores decrease, then occupational differences probably contribute to the differences in scores. If, however, the original differences between groups increase, then the occupational differences were probably masking the true extent of the impact of education.

In general, this is the procedure we shall follow for all six factors, with two exceptions. First, instead of taking all the findings from the analysis of education in Chapter Four, we deliberately select three whose significance seems greatest and which emerge as major findings in other analyses to follow. Second, instead of comparing scores on five scales, we focus alone on the scores on Image and School Desegregation. The former represent the fullest expression of the private world of belief. The latter are the closest approximation to a probable public action we can devise.

The three findings from the educational analysis in Chapter Four which will be resubmitted to further scrutiny are:

1. The higher the education, the more favorable the Image, but the differences between groups are not significant.

2. The higher the education, the more ready for desegregation of the Schools, and the differences between groups tend most frequently to be significant.

3. Each of the groups is more favorable to the Negro on the School Desegregation scale than on the Image scale. In reverse, the private view is more unfavorable than the probable public action would suggest.

The six factors whose possible influences on attitudes will be examined are:

1. *Occupation,* i.e., blue- versus white-collar;

2. *Income,* i.e., those who earn under $5,000.00 a year versus those who earn $5000.00 or more.

3. *Urban versus rural residence.* Simple census classification of over and under 2500 residents is used here.

4. *Religiosity.* Here we distinguish (a) those who go to

church once a month or less (low religiosity); (b) those who go more than once a month but less than once a week (medium); (c) those who go once a week or more (high).

5. *Exposure to the mass media.* The distinction here is between a group called "high exposure" because its members listen to or watch three or four media of mass communication several times a week, and a group called "low exposure" because its members are exposed to two or fewer media several times a week.

6. *Number of children.* Here we make three distinctions: those with no children; those with one to three children: those with four or more.

In Appendix D will be found the details of the statistical analysis of what happens to the differences between the scores of educational groups when we hold each of the six other factors constant in turn. In Table 37 we present a summary of that analysis.

Now we may comment briefly on this summary, with specific attention to the violated findings.

1. HOLDING OCCUPATION CONSTANT. With one inconsequential exception, holding occupation constant does not seriously alter the significance of education for attitudes toward Negroes and Desegregation. The exception is the highly unfavorable attitudes of the college educated, blue-collar group. We judge this inconsequential, or, at least, indecisive, because there are only four persons in this group, and an average score calculated for four people does not have much meaning. If one were to read meaning into this finding, one could say that a group whose educational status is so high but whose occupational standing is so relatively low ought to be expected to be rather deviant.

In summary, similarities and differences among our respondents in their occupational standings do not seem to be strong enough to change the ways in which their attitudes are effected by their educational similarities and differences.

2. HOLDING INCOME CONSTANT. The first finding has to be modified. The previously insignificant differences between the college and grammar school groups on their Image scores now prove to be significant when both groups earn over

98

Education and Attitudes: Other Factors Constant

TABLE 37

Results of Analysis of Differences among Three Educational Groups
(Grammar School vs. High School vs. College) on Two Scales
(Image and School Desegregation), Holding Constant,
in Turn, Each of Six Other Factors.

| | | | Factors Held Constant | | | |
| | 1 | 2 | 3 | 4 | 5 | 6 |
Findings	Occupation	Income	Urban-Rural Residence	Religiosity	Mass Media	Number of Children
Finding 1: The higher the education, the more favorable the Image of the Negro, but the differences between scores measuring Image are not significant.	+	+ −	+	+ −	+ −	+
Finding 2: The higher the education, the more ready for desegregation of the public schools, and the differences tend toward significance.	+	+ −	+ −	+ −	+ −	+ −
Finding 3: The scores of each group on the Scale measuring readiness for desegregation of the school are more positive than are the scores on the scale measuring Image of the Negro.	+	+	+	+	+	+

Code: + = Finding largely confirmed
− = Finding largely violated

$5,000.00 a year. This is not true for the groups which all earn under $5,000.00.

This alteration tells us that high income adds to the effects of high education. Low income, however, does not seem to detract from the influence of education, at least on Image scores.

Finding 2 also must be modified. Within the "under $5000.00 a year" group, the differences between educational groups on Scale V that were formerly significant are now reduced to insignificance. And the differences between the high-income groups are much greater than the differences between the low-income groups.

In short, the combination of high income and high education produce more striking differences in attitudes than does

99

education by itself; and, some of the differences due to education vanish when all the respondents are at a low-income level.

Income thus has variable significance with respect to the influence of education. On the dimension of Image, only high income seems to make a difference. On the dimension of School Desegregation, differences appear both at low- and high-income levels.

3. HOLDING RESIDENCE CONSTANT. Finding 2 once again is modified as place of residence is held constant. The differences between the educational groups, on their School Desegregation scores, are greater in the rural area than in the urban area. This suggests that differences in education are more consequential for attitudes in rural than in urban areas. Conceivably, also, this implies that common sharing of urban residence helps to reduce differences in attitudes between different educational groups. Exposure to the urban environment seems to matter.

Another change in findings concerns the differences between grammar and high school groups. These differences are reduced and insignificant when residence is held constant. Only the college group stands off significantly.

Could it be that the true cut-off point is the college level, and that until this level is reached, neither education by itself nor in combination with other factors can powerfully effect attitudes? Our findings come increasingly to suggest this generalization.

4. HOLDING RELIGIOSITY CONSTANT. Significant anomalies are introduced into our findings when religiosity is held constant.

1. Within the low religiosity group, the high school people have the most favorable Image of the Negro. College and grammar school respondents have virtually identical unfavorable scores. By contrast, within the same low religiosity group, the high school people are most resistant to desegregation of the schools. (What can it mean that infrequent attendance at church tends to decrease the prejudice against the Negro and increase the resistance to desegregation of schools?)

100

2. Within the medium religiosity segment, the grammar school group has the most favorable Image of the Negro.

3. Within the high religiosity segment, the findings remain relatively unaltered.

The suggestion arising out of these findings is that only within the high religiosity group can one count on educational differences persisting in their impact on attitudes. Namely, frequent church attendance is required to reinforce the effects of education.

If this were so, one ought to expect persons with little education but who are frequent church attenders to be more favorable toward Negroes than those with little education who attend church infrequently. In fact, however, this is not true. The high-religiosity, grammar school people have the second most unfavorable Image of the Negro and the second highest resistance to desegregation.

We are forced to fall back on the hypothesis that frequency of church attendance serves to produce a more favorable attitude to Negroes only among those who are also college educated. But outside the ranks of the college persons, the frequency of church attendance is very variable in its importance. This hypothesis tallies well with our finding earlier which suggested that church attendance is not seriously to be taken into account.

Once again, in summary, such factors as can set our respondents' attitudes off from each other clearly and significantly do not seem to have much effect until they have a base of college education upon which to build. In turn, the influence of college education does not make itself felt as well on its own, as when it is reinforced by such other factors as high occupation, high income, and high frequency of church attendance.

5. HOLDING EXPOSURE TO MASS MEDIA CONSTANT. Now finding 1 is violated. Within the low exposure group, the high school people have a more unfavorable Image than the grammar school people.

Finding 2 is violated by precisely the same reversal. Moreover, within the high-exposure group, the difference between the 1–8 and 9–12 segments is reduced and insignificant. Only the difference between the college and 1–8 people remains significant.

Exposure to mass media obviously has effects. The greater the exposure, in general, the more favorable the attitudes, with one notable exception, namely, the low-exposed people who are also college educated. Of all the groups, theirs has the most favorable Image of the Negro. By contrast, of all the groups, the greatest readiness for desegregation is found among the high-exposure, college educated.

The following general trends seem to emerge:

1. Low exposure to the mass media does not seriously detract from the influence of education upon attitudes, except at levels of low education.

2. High exposure to mass media definitely contributes the same favorable effects as high level education.

Once again, a college-level education seems to be required as a base on which other factors can work, and, once again, high levels of other factors can and do add to the favorable influences of college education.

6. HOLDING NUMBER OF CHILDREN CONSTANT. Only within the one-to-three-children group do the differences produced by education hold up, and here the only significant difference is between the college and grammar school segments. Not only do the previous differences become smaller, but there are some surprising reversals. For instance, in the group with four or more children, the college people are more resistant to desegregation than the high school people. And, in the no-children group, the grammar school people are more favorably disposed to desegregation than the college people.

Of all the factors, "number of children" seems to be most powerful in wiping out the influence of education, particularly when one is dealing either with those who have no children or who have four or more. (We shall have a chance later on to speculate about the possible meanings of childlessness and large families.)

Now we can state briefly what we have learned about the interplay between education and other characteristics of our groups. In general, the following things seem to be true when we measure the impact of education, while holding other variables constant:

1. The educational groups continue to remain insignificantly different from each other on their Images of the Negro.

2. The direction of differences, on Image score, namely, that the higher the education the more favorable the Image, generally persists, but is also sometimes reversed.

3. Some of the significant differences between educational groups on School Desegregation become diminished, some to the point of statistical insignificance.

4. The expected direction of differences on School Desegregation is sometimes reversed, though not frequently enough to surrender the generalization that, by and large, the more education, the more ready for desegregation of the schools.

5. Perhaps the most consistently supported finding is the disparity between the scores of any group on Scales I and V. Almost without exception, the groups always appear to be more desegregationist on Scale V than on Scale I. This bears out earlier assertions that the questions on Scale V require choices of courses of action and thereby tend to produce "more realistic" answers than are given when one asks for the Image of the Negro, where no consequences need to be considered.

6. The combinations which seem to produce the most favorable Images of the Negro and the greatest readiness for desegregation of the public schools are high education (college level) in conjunction with a high level of such other factors as occupation, income, and exposure to the mass media.

Summary

1. A number of factors, principally, education, occupation, income, and exposure to the mass media exert a positive influence on the development of favorable attitudes toward Negroes and School Desegregation.

2. None of these by itself is as strong in its influence as when it is supported by at least one other.

3. The effects of a high level of any one of the factors can

be virtually eliminated if it is found in association with a low level of any other.

4. The strongest single factor is college level education. Its effects tend to persist even under adverse circumstances.

5. College education may therefore be said to be generally required but by itself not sufficient to produce favorable attitudes toward the Negro.

6. The factors which most severely reduce the impact of high-level education are childlessness and large (four or more children) families.

7. Whatever the Image of the Negro or attitude toward desegregation, the latter tends to be more generally favorable, i.e., for desegregation, than the former. Almost invariably, the type of action the person seems willing to take to prevent desegregation is more moderate and restrained than one would have predicted from a knowledge of his Image of the Negro.

CHAPTER SIX

EXPOSURE TO MASS MEDIA AND ATTITUDES
TOWARD DESEGREGATION

IN the minds of many people in the northern sections of the United States there exists an image of the South as a single, homogeneous body of people, all of whom do about the same thing in about the same way for about the same reasons and with about the same feelings. But no region as large and diffuse as what is called the South could reasonably be expected to be homogeneous on any but the most general and abstract issues. When the matter is so specific as "race relations," even taking into account the long-standing traditions of the southern region, one must be prepared to make distinctions at least between hard core states and border states, and between the so-called Deep South and other Southern regions. For it is clear that readiness and resistance to desegregation are highly variable throughout the South.

The fact that a prevalent distinction sets so-called border states apart from others with respect to Negro-White relations and attitudes indicates a belief that nearness and exposure to northern states have influences upon attitudes. Implicit here is the idea that somehow the resistance to equality for the Negro will undergo erosion and attrition when Southerners are exposed to the feelings, beliefs, and practices of persons of the North. There is also implicit here the idea that the South is a region which stands against the rest of the nation, and not simply the North, in that it holds firmly to a set of traditions which the rest of the nation has shown greater willingness to change.

The more the traditions of any region are compared with alternative possibilities, the more likely they are to change. Ignorance of alternatives is an insulator and a guardian of tradition.[1] Such ignorance can be maintained either by isola-

---

[1] See, for instance, Wilbert E. Moore and Melvin M. Tumin, "Some Social Functions of Ignorance," *American Sociological Review*, XIV, 6, December 1949.

tion from knowledge of alternatives, or by a selective rejection of the kind of knowledge and awareness that could be effective in shaking traditional beliefs.

On these grounds one would expect that Southerners' resistance to desegregation should vary with their awareness that practices in other areas are very different. This awareness of what the rest of the nation thinks, feels and does should be very effective in increasing the readiness for desegregation, when it is accompanied by some sense of need to conduct oneself as a member of a larger society and not simply as a member of one's own local group. By contrast, those who either do not know what the rest of the nation feels, or do not care about their membership in the larger society, or neither know nor care, are likely to remain most resistant.

In our mass society, awareness of events all over the nation is brought to us almost immediately by the media of mass communication—newspapers, magazines, radio and TV. These are the four primary instruments by which regions in the United States are kept in touch with each other and with the culture of the total society. Through these impersonal media, perhaps more than through personal contact, the kind of knowledge of alternatives which can be effective in changing attitudes and actions is brought into a local area. Therefore, if Southerners differ in their exposure to mass media, there ought to be a corresponding difference in their acceptance or rejection of the traditional pattern of segregation.[2]

One circumstance could prevent the exposure to mass media from making the expected difference. This would be when and if those media become "adapted" locally so that they lose their "mass" quality and become reinforcers of local

[2] The number of variables which must be controlled before any definitive testing can be carried out, and the number of different kinds and intensities of impact which are possible, make the study of mass media, and the more general study of the "flow of influence," both fascinating and tormenting. A remarkably cogent ordering of the field and summary of findings has been achieved by Carl Hovland in his "Effects of the Mass Media of Communication," *Handbook of Social Psychology*, Vol. II, ed. by Gardner Lindzey, Cambridge, Addison-Wesley, 1954, pp. 1062–1103. It is the kind of summary which not only lists and categorizes but makes a significant contribution to the building of a theoretical structure for the field.

traditions. This could happen without the intervention of any organized editorial influences. For, as we know, people tend to see and hear what they want to see and hear.

We do not have the data required to test whether there was selective perception of the media by members of our sample. But we do have information about whether the mass media in general are distorted or biased in Southern cities. Professor Roy Carter, Jr., of the University of North Carolina, has made a study of a selected sample of newspapers from Southern states and his analysis reveals that the content of those newspapers is about evenly divided in its support and opposition to segregation. He notes:

> When content was classified by 'direction,' space allocations in the twelve Southern newspapers included in the study were as follows: Pro-integration 27 per cent, pro-gradualism 12 per cent, pro-segregation 30 per cent, neutral 31 per cent. The combined pro-integration and pro-gradualism space totals for all but one newspaper exceeded the pro-segregation total. In that one instance they equalled it . . . all material overtly favoring integration, but not immediate integration, was coded as pro-gradualism.[3]

In a region where the major traditional strain has been toward some ideal version of total segregation, the roughly 50-50 split in space allocations on segregation issues constitutes a major deviation, and the half of the newspapers who are anti-segregation or non-segregationist properly act as important stimuli to changes of the traditional pattern.[4]

---

[3] Roy E. Carter, Jr., "Segregation and the News: A Regional Content Study," *Journalism Quarterly*, Winter 1957, pp. 3–18.

[4] Relative to the state of Negro-White relations, for instance, in Chicago or New York, how effective in increasing or reinforcing sentiment for segregation is any single spectacular crime report in which the assailant is identified clearly as Negro? The local balance of readiness and resistance to desegregation, while variable by region, may be more easily and more seriously knocked off balance in the less-segregationist states than in the states more traditionally segregationist. Conversely, what would scarcely pass even for news in a northern state, much less in any way alter the balance of segregation-desegregation sentiments, might very well be a very significant piece of news and a very effective stimulus to new patterns, in the more traditionally segregationist states.

Exposure to Mass Media and Attitudes

We also have data about the mass media other than the newspapers. In our interviews, we asked about the radio listening, TV viewing, and magazine reading habits of our respondents. We wanted to know whether they were exposed to only locally-originating materials, or whether they were sharing with the rest of the United States certain society-wide news, editorial opinion, and general cultural materials.

We found that 110 out of our 287 respondents listened to radio news analysts. Of these 110, some 89, or 80.9 per cent, most often tuned in a national network program originating in a northern state.

As for TV news, 212 out of 287 respondents listened regularly to a TV news analyst. Of these 212, some 206, or over 97 per cent, most frequently tuned in a news analyst originating in a northern state.

With regard to magazines, we found that 197 out of our 287 respondents regularly read a national weekly magazine. Of these, more than 94 per cent devoted their primary magazine-reading time and attention to news and photo magazines, mostly *Time* and *Life,* and other national circulation journals with no identifiable pro-segregation bias.

As a further safeguard against the possible influence of biased media content, we compared the attitudes of those who regularly were exposed to media originating locally against those who were primarily exposed to media originating in the North or other regions. We found that the differences in attitudes are insignificant and unpatterned.

It is safe to assume, then, that the majority of the mass media materials come into the South relatively unaltered, except for those types of local adaptions which every region practices, but which are not here relevant to attitudes toward desegregation. Moreover, it seems of little moment that there are minor alterations or that some of the respondents are more exposed than others to locally originating materials. If the mass media have an influence it is probably due to the sheer exposure to news and information.

Now we can surmise as follows:

If a person shows an interest in what is going on outside his own immediate social world by exposing himself to mass media, he is likely to exhibit a more favorable set of attitudes toward Negroes, and a greater readiness for desegregation than the person who is more self-oriented and more focused upon the immediate events of his immediate locality.

To test this assertion, we asked all respondents how frequently they listened to radio and TV news analysts, and how frequently they read newspapers and magazines.

On the basis of their responses, we scored them into the following "exposure groups:" (a) those who were exposed to no media; (b) those exposed to one, and so on, until we reach the group exposed to four media. A respondent was defined as "exposed" to TV, radio or newspapers if he read or watched a "couple of times a week or more." In the case of magazines, a person was considered "exposed" if he read at least every other issue of at least one magazine containing news items.

Those who are exposed to none of the media are called the 0 group; those exposed to only one, the 1 group; and so on, to those who are called the 4 group because they are exposed to all four of the media.

For the total sample of 287 persons, the distribution of exposure types is shown in Table 38.

TABLE 38
Exposure to Mass Media

Number of Media Exposed to	Number	Per Cent
None	9	3.14
One	38	13.24
Two	89	31.01
Three	110	38.33
Four	41	14.28
TOTAL	287	100.00

We may now examine the way in which the different exposure groups score on the different aspects of readiness and resistance to desegregation.

Exposure to Mass Media and Attitudes

In Table 39 are seen the mean scores on the five scales for the five exposure groups.

TABLE 39
Mean Scores on Five Scales for Five Exposure Groups

Exposure Group		I Image (0–4)	II Ideology (0–6)	III Sentiment (0–6)	IV General Action (0–6)	V Specific Action (0–4)
0[a]	$\overline{X} =$	2.77	5.60	5.33	4.33	2.55
	$\sigma =$					
1	$\overline{X} =$	2.84	5.00	4.78	4.15	2.73
	$\sigma =$	1.48	1.35	1.75	2.18	1.15
2	$\overline{X} =$	2.80	4.01	3.64	3.08	2.23
	$\sigma =$	1.45	2.00	2.19	2.31	1.43
3	$\overline{X} =$	2.74	3.94	3.28	2.81	1.81
	$\sigma =$	1.58	2.01	1.76	2.27	1.30
4	$\overline{X} =$	2.58	3.34	2.87	2.53	1.65
	$\sigma =$	1.59	2.27	2.42	2.21	1.23

[a] The mean for the 0-group is reported here only *pro forma*. The small $N = 9$ forbids any use of this group in subsequent analysis.

The most important findings contained in the table above are as follows:

1. In each of the five scales, the higher the degree of exposure to the mass media, the more favorable the attitude. This holds true even in Scale I, Image. The differences between the means on this scale are small, but they are consistent and in the expected direction.

2. All of the means move from the segregationist toward the desegregationist end of the scale, as one goes from the idealized version of how situations ought to be handled in general (Scale II), to the more realistic situation of how one would feel if he were confronted with situations of contact (Scale III), and finally to the question of what one would do in the face of contact with the Negro (Scale IV).

3. All of the groups move about the same amount from

110

their relatively high pro-segregation scores on Ideology to the lower scores on General Action. Moreover there are no reversals. The rank order of the exposure groups remains the same on all three scales. If exposure is what makes the difference between the groups, it makes the difference in the same way through all three dimensions as measured by Scales II, III, and IV.

4. The greater the exposure to mass media, the greater the difference between the scores on School Desegregation and Image. Notice, for instance, that exposure group 1 goes from 2.84 on its Image to 2.73 on Specific Action, i.e., the schools. By comparison, exposure group 4 goes from 2.58 on its Image to 1.65 on its Specific Action. In short, the same effects noted earlier for education seem true for exposure to the mass media as well.

Finally, though the lower exposure groups do not alter their scores very sharply between Scales I and V, they do become more favorable. This conforms with the general expectation that at least some influence is exerted by the question itself when concrete action rather than some cost-free image is called for.

The interpretation of the findings so far has relied heavily on the size of the means and the direction and consistency of the changes in the sizes of the means. This interpretation ought now to be checked against the findings which emerge when we test for significance of difference between the means.

Table 40 shows the outcome of the tests of significance applied to the mean scores for each of our four exposure groups on each of the five scales.

The most significant findings shown in Table 40 are as follows:

1. Of the six comparisons of scores on Images of the Negro, only one difference, that between groups 1 and 4, is statistically significant. That is, the Image of the Negro held by the group which is exposed to only one mass medium is significantly different from that held by the group which is exposed to four of the mass media. None of the other groups differ from each other as much.

2. On each of the other four scales, at least three of the six

111

TABLE 40

Tests of Significance of Difference Between Mean Scores
of Four Exposure Groups on Five Different Scales

Scale	Groups Compared	dm	t	p <
I. Image (0–4)	1 , 2	0.04	—	n.s.
	1 , 3	0.10	0.36	n.s.
	1 , 4	0.26	2.39	.02
	2 , 3	0.06	—	n.s.
	2 , 4	0.22	0.75	n.s.
	3 , 4	0.16	—	n.s.
II. Ideology (0–6)	1 , 2	0.99	3.05	.01
	1 , 3	1.06	3.60	.001
	1 , 4	1.66	3.96	.001
	2 , 3	0.07	—	n.s.
	2 , 4	0.35	0.84	n.s.
	3 , 4	0.60	1.59	n.s.
III. Sentiment (0–6)	1 , 2	1.14	3.11	.01
	1 , 3	1.50	4.17	.001
	1 , 4	1.91	4.04	.001
	2 , 3	0.36	—	n.s.
	2 , 4	0.77	1.74	.10
	3 , 4	0.41	0.87	n.s.
IV. General Action (0–6)	1 , 2	1.07	2.49	.02
	1 , 3	1.34	3.23	.01
	1 , 4	1.62	3.28	.01
	2 , 3	0.27	—	n.s.
	2 , 4	0.55	0.65	n.s.
	3 , 4	0.28	—	n.s.
V. Specific Action (0–4)	1 , 2	0.50	2.07	.05
	1 , 3	0.92	4.08	.001
	1 , 4	1.08	4.41	.001
	2 , 3	0.42	—	n.s.
	2 , 4	0.58	2.37	.02
	3 , 4	0.16	—	n.s.

differences are significant. This suggests that the sample is relatively homogeneous in its Image of the Negro as compared to the other aspects of its attitudes toward the Negro and segregation. Here, again, it seems that when it is a question of the vision of the Negro that the White carries around in his head, the whole sample is relatively uniform.

3. On Scales II, III, IV, and V, the lowest exposure group differs significantly from the other three groups. This suggests that there is a critical point reached at exposure to two mass media a week, the achievement of which sets the person off in his attitudes from all persons with less exposure. Once this level is reached, there appears to be a definite turning to more favorable attitudes toward the Negro. But until this level is reached, the hard and fast Image of the Negro as an inferior person tends to become translated with relatively little change into an Ideology, a Sentiment, and a series of action-orientations which tend to match the Image itself.

4. The only other significant or near-significant differences occur between exposure groups 2 and 4 on Sentiment and on Specific Action.

5. Between groups 2 and 3, there are no significant differences to be found anywhere in our testing.

Here, then, is a clear-cut type of polarization between the relatively high segregationism of the lowest exposed group, on the one hand, and the relatively low segregationism of the three other exposure groups. The fact that *some* of the differences between groups 2 and 4 are significant indicates that we are probably right in thinking of the exposure to the mass media as a *continuous* variable. That is, the more the exposure to the mass media, the greater the readiness for desegregation.

If we now combine the observations derived from Tables II and III, the following generalizations can be made:

1. Increases in exposure to mass media are associated with small but consistent increases in readiness for desegregation.

2. These small differences become larger and reach statistical significance when the extremely low exposure group is compared with all other exposure groups.

3. There are no significant variations on these general themes. No reversals of any importance are encountered.[5]

---

[5] In this regard, see the well-founded doubts regarding the impact on attitudes of a variety of "informational" material which are expressed by Simon Marcson in his, "Research on Informational, Educational, and Propaganda Effects on Attitude Change," *Phylon*, Vol. 17, 1956, pp. 119–128.

The word "relatively" must be very heavily stressed. If we look back at Table 39, we see that in only a few cases does the score of any group on any of the scales go beyond the 50 per cent point of possible favorableness toward the Negro. For instance, on Scale I, which is a five-point scale ranging from 0 to 4, no group has less than a score of 2.50. In short, no group gets even as far as the 50 per cent line if we take the score of 2 to be the middle point between 0 and 4.

Yet, there are *relative* differences. The Image score of group 4 is smaller than that of group 1. So, too, with the scores on Ideology. These range from a high of 5.0 for group 1 to a low of 3.34 for group 4. Again no group reaches even the 50 per cent point of favorableness. Exposure group 4 comes close to it with a score of 3.34 but does not achieve it. But group 4 is significantly more ready for desegregation than group 1. In short, while one cannot say that there is *absolute* readiness for desegregation, one can talk sensibly about the greater and lesser degrees of readiness and resistance.

The 50 per cent line is reached or passed only by group 4 on Scales III, IV, and V, and by group 3 on Scales IV and V. These most highly exposed groups tend most strongly toward the desegregationist end of the scale limits, and each increase in exposure brings the scores closer to that limit. Here then is a definite strong relationship between exposure to the mass media and readiness for desegregation.

This generalization must be viewed in a context of what one might in general have expected in a region where the major traditions support some form of segregation, and where deviation from these expectations and traditions often proves costly to the deviator. Could one reasonably expect the arrays to be more widespread?

It is true that what occasions surprise to an observer can be as much a function of his own value inclinations as of his theoretical expectations. It would be difficult for any observer to ignore the fact that the spread of respondents through the various scale scores includes such prominent percentages in the lowest scores, and that three of the five means on the scales which measure "what would you do" are at or below a middle point of 3. This is hardly what one would expect in a culture whose central strain is toward preservation of a traditional pattern best expressed by scale scores of 5 and 6.

One has the sense from these findings that about as much difference as can be safely expressed has turned up, and that exposure to mass media is a differentiating indicator of where these differences are to be found.[6]

Moreover, exposure to mass media appears to be most influential when issues such as choice between competing values and the cost and profit of discrimination is implied (Scale V). By contrast, such exposure is least influential when it comes to the White's Image of the Negro. *In short, though the various exposure groups hardly differ in how they think of the Negro, they differ substantially in how forcefully they insist upon segregation in the schools.*

Could the true difference be one in recklessness versus deliberateness, a difference in inclination and ability to see the situation as one of alternative and competing choices and values? Persons who are more exposed to the mass media seem also to be able to perceive more fully the interplay of competing choices and to calculate the consequences of their actions more fully. This in turn suggests that they differ from the less-exposed group in other characteristics of their lives which involve the capacity to see situations in terms of alternative and competing values.[7]

[6] An attempt at accounting for differential changes in opinion about ethnic groups, as a result of exposure to communication, is offered by Lawrence Schlesinger in a paper presented at the 1956 meetings of the American Psychological Association, and entitled, "The Influence of Social Communication on Ethnic Opinions." Our own findings and those of Schlesinger can be brought into consonance if we introduce the notion that the "exposed" groups are more sensitive to the opinions of non-Southerners, as well as being more aware of them.

[7] This interpretation tallies neatly with that offered in Bradbury's "economistic hypothesis." See, W. C. Bradbury, "Evaluation of Research in Race Relations," *Inventory of Research in Racial and Cultural Relations,* Vol. 5, 1953, pp. 99–133.

CHAPTER SEVEN

EXPOSURE TO MASS MEDIA AND ATTITUDES,
WITH OTHER FACTORS HELD CONSTANT

DO the respondents who are more favorable to the Negroes and more frequently exposed to the mass media differ from the less favorable, less exposed respondents in other characteristics? This is the suggestion we made at the end of the last chapter, and we turn in this chapter to see how true this is.

For convenience, the four mass media exposure groups have been condensed into two, "high" and "low." The "high" are those exposed several times a week or more to three or four of the mass media. The "low" are those exposed to only one or two media several times a week.

Table 41 has an array of certain selected characteristics of these two exposure groups.

The low and high exposure groups differ substantially from each other on all features, except for the per cent who have 1–3 children. The high exposure group has nearly three times the number of college educated people. Over 45 per cent of its people go to church once a week or more, compared to the less than 30 per cent of the low exposure group. More than twice as many high exposure persons live in urban areas. More than twice as many members of the high exposure group earn over $5000 a year. Finally, the per cent of persons in the high exposure group who hold white-collar jobs is over 71 per cent compared to over 43 per cent of the low exposure group.

In sum, the high exposure group is significantly better educated, more religious, more urban, better paid, and holds better jobs.

Do these different characteristics influence attitudes toward the Negro? If so, in what way? To answer this question, we now must examine the difference in scores between high and low exposure people, holding constant each of the other characteristics in turn. This is the same procedure we followed in the case of education.

116

TABLE 41

Selected Characteristics of Mass Media Exposure Groups

Mass Media Groups	College Educated Num-ber	College Educated Per Cent	Have 1–3 Children Num-ber	Have 1–3 Children Per Cent	High Religiosity (Once a week or more) Num-ber	High Religiosity (Once a week or more) Per Cent	Residence Num-ber	Residence Per Cent	Over $5000 Income Num-ber	Over $5000 Income Per Cent	White-Collar Jobs Num-ber	White-Collar Jobs Per Cent
Low Exposure[a] (N = 136)	19	13.97	93	68.38	48	29.41	44	32.35	30	22.06	59	43.38
High Exposure[b] (N = 151)	56	37.08	106	70.19	69	45.69	107	70.86	67	44.37	108	71.52

[a] Low Exposure = exposed to 1 or 2 media several times a week.
[b] High Exposure = exposed to 3 or 4 media several times a week.

Four major findings from our last chapter can be put to test, as follows:

(1) The more the exposure to the mass media, the more favorable the Image of the Negro, but the differences among the exposure groups are generally not significant.

(2) The more the exposure to mass media, the greater the readiness for desegregation of the public schools; and the differences between the exposure groups tend to be significant, especially when the lowest exposure group is involved in the comparison.

(3) For each of the exposure groups, the score on the Scale of Image expresses more anti-Negro attitudes than does the score on School Desegregation.

(4) The differences between the scores on Scales I and V are greater for the high exposure groups. That is, the disparity between the Image of the Negro and the readiness for desegregation is greater for the highly exposed persons.

Before proceeding to see how well these findings hold up, it should be noted that we ought reasonably to expect some of the differences to diminish because of the fact that we have joined to the lowest exposed persons in group 1 those who are in exposure group 2, to form the new group called "low exposed."

The statistical details of the tests are to be found in Appendix E. The material in Table 42 summarizes the outcome of the tests.

1. HOLDING EDUCATION CONSTANT. Finding 1 is in part confirmed and in part violated. Only within the high school group does the more highly exposed group have a more favorable Image of the Negro. In the grammar school and college groups, the highly exposed have a more unfavorable Image of the Negro. This reversal goes far beyond expectations. We expected differences between the groups to be diminished when we held education constant. But we scarcely expected that the direction of differences would be reversed. Moreover, we do not have even a sound guess as to why the difference between high and low exposure holds in the expected way only for the high school group.

What we may have here is further evidence that the con-

118

TABLE 42

Results of Analysis of Differences Between High Exposure to the Mass Media and Low Exposure on Two Scales (Image and School Desegregation), Holding Constant, in Turn, Each of Six Other Factors

			Factors Held Constant			
	1	2	3	4	5	6
Findings	*Education*	*Number of Children*	*Religiosity*	*Residence*	*Income*	*Occupational Status*
1. The more the exposure to the mass media the more favorable the Image of the Negro, but the differences among the exposure groups are generally not significant.	+ −	+ −	+ −	+ −	+	+ −
2. The more the exposure to the mass media, the greater the readiness for desegregation of the public schools, and the differences between the exposure groups tend to be significant, especially when the lowest exposure group is involved in the comparison.	+ −	+ −	+ −	−	+ −	+ −
3. For each of the exposure groups the score on the Scale of Image expresses more anti-Negro orientation, or, put in other terms, is closer to the segregationist extreme than is the score on school desegregation.	+ −	+	+	+	+	+
4. The differences between the scores on Scales I and V are greater in the high-exposure groups than in the low-exposure groups; that is, there is more disparity between the Image of the Negro and the readiness for desegregation among the high-exposed persons than among the low-exposed persons.	+ −	+	+	+	+	+

+ = Finding confirmed
− = Finding violated

sequence-free Image is much less subject to influence by otherwise important factors. That is, the idea of the Negro as an inferior creature seems to be pretty evenly distributed, so that sometimes the better educated and higher income groups have an even more unfavorable Image than their less well-educated or lower-income neighbors. Exposure to the mass media is not likely, under the circumstances, to prove very forceful in altering their Image of the Negro.

When we look at the results on finding 2 the picture changes somewhat. For now the groups do differ from each other in the expected way on Scale V. The highly exposed groups show greater readiness for desegregation than low-exposed groups within each of the three educational categories. However, within both the grammar school and college groups, the differences between the scores of the two exposure groups are as large as before. Only within the high school group does the difference between the two sets of scores tend to approach significance.

These findings suggest that the effects on readiness for desegregation which are produced by exposure to mass media tend to persist even when the possible effects of differences in education are eliminated. In short, exposure to mass media exerts its own influence. This conclusion is even more credible if we bear in mind the fact that combining groups 1 and 2 into a new low exposure group may be responsible for reducing the sizes of the differences.

Findings 3 and 4 are confirmed in each instance without any exception.

We can summarize these findings by noting that when education is held constant, the differences between the exposure groups on their Image of the Negro tend to deviate sharply from the previous results. The scores on School Desegregation, however, tend to hold up, though some of the differences diminish. Each group holds up in being more favorable in its attitudes toward school desegregation than in its Image of the Negro. Finally, the more-exposed groups change more markedly from their relatively high segregationist Image to their relatively low resistance to desegregation of the schools.

2. HOLDING NUMBER OF CHILDREN CONSTANT. The two exposure groups do not differ significantly from each other in the percentage of their members who have one-to-three children. We should therefore not expect any significant deviation in our findings when we measure attitudes while holding constant the factor of number of children. In fact, this is what we

discover, at least within the group having one-to-three children. All four findings hold up without exception.

However, in both the other groups, i.e., those with no children and those with four children, there are deviations from our general findings.

In the group with four children, every finding is violated. The high exposure group has a more unfavorable Image of the Negro; the readiness for desegregation of the schools is virtually identical for both the low and high exposures; the scores of the low exposure people are more unfavorable for school desegregation than on Image; there is virtually no difference in the scores on these two scales for the high exposure group; and finally, there is more disparity between these two scale scores for the low exposure people than for the high exposure group.

Here then is a group–those with four children–whose reactions are almost totally opposite to our expectations with regard to the possible impact of exposure to mass media. In so doing, they also tell us quite clearly that such exposure, or any such "horizon-broadening" influence, cannot be expected to have an effect until a certain level of preparedness is reached and/or a certain stake in the system is developed.

The social characteristics of the group with four children help account for the way in which this group scores on Image and School Desegregation. Some 71.5 per cent of the people in this group have grammar school education or less. By contrast, in the group with two children, 40 per cent have grammar school educations, and this is the closest which any group comes to the 4-child group in this characteristic. Clearly, the 4-child group is a predominantly and distinctively low-educated group.

The figures on income and white-collar jobs support those on education, though not so strongly in the case of income. The 4-child group has 64.7 per cent blue-collar workers to 36.23 per cent for the 1–3 child group, and 35.29 for the no-child group. On income, the 4-child group has 81.25 per cent who earn under $5000 a year, compared to 56.2 per cent of the 1–3 child group and 73.3 per cent of the no-child group.

While the differences on income are not striking, the educational and status differences are clearly polarized, with the 4-child group at the low end and the other groups far away from it. We have already seen how differences in education, occupation, and income matter in regard to attitudes. We can therefore understand why the 4-child group should exhibit toward the Negro and toward desegregation the kinds of attitudes we have come to expect from those who feel no stake in the system and who have not reached the point at which countervailing perspectives can have an influence.

The group with no children is in some ways also anomalous. Finding 2 is violated to the extent that the score of the high exposure segment on desegregation is more unfavorable than is its Image of the Negro. And Finding 4 is violated in that there are no differences in the disparity between scores on Scales I and V for the low and high exposure groups. Both groups move away about equally from their Scale I scores.

In the case of this no-child group, there are no significantly different social characteristics which would help us account for the deviant behavior. The only clue we have is that they do not have children. Could it be that because of this the no-child group can afford to be ideologically consistent in its attitudes toward desegregation, without having to worry about the consequences for their children of their active resistance to desegregation of the schools? Enjoying the luxury of freedom from concrete consequences, they can afford to call for or support that kind of action about which parents with children, and with other stakes in the system, feel apprehensive. These findings lead us to suggest that the influence of exposure to the mass media on attitudes varies with the receptivity of those exposed. This receptivity is itself dependent upon either or both of the following conditions: (a) that the person has a profitable position which he desires to maintain and therefore has a stake in the society; (b) that through formal education he has previously been exposed and sensitized to the importance of being alert to the needs, wishes, and customs of others. This sensitivity includes, as we see from our previous materials, a sense for long- versus short-term consequences; a felt need to bargain and compromise the demands of one aspect of oneself against others; and a willingness to consider as legitimate and moral the stands which others take in opposition to one's own position. These are the ingredients of what we have previously termed a sense of perspective.

Those with four-or-more children appear to have little of this perspective and little sense of a stake in the society. The absence of perspective and the lack of a sense of stake seem to be due to a degraded social position and inadequate exposure to school. In the case of those with no children, the most important factor seems to be the absence of children who might function as concrete hostages to fortune.

3. HOLDING RELIGIOSITY CONSTANT. With only two exceptions the findings remain unchanged.

The first exception occurs in the medium religiosity group. Here those with high exposure to mass media have a more unfavorable Image of the Negro.

The second exception is in the high religiosity group, where the differences between the scores on readiness for desegregation of the schools of the low and high exposure groups are not significant, even though the difference is in the expected direction.

This suggests that high religiosity may have a sufficiently strong influence to overcome and reduce whatever disparities in attitudes might arise from differences in exposure to mass media. But one must offer this suggestion very tentatively. For, in every case except that noted above, high exposure yields scores consistently lower than those of the low exposure groups. Moreover, the group which has high exposure and low religiosity shows least resistance to desegregation of the schools. A finding such as this makes one cautious about ascribing to high religiosity the ability to override differences due to exposure. On the other hand, the low religiosity group, except for the score on Scale V of the low religiosity-high exposure segment, is consistently unfavorable in its Image of the Negro and its strong resistance to desegregation.

We have here such a mixed-up set of findings about the interplay between religiosity and exposure to mass media that one is led to suspect that other factors, not held constant and not analyzed, are at work. If one must be cautious about talking about the influence of high religiosity in one context, but ascribe considerable influence to such religiosity in another context, then, obviously, the results cannot be satisfactorily dealt with in terms of religion and exposure alone.

Probably, therefore, nothing decisive can be said about the interplay between religiosity and exposure to mass media. What we have learned about the influence of the exposure to mass media, without holding religiosity constant, is probably as good an approximation of the actual state of attitudes as what we have newly learned by holding religiosity constant.

4. HOLDING RESIDENCE CONSTANT. The findings about the influence of exposure to mass media are violated to a considerable degree. Within both urban and rural groups, the differences between the low and high exposure groups are insignificant. Generally, the high exposure group in the urban area has a more unfavorable Image of the Negro.

How can we account for these two deviations?

The reduction to non-significance of the differences on Scale V tells us nothing about the possible effects of residence, since this reduction takes place for both the rural and the urban groups. Once again, it seems that other variables are at work producing these modified results, but not showing themselves clearly.

The finding that the high exposure-urban group has a more unfavorable Image of the Negro suggests that the urban influence overrides the influence of exposure to mass media. But this does not occur on the scores for Scale V, and, in general, it has not appeared that residence in the urban area leads to more unfavorable attitudes.

Probably the best judgment about the meaning of residence as a factor in attitudes toward the Negro and desegregation, is that, by and large, residence is irrelevant, and that such differences as we found earlier between low and high exposure groups can be trusted to be reasonably good approximations of the actual case.

For in one context we find more favorable attitudes among rural residents. In another, the urban people are more favorably disposed to Negroes and desegregation. These contradictory findings urge great caution in using residence as an explanation.

5. HOLDING INCOME CONSTANT. The findings hold up in all but one instance. This is the case of the scores on Scale V, where the low and high exposure people who both earn under $5000 a year are not significantly different, though the difference is in the expected direction. The reduction of the difference to insignificance suggests once again that unless several factors act in unison, that is, unless high education is accompanied by high exposure or high income or high status, the influence will tend to be diminished seriously. We are borne out in this interpretation by the fact that in the group over $5000 there is a very large and statistically significant difference between the scores on Scale V of the low and high exposure groups. The reinforcement which high income gives to high exposure is clearly at work.

6. HOLDING OCCUPATIONAL STATUS CONSTANT. Here, too, deviations from our findings are recorded. First, the low status-high exposure group has a more unfavorable Image of the Negro than the low status-low exposure group. The difference is small and statistically insignificant, but it is nevertheless there. One could either write off the difference as being inconsequential, or, note that the absence of a high-status reinforcement for the influence of high exposure reduces the influence of that exposure. This latter interpretation is borne out by the fact that within the low-status group the difference between the low and high exposure groups on Scale V are reduced from significance to insignificance. Again we see the consequences of the failure to have high-status reinforcement of high exposure. And once again, finally, this interpretation is lent credence by the fact that within the high-status group, the high exposure people differ significantly from the low exposure people in their readiness for desegregation.

Summary

The most general findings of this analysis of the influence of mass media with other variables held constant can now be put in summary form.

Mass Media with Other Factors Constant

1. First, we encountered a reduction in differences between group scores. Probably most of this reduction is due to the way we combined exposure groups. In this combination, we added to the lowest scorers certain persons with slightly more favorable attitudes, and added to the higher scorers a group with somewhat less favorable tendencies. Any such combination would tend naturally to reduce the differences which we found earlier.

2. There is considerable ambiguity about the influence of religiosity and of urban or rural residence. In order to account for the deviations from our findings, we had to evoke alternative and contradictory theories of the possible influence of these two variables. In general, then, this leads us to be more cautious about the possible significance of these variables.

3. The number of children is decidedly influential. Those with no children and those with four children or more are both anomalous, but in different ways and probably for different reasons. However, their deviations from our findings only help strengthen our notions regarding the importance of the concept of the stake in society and the achievement of a perspective on the self and others.

4. We had continuously verified for us the previous contention that *the combination of high status, high income, high education, and high exposure are powerful in their influence on readiness for desegregation and in the development of a more favorable image of the Negro.* Any two of these factors together yield our expected findings more readily and more clearly than any one factor alone. *The reinforcement which any two of these lend to each other appears to be critical in the maintenance of the kinds of Image of the Negro and the attitudes toward desegregation which we sum up under the term readiness.*

CHAPTER EIGHT

OCCUPATION, MOBILITY, AND ATTITUDES
TOWARD DESEGREGATION

IT is now well accepted that social status and social mobility can exert powerful influences on attitudes and behavior.[1] Status refers to position in a social order, and mobility refers to changes in such positions. Different positions tend almost always to enjoy different perquisites and prestige. Persons at different statuses usually feel unequally valued by their social order, and, in turn, act as if they were unequally satisfied with this society and its standards.

If, therefore, proposals are made to undertake certain social changes, and if these changes imply threats to existing status arrangements, the proposals ought to be met with different degrees of alarm and resistance.

Desegregation, as it refers to the promised amelioration of the positions of Negroes in our society, is one such major change. Reactions to desegregation vary in degree and quality of resistance, and in this chapter we shall examine the extent to which differences in attitudes toward desegregation are related to differences in status and mobility.

We use the term "status" here to refer simply to the occupational position of the respondent, that is, whether he holds a blue-or a white-collar job. The former are called "low status" and the latter "high status." The occupational classifications which we have fit into these two categories are:

High status: Professional, technical and kindred
Managers, officials, and proprietors (except farm)
Clerical and kindred
Sales workers
Craftsmen, foremen, and kindred

---

[1] For a selective review of the literature see Chapter I, in E. A. Suchman, P. P. Dean, R. M. Williams, Jr., *et al, Desegregation: Some Propositions and Research Suggestions,* New York, Anti-Defamation League, 1958.

See, also, Melvin M. Tumin, *Segregation and Desegregation,* New York, Anti-Defamation League, 1957.

Low status: Farmers and farm managers
Protective service workers
Operatives and kindred workers
Farm laborers and farm foremen
Service workers (except protective and house-hold)
Laborers (except farm and mine)

The division into high and low status was made mostly on grounds of convenience, but partly, also, because this line of distinction corresponds approximately with how the people in the area themselves rank jobs. We do not claim that these distinctions are accurate reflections of some well-calibrated scale of prestige. Rather, we are interested in discovering, once we divide our respondents in this way, if we can then make some organized sense out of the differences in their attitudes toward desegregation.

On the basis of a distinction between high and low status, we get a fourfold classification when we compare respondents with their fathers, as follows: (1) high-status sons of high-status fathers—this group will be termed "High Stationaries"; (2) high-status sons of low-status fathers, or "Upward Mobiles"; (3) low-status sons of low-status fathers, or "Low Stationaries"; (4) low-status sons of high-status fathers, or "Downward Mobiles." The number and per cent in each of these groups is reported in Table 43. Certain other information about each of these groups is shown in Table 43A.

TABLE 43
Distribution of Mobility Types

Mobility Types	Number	Per Cent
(1) High Stationaries	92	33.09
(2) Upward Mobiles	72	25.90
(3) Low Stationaries	86	30.94
(4) Downward Mobiles	28	10.07
TOTAL	278	100.00

128

TABLE 43A
Educational, Income, Age and Residence
Characteristics of Mobility Groups

	Median Education	Per Cent Earning Over $5000 Per Year	Median Age	Per Cent Stable Urban Residence	Per Cent Stable Rural Residence
(1) High Stationaries	11.0	60	39.8	59	18
(2) Upward Mobiles	9.5	42	41.2	50	35
(3) Low Stationaries	7.2	7	45.4	40	50
(4) Downward Mobiles	8.8	18	34.1	64	21

From Table 43A one sees that the High Stationaries have the highest median education, the highest per cent of members earning over $5000 a year, the second highest per cent of persons whose residence in the urban area is stable (i.e., have lived in the area five years or more), and the lowest per cent of people whose residence in rural areas is stable.

At the lower end of the distributions stand the Low Stationaries whose median education is lowest of the four groups and whose per cent of persons earning over $5000 a year is also at the bottom. Moreover, the average age of this group is older, and it has the lowest percentage of persons with stable urban residence.

Group 2, the Upward Mobiles, and Group 4, the Downward Mobiles, are intermediary between the High and Low Stationaries on all but one of the five items.

These facts lead us to suggest a series of hypotheses about probable rank orders on attitudes toward segregation.

It is here suggested that the rank order of readiness for desegregation will be as follows:

Rank Order of Readiness	*Mobility Group*
1	High Stationaries
2	Upward Mobiles
3	Low Stationaries
4	Downward Mobiles

129

Occupation, Mobility, and Attitudes

We may now turn to the data to test these hypotheses. In Table 44 are shown the mean scale scores for each of the four mobility groups on each of the five measures of readiness for desegregation described above. In Table 45 are presented the results of tests of significance of differences between the means.

TABLE 44
Mean Scores for Four Mobility Groups on Five Scales

Mobility Group	I Image 0–4	II Ideology 0–6	III Sentiment 0–6	IV General Action 0–6	V Specific Action 0–4
High Stationary	2.55	3.41	2.95	2.66	1.65
Upward Mobile	2.80	3.88	3.31	2.75	1.98
Low Stationary	2.95	4.82	4.19	3.69	2.45
Downward Mobile	2.64	4.35	4.39	3.28	2.39

TABLE 45
Tests of Significance of Difference Between
Means of Mobility Groups

Mobility Group	I Image	II Ideology	III Sentiment	IV General Action	V Specific Action
High Stationaries *vs.* Upward Mobiles	n.s.	n.s.	n.s.	n.s.	n.s.
High Stationaries *vs.* Low Stationaries	n.s.	.001	.001	.01	.01
High Stationaries *vs.* Downward Mobiles	n.s.	.05	.01	n.s.	.02
Upward Mobiles *vs.* Low Stationaries	n.s.	.001	.02	.01	.05
Upward Mobiles *vs.* Downward Mobiles	n.s.	n.s.	.05	n.s.	n.s.
Low Stationaries *vs.* Downward Mobiles	n.s.	n.s.	n.s.	n.s.	n.s.

The data presented in the foregoing two tables enable us to state the outcomes of some of our hypotheses.

Comparison 1: High Stationaries versus Upward Mobiles. On all five scales the High Stationaries are more ready for desegregation, but none of the differences reaches significance.

Comparison 2: High Stationaries versus Low Stationaries. On all five scales the High Stationary group is more ready for desegregation, and four of the five differences are significant. The one insignificant difference occurs on Image.

Comparison 3: High Stationaries versus Downward Mobiles. High Stationaries are more ready for desegregation and the differences are significant in all cases except Image and Ideology. In the case of Ideology, the difference is in the expected direction and is close to significant. High Stationaries are apparently more ready for desegregation than Downward Mobiles.

Comparison 4: Upward Mobiles versus Low Stationaries. These two groups differ significantly on all scales except Negro Image, and there the difference is in the anticipated direction.

Comparison 5: Upward Mobiles versus Downward Mobiles. The Upward Mobile group is more ready for desegregation, but only on Sentiment Structure does the difference reach significance. The finding here therefore is suggestive but inconclusive.

Comparison 6: Low Stationaries versus Downward Mobiles. On four of the five Scales (I, II, IV, and V) the Downward Mobiles are more ready for desegregation. The reverse is true on Scale III. In no case, however, does the difference reach the level of significance. This may be taken as a tentative indication of greater readiness for desegregation in the Downward Mobile group.

Comparison 7: Stationary versus Mobile. Table 46 below reveals the mean scale scores for all mobiles versus all stationaries. The differences between the means are unpatterned and insignificant. None of the differences even approaches significance. Mobility seems not to matter.

Comparison 8: High Status versus Low Status. Tables 47 and 48 below present the mean scale scores and the differences for all High Status people (High Stationaries and Upward Mobiles) and for the Low Status group (Low Stationaries and Downward Mobiles).

TABLE 46
Mean Scores for Two Mobility Groups on Five Scales

Mobility Group	I Image 0–4	II Ideology 0–6	III Senti-ment 0–6	IV General Action 0–6	V Specific Action 0–4
Mobile Groups (2 and 4)	2.76	4.02	3.62	2.90	2.10
Stationary Groups (1 and 3)	2.75	4.09	3.56	3.16	2.04

TABLE 47
Mean Scores for Two Status Groups on Five Scales

Group	I Image 0–4	II Ideology 0–6	III Sentiment 0–6	IV General Action 0–6	V Specific Action 0–4
High Status	2.66	3.62	3.12	2.70	1.68
Low Status	2.88	4.71	4.24	3.59	2.44

TABLE 48
T-Tests of Significance of Difference Between Mean Scores
of Two Status Groups on Five Scales

Group		I Image	II Ideology	III Sentiment	IV General Action	V Specific Action
High Status *vs.* Low Status	p =	n.s.	.001	.001	.001	.001

The sizes of the means all favor the High Status group, so far as readiness for desegregation is concerned, and all differences are significant except those on Image.

In view of the outcomes of these comparisons, our hypothesized rank order of readiness for desegregation must be revised as follows:

Rank Order of Readiness	Mobility Group
1	High Stationaries
2	Upward Mobiles
3	Downward Mobiles
4	Low Stationaries

Occupation, Mobility, and Attitudes

The one significant change finds Downward Mobiles more ready for desegregation than Low Stationaries.

Some Intervening Variables

Our findings strongly suggest that though status seems to have more influence than mobility on attitudes toward desegregation, some importance must be ascribed to the historical background of the status. The High Stationaries are more favorable than Upward Mobiles, and Downward Mobiles more than Low Stationaries. This implies that two generations of high status (i.e. High Stationaries) lead to more favorable attitudes toward Negroes than one generation of such status (i.e., Upward Mobiles). Similarly, the fact that Downward Mobiles are more favorable than Low Stationaries suggests that one generation of low-status experience produces less resistance to desegregation than two generations (i.e. Low Stationaries).

There is also a strong suggestion that the differences may be found in the degree of anxiety about status. If this is so, it should reflect itself in different attitudes toward social norms, expressed in terms of differences in a man's sense of his place in society.

To test this possibility, a series of five questions, which roughly satisfy the requirements of a scale (coefficient of reproducibility = 90.32) were asked of the respondents. They were all asked to approve, disapprove, or express indecision about the following five statements:

(a) There's little use in trying to influence public officials these days, because often they aren't interested in the problems of the average man.

(b) Nowadays a person has to live pretty much for today and let tomorrow take care of itself.

(c) In spite of what some people say, the situation for the average man is getting better all the time.

(d) It's hardly fair to bring children into the world today, with the way things look for the future.

(e) These days a person really doesn't know whom he can count on.[2]

[2] These test items were first developed by Professor Leo Srole.

Occupation, Mobility, and Attitudes

Table 49 shows the per cent of positive responses given to each of these items. We sum up the meaning of these items in the term "anomie," meaning alienation from accepted social standards as opposed to integration with the norms.

Table 50 presents the mean scores on anomie for the four mobility groups.

TABLE 49

Per Cent Positive Responses to Anomie Questions

Anomie Questions	Per Cent Positive Responses
Situation for average man getting better	76.57
Hardly fair to bring children into world	75.87
Must live pretty much for today	72.37
Little use in trying to influence public officials	56.64
A man doesn't know whom he can count on	47.90

TABLE 50

Mean Anomie Scores for Four Mobility Groups

Mobility Group	Mean Anomie Scale Score[a]
High Stationaries	4.05
Upward Mobiles	3.61
Downward Mobiles	2.92
Low Stationaries	2.54

[a] Scale limits are 0–5. The higher the score the greater the normative integration; the lower the score the greater the anomie.

From Table 50 we see that the rank order of readiness for desegregation corresponds with the rank order of satisfaction with the norms, or "normative integration." To put it in reverse terms, the higher the anomie, i.e., the greater the dissatisfaction with the socal norms, the greater the resistance to desegregation.

In Table 51 are seen the results of tests of significance of difference on the mean scores on the scale of anomie.

TABLE 51

T-Tests of Significance of Difference Between Mean Scale Scores of Mobility Groups on Anomie Scale

Mobility Groups	*p*
High Stationaries *vs.* Upward Mobiles	.05
High Stationaires *vs.* Downward Mobiles	.01
High Stationaries *vs.* Low Stationaries	.001
Upward Mobiles *vs.* Downward Mobiles	.01
Upward Mobiles *vs.* Low Stationaries	.001
Downward Mobiles *vs.* Low Stationaries	n.s.

All the differences are significant except between Downward Mobiles and Low Stationaries. Here the difference is in the expected direction but is not statistically significant.

In general, these findings may be summarized as follows:

1. There is a positive relationship between normative integration, i.e., acceptance of social norms, on the one hand, and readiness for desegregation on the other. The higher the acceptance, the greater the readiness.

2. There is a patterned relationship between mobility-type and normative integration.

3. There is a patterned relationship between mobility-type and readiness for desegregation.

If we carry through with an earlier assumption, we can relate these three findings. The assumption was that the degree of normative integration would vary directly with the highness or lowness of one's status or position, and with the number of generations (one *vs.* two) during which the position had been occupied. That is, High Stationaries, (i.e., persons who had been high status for two generations) ought to be most satisfied with their positions. By contrast, Low Stationaries, (ie., those at low status for two generations) should be most dissatisfied.

If this assumption is correct, then we can say that different

135

mobility types tend to show different degrees of satisfaction with the social norms. In turn they also exhibit different attitudes toward Negroes and desegregation. The high status and hence the satisfied persons seem to feel least threatened by the changes implied in desegregation. The low-status persons, by contrast, seem most discontent with the norms and, in turn, most resistant to desegregation.

The two relationships we explored but could not document are those between mobility and anomie, and between mobility and attitudes toward Negroes. Whether a man has moved up or down from his father's status does not seem to matter. It is the status itself and the length of time in the status which matters much more.

That mobility should prove to be relatively insignificant is a disturbing finding. Some of the research evidence suggests a strong positive relationship between mobility and various types of social satisfaction. Other research suggests strong relationships of another kind; that is, the mobile persons tend to show certain anxieties which are not displayed by those who have remained stable. But there are almost no studies in which mobility turns out to be unimportant either way.

Therefore, when the analysis of our data showed mobility to be insignificant, we decided to explore further along several lines. First, are there substantial differences in actual occupational change between the mobile and stable persons? Second, if there are such differences, do the persons themselves reflect this change in what they say about their present standing compared to their fathers'?

The first question can be answered by finding out the average number of occupational positions moved by the upward and downward mobiles, assuming that the range of eleven occupations which we originally set up constitutes some kind of a ladder. When we compute the average number of moves, we find that the Upward Mobiles have moved an average of 3.44 positions above the occupations held by their fathers. The Downward Mobiles have, in turn, sunk an average of 4.39 occupational steps. Since there are only 11 steps in all, these constitute very substantial average moves. Our first question is therefore answered affirmatively.

Occupation, Mobility, and Attitudes

To discover whether the persons involved in these moves reflect their movement in their feelings about their jobs compared to those of their fathers, we asked all our respondents to state how well off they felt compared to their fathers. Table 52 shows the number and per cent of each of the four mobility types who felt better off or worse off than their fathers.

TABLE 52
Father-Son Comparison

Mobility Group	Feel Better Off		Feel Worse Off	
	Number	Per Cent	Number	Per Cent
Upward Mobiles	51	71	6	8
Low Stationaries	50	58	14	16
High Stationaries	50	54	19	21
Downward Mobiles	9	32	7	25

The findings are once again surprising. Now the fact of mobility comes through clearly. Those who have experienced upward mobility have by far the highest per cent who say they feel better off than their fathers. By contrast, those who have been downwardly mobile have the lowest per cent of persons who feel better off and the highest per cent who feel worse off. The two stationary groups fall between these two extremes on both counts.

Now we know that the objective facts of mobility, as measured by average number of moves, is matched by the subjective experiences and feelings of the persons involved, at least when they compare themselves to their fathers. But we also know, from our previous analysis, that whether the person has moved does not seem to influence either his satisfaction with the social norms or his attitudes toward Negroes and desegregation. It therefore seems quite clear that a person can feel better off than his father, when comparing jobs, and still feel considerably dissatisfied with his position. This suggests strongly that his satisfaction with his position depends on how well off he feels compared to somebody other than his father.

With whom else could these persons reasonably compare themselves to get some sense for how well off they are? What

137

are their standards of comparisons? Who are their reference groups? Who are the people whose positions they take as a measure of where they themselves ought to be?

A number of possibilities suggest themselves. We can compare present positions with earlier positions held. Or we can compare present positions with those presently held by friends and associates of earlier years. Or, we can compare present situations with those now enjoyed by persons in the same nominal positions. That is, if one is a doctor, he may use the average situation of all other doctors as his basis for judging how well off he is.

We asked our respondents about each of these possibilities. First came the comparison of their present jobs with the jobs they held when they originally started working. The number and per cent of each mobility group who said they were better off now than when they first started to work was as follows:

1. High Stationaries   82 out of 92, or 89%
2. Upward Mobiles   63 out of 72, or 88%
3. Downward Mobiles   19 out of 28, or 68%
4. Low Stationaries   57 out of 86, or 66%

Once again the influence of mobility seems much weaker than that of status. Groups 1 and 2, both high status, but one of which is mobile and one stationary, have virtually identical scores. Similarly, groups 3 and 4, both of whom are low status, but one mobile and the other stationary, also have nearly identical scores. But these are both considerably lower than those of the high-status groups.

The next comparison tried was that between the present situation enjoyed by the respondents and the average present situation of friends and acquaintances of earlier years. When we asked the respondents to evaluate themselves in these terms, the number and per cent who said they were better off was as follows:

1. High Stationaries   39 out of 92, or 42%
2. Upward Mobiles   21 out of 72, or 29%
3. Downward Mobiles   5 out of 28, or 18%
4. Low Stationaries   13 out of 86, or 15%

Occupation, Mobility, and Attitudes

Here the picture changes somewhat. The High Stationaries stand out in the per cent of their group who feel better off. But now among the Upward Mobiles, the per cent who have this attitude, though still significantly larger than that of the two low-status groups, is also considerably smaller than that of the High Stationaries.

Perhaps the most significant difference between this comparison and the earlier ones cited is that while virtually no one says he is worse off, a significantly larger per cent of the total sample judges itself to be *as well off* as the early associates with whom they were asked to compare themselves. The numbers and per cents are as follows:

1. High Stationaries   28 out of 92, or 30%
2. Upward Mobiles   30 out of 72, or 42%
3. Downward Mobiles   16 out of 28, or 57%
4. Low Stationaries   51 out of 86, or 59%

Altogether 125 out of 278, or almost 45 per cent, say they are as well off. By contrast, only 78 out of 278, or just 28 per cent, say they are better off. The real difference between high- and low-status groups here, then, is in the per cent of the former who say they are better off, and the per cent of the latter who, though not better off, prefer to think of themselves as being as well off as early associates.

Again, then, it is status and not mobility which cuts the sample and divides it into different attitude groups.

The last comparison tried was between the present situation of the respondent and that of his contemporaries who hold the same kind of job. Each respondent was asked to say whether he felt himself better, the same, or worse off than men in the same job categories.

The number and per cent for each mobility group was as follows:

Mobility Group	Better Off Number	Better Off Per Cent	The Same Number	The Same Per Cent	Worse Off Number	Worse Off Per Cent
1. High Stationaries	28	30	38	41.3	8	9
2. Upward Mobiles	19	26	39	54.2	1	1
3. Downward Mobiles	7	25	14	50.0	1	4
4. Low Stationaries	12	14	55	63.9	4	5

139

Occupation, Mobility, and Attitudes

Once again the high- and low status people are at the two extremes. This time, however, there is a bunching toward the upper end of the percentages. As in the last set of comparisons, far many more persons prefer to think of themselves as being as well off as their contemporaries.

What we can now see is that the sharpest differences between mobility groups occur when we ask them to compare themselves with the jobs their fathers had. But, as will be recalled, this difference does not carry through to differences in social satisfaction (the anomie scale) or in attitudes toward Negroes and desegregation. The most significant facts about occupations, as we have analyzed them, is whether they are blue- or white-collar and whether these statuses have been occupied one or two generations. It is status and not mobility which is consequential in this context.

Summary and Conclusions

In this chapter, we have examined the connections between certain measures of occupational status and mobility and certain attitudes toward desegregation. It has been found that mobility is a weaker differentiator of attitudes than is status. When historical dimensions of status are taken into account, particularly the number of generations during which a respondent has occupied a given level, some more subtle effects of status are made clearer. In general, with regard to attitudes toward desegregation, the rank order of readiness for desegregation is (1) high status, two generations (father and son); (2) high status, one generation (father low, but son high); (3) low status, one generation (father high, but son low); (4) low status, two generations (father and son both low).

Certain relationships are also revealed between status and anomie; and between anomie and readiness for desegregation. In general, the higher the status, the lower the anomie; and, the lower the anomie, the higher the readiness for desegregation.

Again, with regard to anomie, the experience of upward mobility does not seem to be as influential as the experience of two generations of high status; and the experience of downward mobility does not seem as destructive of social morale as the experience of two generations of low status. Not even when the objective experience of upward mobility is accompanied by a subjective expression of improvement in life circumstances is the fact of this mobility more influential than the fact of stable high status.

If we now try to bring some of these findings into consonance with those provided by the analyses of education and exposure to mass media, we can assert that four major findings hold true for status differences:

1. The higher the status, the more favorable the Image of the Negro, but the differences are generally not significant.

2. The higher the status, the greater the readiness for desegregation of the schools, and the differences are significant.

3. For both the low- and high-status groups, the score on Image is more segregationist than the score on School Desegregation.

4. The differences between the scores on Scales I and V for the high-status group is greater than the corresponding difference for the low-status group.

Again we see that status differences work in the same way as differences in education and exposure to mass media. Again, therefore, we must see to what extent these findings hold up when we hold constant the possible effects of a number of other variables.

CHAPTER NINE

OCCUPATION, MOBILITY, AND ATTITUDES
WITH OTHER FACTORS HELD CONSTANT

WILL the influence of status persist when we set a control for the possible effects of other variables? This is the central question of this chapter.

We know that the high-status group has a significantly higher proportion of people who are well educated, have high income, and are highly exposed to mass media. We know also that these factors tend to influence attitudes in the same way as high status. That is, the more education, income, and exposure to mass media, the more favorable the Image of the Negro and the more ready for desegregation of the schools. Therefore, when we control for the effects of these variables, we ought to find that the high-status people become somewhat more like the low-status people in their Images of the Negro and their scores on readiness for desegregation.

We cannot state clearly our expectations about the effects of such other variables as the number of children, religiosity, and residence. We have seen in previous analyses that there is great variability in the way in which these factors relate to attitudes.

A summary of the analysis is presented in Table 53 on p. 143. Details will again be found in the Appendices.

1. HOLDING EDUCATION CONSTANT. One curious deviation from Finding 1 emerges. In the grammar school group the white-collar people have a more unfavorable image of the Negro than their blue-collar counterpart.

Finding 2 suffers only one exception, to wit, within the grammar school group the difference between high- and low-status people is not significant.

Findings 3 and 4 are sustained without exception.

Our general impression that a high status must be reinforced by high education, and vice versa, before significant differences in attitudes result is once again borne out. For instance, at the grammar school level, status does not relate

Occupation with Other Factors Constant

TABLE 53

Results of Analysis of Differences Between Status Groups on Two Scales (Image and School Desegregation), Holding Constant, in Turn, Each of Six Other Factors.

Findings	Factors Held Constant					
	1	2	3	4	5	6
	Education	Number of Children	Religiosity	Residence	Income	Exposure to Mass Media
1. The higher the status, the more favorable the Image of the Negro, but the differences are not significant.	+ −	+ −	+ −	+ −	+ −	+
2. The higher the status, the more ready for desegregation of the schools, and the differences are significant.	+ −	+ −	+ −	+ −	+ −	+ −
3. For both low and high status groups, the score on Image is more pro-segregationist than the score on school desegregation.	+ −	+	+	+	+	+
4. The difference between the scores on Scale I and V for the high status group is greater than the corresponding difference for the scores of the low status group.	+ −	+ −	+	+	+	+

+ = Findings confirmed
− = Findings violated

itself as significantly or in the same way to attitudes toward the Negro as at the high school or college level. And once again, the college-education, high-status people have by far the lower (more favorable) scores both on Image and on readiness to desegregate the schools.

It is also clear from our findings that the status differences themselves are important. The reduction in the size of the differences between white- and blue-collar workers has not been nearly as great as anticipated.

Why should persons in white-collar jobs have different attitudes and greater readiness than those in blue-collar jobs? It is clearly not the fact of employment alone, nor the type of work alone. Probably, occupational status gives the individual a sense of a stake in society, a sense of a favored position which is worth protecting. At this level, men seem to be aware that there are numerous values which have to be compromised, and that it is important for themselves as well as for others that decent social relationships should be enjoyed by everyone in the community.

2. HOLDING NUMBER OF CHILDREN CONSTANT. On Finding 1, the group with four-or-more children is deviant once again. The white-collar segment within this group has a more unfavorable Image of the Negro than the blue-collar segment. The differences are small, to be sure, but they are there, and they are in the "wrong" direction. By now, however, we are not surprised at the way in which this group with four-or-more children reverses our ordinary expectations.

Finding 2 is violated now by the group with no children. Though the white-collar segment of this group is more ready for desegregation, the difference between it and the blue-collar segment is small and insignificant. Again, those with no children seem to be much less concerned about disruption of the schools than is exhibited by other groups.

Finding 3 is sustained in all cases except that of the group with four-or-more children. Here, in fact, the blue-collar group is even more segregationist in its School Desegregation score than on its Image score.

We know that in general those with four-or-more children constitute the economically and socially most depressed group in the total sample. While the white-collar segment of this group is nearer the average of the total sample, the blue-collar segment seems to be resolutely determined to prevent desegregation in the schools. The combination of four-or-more children and blue-collar occupational status seem to work hand in hand to produce the most resistant group in our total sample.

With respect to status, finding 4 is violated in two of the three groups. Among the childless and those with four-or-more children, the fact of high status does not produce the disparity between the scores on Image and desegregation that we anticipated.

Only in the group with one-to-three children do all the findings hold steady. This group has shown these same characteristics throughout our analysis. This is the group that has the highest means on education, income, and other such measures of position and stake in the society.

3. HOLDING RELIGIOSITY CONSTANT. Only in the low-religiosity group (those who go to church less than once a month) do the findings about the influence of status hold. The medium-religiosity group, (less than once a week but more than once a month) and the high-religiosity people (once a week or more) violate several of our findings.

For the medium-religiosity people, the violations are as follows. First, the white-collar segment has a noticeably more unfavorable Image of the Negro than its blue-collar counter-part. Second, the difference between the blue- and white-collar segments on readiness for desegregation, though in the expected direction, is not statistically significant.

The high-religiosity group violates findings 2 and 4 as follows. First, the difference between the blue- and white-collar groups on readiness for desegregation is not as significant as it formerly was. Second, the difference between the scores on Scales I and V of the high-status group is not greater than the corresponding difference in the scores of the low-status group. Particularly noteworthy is the fact that the white-collar, medium-religiosity group drops more than a full scale point from its unfavorable Image of the Negro to its relative readiness for desegregation of the school. To be sure, it shows greater resistance to desegregation than either of the other two white-collar groups. But the drop in its scores is the sharpest found anywhere in our figures.

Once again we are unable to generalize about the bearing of religiosity upon attitudes toward the Negro and desegregation of the schools. The low- and high-religiosity groups are more alike than is either one of them like the medium-religiosity group. There is no way of saying, then, that the more religion, or the more attendance at church, the more favorable the Image, or the greater the readiness for de-segregation. Our data simply will not support this kind of contention.

The high and low religiosity people form two groups who tend to be more favorable in their Image of the Negro and more ready to desegregate the schools but for very different reasons, apparently. Those who have no formal religious inclinations, at least not expressed in church attendance, might, to that extent, be considered as "independents" or "deviants" relative to the church-going norms of the community. If this is the case, it would not be unreasonable to expect them to be independent or deviant with regard to the traditional norms of segregation as well. On the other side those who attend church most frequently may be expressing in their favorable attitudes certain religious ideologies and convictions about the brotherhood of man.

4. HOLDING RESIDENCE CONSTANT. The rural group once again confuses the picture. The white-collar residents of the rural area have a more unfavorable Image of the Negro than their blue-collar co-residents. Moreover, though the former are more ready for desegregation of the schools, the difference between them and the blue-collar, rural segment is not significant.

Contrary to our findings on exposure to mass media, the urban group does show the desegregationist tendencies which our earlier analysis had led us to expect. But we cannot make firm claims about the impact of urban residence in view of the fact that the influences over the range of variables have been so different. To say that urban residence exerts one kind of influence in combination with status, but quite an opposite influence in combination with exposure to the mass media, is simply to state a problem and not solve one. We therefore conclude that urban and rural residence do not play significant and steady roles.

5. HOLDING INCOME CONSTANT. Those who are white-collar and earn under $5,000.00 a year violate our expectations in precisely the same way as did the rural group just examined. Their Image of the Negro is slightly more favorable than the Image of those who are white-collar and earn over $5,000.00. Second, though their readiness for desegregation of the schools is somewhat greater than the blue-collar group, it is not significantly greater.

Once again this is a case of the influence of a "high" on one variable, such as status, being diminished by the opposite play of a "low" on another, such as income. Just as *high income reinforces high status* in producing the most favorable images of the Negro and the greatest readiness for desegregation, so *low income works against high status* and reduces the scores on Image and readiness for desegregation to a point where the high- and low-status groups are virtually indistinguishable.

6. HOLDING EXPOSURE TO MASS MEDIA CONSTANT. The single deviation here is within the low exposure group, where the differences between the low- and high-status group on Scale V are not as significant as they previously were. Still, the scores are sufficiently far apart (2.55 *vs.* 2.17) to suggest that this may be an insignificant deviation.

The fact that our findings are otherwise confirmed here is something of a surprise. For, it will be recalled that when we condensed the four exposure groups into two, joining the two lowest together into one new group called *low,* and the two highest into a new group called *high,* we expected some of the differences to be reduced. In fact, however, status differences hold up, even when we control for the factor of exposure. The significance of status is thereby well documented. This finding somewhat undercuts our notion about the required mutual reinforcement of these major variables.

Summary and Conclusions

In general, we can conclude from this analysis that status is a powerful differentiator even when we distinguish only between white- and blue-collar positions. We noticed, for instance, how the differences that status made by itself continued to hold even when we controlled for the effects of education, income, and exposure to mass media. The deviations from the findings are comparable to those we found when we tested for the influences of education and exposure to mass media while holding other variables constant. We may judge fairly, then, that each of these variables is truly a major variable. Some diminution of their effects results when one controls for the influence of each upon the other. But by and large they each tend to be reasonably good single predictors

147

of the kinds and relative sizes of scores of the different groups involved.

Position in the white-collar segment, though this includes everything from clerks through judges, seems to invest the individual so defined with a social rank of some worth. At the least, it appears to identify that kind of an individual who feels bound to the legal and social norms, not alone of his immediate and parochial subgroup, but of the larger society as well. *In short, occupational status is another indication of "stake," and seems closely related to perspective. We have seen how the sense of a stake and the acquisition of perspective both lead the individual to entertain a somewhat more favorable Image of the Negro and to be somewhat more ready to desegregate the schools.*

CHAPTER TEN

THE QUALITY AND ROLE OF LEADERS
IN THE PROCESS OF DESEGREGATION

NOW we see that education, exposure to the mass media and occupational status have a modest impact upon one's Image of the Negro and a decidedly strong influence upon one's readiness for desegregation of the schools. When high education and high exposure are combined with white-collar occupation, the most favorable Image of the Negro and the greatest readiness for desegregation are present.

These are "relative" statements. They do not help us identify the "absolute" Image or the "absolute" level of readiness. But it is hard to visualize how such absolute levels could be specified. The level of readiness and the Image are meaningful measurements relative to some other condition. For instance, if we ask whether the majority of our respondents could conceivably be expected to invite Negroes to dinner tomorrow, the answer is obviously "no." If we ask whether that same majority could conceivably be expected to accept Negroes as working partners tomorrow the answer is probably "yes." If we ask, finally, whether that majority would send their children to desegregated schools tomorrow, the answer would seem to lie somewhere in between the highly probably "yes" and the almost certain "no." As our rank orders of resistance have shown, the quality and importance of the Image of the Negro depends on the context, and this dependence on context is even more applicable to the level of readiness for desegregation.

Moreover, the particular situation is not the only important consideration. Surely much depends in *any* situation on how the proposal is introduced, and by whom. A great deal also seems to depend upon the ratio of Negroes to Whites in the area. Whether the region has been prosperous or has been suffering economic turndown or recession seems also to matter. To make predictions about a particular situation, in a particular place and at a particular time, one must know more than our study reveals about the quality of attitudes.

Some general assessments, however, can be made. Barring unforeseen events, it is most likely that the population of the South will, on the average, become more educated and more exposed to mass media, and a higher percentage of its work force will move out of the blue-collar and into the white-collar occupations. These developments seem assured by the predictable increase in urbanization and industrialization of the South and by the general economic movement of the entire society.

If our analysis of the impact of education, mass media, and high-status jobs upon attitudes toward desegregation is correct, and if one can generalize from our North Carolina sample to the whole South, then we can expect some modest amelioration of the White's Image of the Negro, and a more pronounced increase in readiness for desegregation, especially in the public schools.

But this is a process and not a quick turn of events. Any social process which involves as much basic change as is implied in the term desegregation is sure to produce some conflict, some struggle back and forth, possibly some damage to all parties. But the die does seem finally cast. Probably the Supreme Court Decision of 1954 marks the decisive point from which there is no turning back. Whatever setbacks may occur, whatever violent outbursts of resistance, whatever regathering of segregationist forces—these are likely to be short lived; and once they have transpired, the movement toward desegregation and general equality for Negro and White will probably resume.

Along the way, however, there are numerous intermediate costs and consequences. The tempo and pace of the movement toward desegregation is therefore a critical consideration. So, too, is the way in which the changes are brought about, for on this depends the amount of hostility which is engendered, the increment of bitterness which will accumulate, and the character and meaning of the probable new alignments of political forces.

Only from some supremely Olympian point of view can the

intermediate stages and their consequences be dismissed as trivial relative to the final outcome. For the outcome of a social process contains the sum total of all that has transpired and accumulated along the way.

If ever there were any doubts about the significance of intermediate stages and consequences, Governor Faubus of Arkansas has dispelled these doubts once and for all. However one evaluates the Little Rock events, there can be little doubt that Faubus played a highly influential role. And the situation would have been drastically different had Faubus not taken his stand and implemented it as he did.

Other governors and mayors, other officials who have been able to persuade their constituents one way or the other, have also shown us, over the years since the Supreme Court edict, that the roles played by leaders, official and otherwise, can be critical.[1] This is always the case when we are in the midst of a situation where the issues at stake are of deep concern to everyone, and where the competing leaderships are vying for the adherence of a relatively volatile and varied constituency.

The population we have described and analyzed is extremely varied. Certain portions fulfill the stereotype of a hard-bitten, hard-core segregationist South. Others come closer to resembling a northern liberal desegregationist population. There are roughly the same percentages at both extremes: on the one side, those who would use force to prevent desegregation, and on the other those who would do nothing to impede desegregation, or perhaps would even act to facilitate such desegregation. In between stand the large majority, those who view desegregation as undesirable but do not seem prepared actively to impede the process.

If the advantages of local habit, long standing tradition, and regional social pressure lie with the segregationists, the

---

[1] For further study of the roles of power, leadership, and public opinion, see Chapters 2 and 3, in *Desegregation, Some Propositions and Research Suggestions* by E. A. Suchman, J. P. Dean, R. M. Williams, Jr., *et al,* New York, Anti-Defamation League, 1958.

For a more general survey of the role of leadership in social action, see Cecil A. Gibb, "Leadership," Chapter 24 (pp. 877–920) in *Handbook of Social Psychology,* Vol. II, ed. by Gardner Lindzey, Cambridge, Mass., Addison-Wesley, 1954.

advantages of general social pressure, legal injunction, and dominant national trends lie with the group seeking acceptance of desegregation, or at least willing to let it come without resistance.

Again, the large majority appears to stand in between these two sets of attitudes. For while they are habituated to traditional patterns of segregation, they are also accustomed to thinking of themselves as members of the Union, and as men who believe in law and order and who act upon that belief.

It is useful to think of the range of these different attitudes as a continuum, starting with extreme resistance to desegregation on the one side and moving gradually through the milder forms of resistance to the beginnings of acceptance, ending finally in active advocacy of the cause of desegregation. We can then mentally divide the continuum in half and distinguish all those who are resistant to some degree or another from all those who are ready to some extent to accept desegregation.

Corresponding to each of these two sub-ranges of opinion and attitude in the community we studied are two identifiable sets of leaders. These are men of prominence, some of them elected or appointed officials, occupying important public posts, who are built solidly into the community structure of power. They are alike in the legitimacy and important of their positions of influence. They are markedly dissimilar, however, as we shall soon see, in their attitudes toward desegregation.

There is another group of leaders who are not easy to identify and who generally occupy no important posts, nor have they been legitimized in their power and influence in any way. They are almost ephemeral creatures, in a sense, for they emerge only in a time of crisis and usually disappear as quickly as they emerged. These are the men, more often solitary individuals, who come up suddenly from no one knows where, to fill in the vacuum of leadership and power which is created when either the respectable leadership fails to exercise power, or when, as in the case of Little Rock, the respectable leadership is rendered virtually powerless by the executive withdrawal of public power and supervision, and an invitation is extended to the population to come and do as it sees fit with the events of the day.

When such an invitation is extended, there is almost always someone around to take up leadership, and to create new norms of conduct, appealing almost always to the deepest passions of the people and making it virtually impossible for respectable leadership to exert its normal influence.

The audience to whom this emergent leadership most pointedly directs its appeal consists of the most disinherited and alienated members of the social group. These are the poorest, the socially least-prestigeful, the least educated, the persons for whom obedience to law and order has the least appeal for there is so little for them to lose—at least as they see it. Almost always, such a group can be induced to seize the power which has been offered to it and to take violent action against persons or groups whom the emergent leadership identifies as the enemy—those who have either been responsible for the low status of the disinherited ones, or some convenient and powerless scapegoat on whom the cumulated bitterness of the years can be expended without too much fear of subsequent reprisal.

It is the rare moment in human history when an otherwise respectable, law-abiding and community-rooted leader can successfully confront and turn back a group of men who have been incited to act out violently their senses of bitterness and frustration. Normally, the respectable leader does not have the stomach, the skills, or the quick presence of mind for such confrontation. Emotionally aroused groups turn quickly into mobs, and then men behave in fearsome and unpredictable ways. The positive power of the mob and the absence of any effective restraint by the respectable leadership combine to produce troublesome and costly results which sometimes have long-lasting effects.

The effectiveness of the respectable leadership depends upon the assurance that the legal instruments of power will be used to support the law and to maintain a condition under which differing points of view can compete and debate. But the respectable leadership itself helps determine whether such

153

an assurance of legal power will be sustained. Quick and resolute action by such leadership is often of the utmost importance in forestalling and preventing the creation of power vacuums into which mob power flows. Mob sentiment is cumulative; it grows and feeds upon itself. Immediate and effective quelling of initial acts of disobedience and violence has proven to be the best antidote to mob formation. The assurance that any acts of violence will be met by the full force of the law and other instruments of community restraint is a major preventive of lawlessness and the assurance of peaceful public debate. But the satisfactoriness of public debate as a way of resolving issues in conflict depends on the extent to which the major points of view held by various segments of the community are adequately represented. Those who feel unrepresented or unrepresentable are the clients for new leaders or possibly mob action.

Moreover, if there are voices from both sides, and if the speakers are respected and powerful men, then the number of intermediate costs to be paid on the path to desegregation are likely to be reduced, and the exorbitant costs of mob violence are likely not to have to be paid at all.

A crucial question, then, which we directed to our community in North Carolina, concerns the extent to which the competing points of view were adequately represented.

To test whether leadership in the North Carolina community was responsive to the various points of view in the population, we attempted a series of interviews with a selected panel of twenty-eight of the most respected and formally most powerful men in the community.

The Panel

The selection of the panel was not a difficult process. With the advice of one of the local newspaper editors, a small number of men were chosen on the basis of their official positions. Each of these was asked to name others whom he thought constituted the leadership in the community, without regard to the side or stand they took on desegregation. In this way, a group of twenty-eight was finally chosen. Of these, five could not be interviewed. These included the mayor, two businessmen, one clergyman, and one labor leader. Except for the mayor, each of these "unavailable" leaders had an occupational counterpart in the sample who was interviewed. The final panel of twenty-three included two lawyers; three presidents of firms; one bank president; one executive of a business men's organization; five ministers; three college officials of top rank; one executive officer of the public school system; four newspaper editors; one highly placed Federal official; one labor leader; and one regional director of a national service-organization.

The interviews were conducted privately, and ranged in length from one half-hour to three hours. In only two instances was there apparent hesitancy to answer frankly; in only one case was there any noticeable lack of rapport and unwillingness to give specific responses. Generally the same questions were put to each of the respondents, but in some cases certain modifications in phrasing were required to suit the particular occupation of the panel member. The general run of questions was as follows:

(1) How long in present position?

(2) What previous positions held?

(3) Length of residence in the community?

(4) Previous places of residence?

(5) Number of years of school completed?

(6) What public stand, if any, already taken on desegregation?

(7) (For ministers) What stand taken by their parent church bodies?

(8) Was respondent generally accustomed to speaking out publicly on issues?

(9) How influential did respondent feel himself to be, with public at large, or with his own particular public (parish, readers, etc.)?

(10) What impact has he had in past when he has spoken out?

(11) Why do people listen to him on certain issues?

(12) (For ministers) Composition of congregation, and any stands taken by congregation on desegregation?

(13) (For business men) Hiring practices of their companies; their views of future of desegregation in labor force?

Once this background was in hand, the panel was then asked specifically about desegregation of the public school, as follows:

1. What is your view of the future course of desegregation in the public schools in your community? Is it inevitable? Will trouble or violence occur? Was the Supreme Court decision unfortunate? Did it come too soon? How long do you think it will be before the public schools of your community are desegregated?

2. If the Federal Court ordered desegregation of the public schools of the community by September 1957, would you speak out, for or against the ruling? What path of action would you follow? What would you urge others to do? What would be your personal and private reactions?

On the basis of the general run of responses, we divided the panel into those who were for and those against school desegregation. During the rest of this report we will refer to the former as the desegregationists, and the latter as the segregationists. (It should be kept in mind, however, that as used here these terms are not restrictive or absolute; they cover a wide range of readiness and resistance.) The panel divides into fourteen in favor of desegregation and nine opposed to it.

EDUCATION, BIRTHPLACE AND RESIDENCE. Data from the larger sample of the labor force shows that there is a clear-cut relationship between formal education and attitudes toward segregation—the greater the number of years of school completed, the more ready for desegregation. There is also a suggestion of a growing difference between the attitudes of rural and urban dwellers, though this relationship is not nearly as clear-cut nor as regular.

In the leadership panel, these differences become meaningless. For while their attitudes differ, it turns out that thirteen of the fourteen desegregationists and all of the nine segregationists had college education. Ten of the fourteen desegregationists, and eight of the nine segregationists, had been born in the South. The major portion of the lives of all but four of the twenty-three men had been spent in the South, including the years during which they were going to school. Nor did the panel members differ markedly in length of residence in the community. All the business men, segregationists and desegregationists, and all the newspapermen had been long-time dwellers in the city, while the educators and clergymen had spent some fewer years in the area.

On the basis of these data, we cannot account for differences in attitudes in terms of residence and education. Nor ought one to expect these leaders to be differently influential because some are "local boys" and others are not. Those representing each attitude have the necessary qualifications for claiming knowledge of the area and its traditions, by virtue of their own exposure to them, since birth. Both sides can lay matching claims to knowing what is needed, what the people really are like, and what they really want.[2]

DOES RELIGION MATTER? Judging by the responses of our large sample, religion makes no difference of any statistical significance in attitudes toward desegregation. Neither the fact of church affiliation, the particular denomination, nor the frequency of church attendance discriminates cleanly among our respondents. Yet the clergymen in our leadership panel were either openly in opposition to segregation or, at the least, did not speak out publicly in favor of it.

One has to speculate about the significance of religion in the segregation issue. It seems reasonable to assume that the behavior of the ministers at least made it difficult for the seg-

---

[2] More important, still, is the fact that since the desegregationist position implies a larger-than-local perspective, a majority of a panel have arrived at this larger perspective even though nothing special in their educational backgrounds or their patterns of birth and residence impelled them to differ from their segregationist fellow citizens in these regards. This suggests that there is room for the play of ideological conviction in the final shaping of action. Perhaps, even, this play of ideology goes on independent of those forces flowing from vested interests, and concern for material welfare. But it must also be remembered that the impact of ideology is most noticeable at the level of high education, income, and prestige. Can it be, then, that the persuasiveness of principles varies proportionate to the freedom from material want and from concern for status?

regationists to invoke the example of these respected men in support of their positions. Even though the stand of the anti-segregationist ministers could be dismissed as something which ministers *had* to say, the open avowal of desegregation by these spiritual leaders put a damper on any attempt to give a religio-moral tone to the segregationist position.

In the over-all strategy of social change, it appears, leaders are sometimes limited to standing as symbols of the moral right, thereby cutting out the possible appeals to morality by their different-minded adherents. The denial of access to institutional sanction, as effected by the stand of some of the ministers, must be counted as an important element in the total picture.

COMPETING STRATEGIES. Many believe that Southern leaders who favor desegregation are coerced into silence, partly out of fear of reprisal and partly out of fear of losing their positions of leadership. If this is so, a real dilemma is posed. For since desegregation represents the new and the unfamiliar pattern, open and clamorous propagation of this point of view seems required if the leadership is to be effective. A crucial question, then, concerns the extent to which these leaders have spoken out generally in the past, and are speaking out today on behalf of desegregation, and yet are keeping their positions of leadership. Do they, as proponents of the new and the different, speak out more frequently than their segregationist peers who are defending the old and the familiar?

We divided our sample into those who (a) have frequently spoken out in public; (b) those who have not; (c) those who say they *cannot;* and (d) those who refuse to say, or from whom the answer is unclear. Of the fourteen desegregationists, eight have spoken out, one has not, three say they cannot, and two give unclear responses. By contrast, of the nine segregationists, three have spoken out in the past, three have not, two say they cannot, and one refused to say.

These differences are not a function of differences in the leaders' occupations, for the three non-speakers among the segregationists include a business man, a clergyman, and an educator. The two who "cannot" are an editor and one other. Among the desegregationists, an editor, a business organization executive, and one other say they cannot speak out. The nonspeaker is a clergyman.

Of crucial significance is the fact that there were ministers, educators, and newspaper editors who spoke out publicly in favor of desegregation, even though many of their constituent publics, their supervisors, and their boards of trustees were opposed. Two of the ministers have spoken out *on behalf of desegregation* to their own segregated all-White parishes. The educators who favor desegregation do so openly on campuses that are totally segregated. The anomaly is that the only educator who favored segregation was forced by court order to make room in his school for a limited number of Negro students. His reaction to this order is indicated in his statement that he will take only those steps required by law.

The business men in the panel are more diverse in their opinions. They range from frank support of desegregation to equally frank opposition. The stereotyped caution of the business man is expressed only by one man, the owner of the largest plant in the area, who asserts that he does not propose to "lead" on this issue. The policy of his company is one of following the trends in the area. At the same time, in at least some job-categories in his plant, Negroes and Whites work side by side on equal status levels.

The union has not taken any stand on the issue because its parent State body has not, and because its local position is too weak, organizationally, and in terms of its membership. Yet the union organizer favors integration, and, along with other union leaders, has managed to maintain a desegregated union hall, and to have several Negro shop stewards representing both White and Negro workers in their plants. *It seems eminently possible, then, for Southern leaders who favor desegregation to speak out on behalf of desegregation and still continue in their positions of leadership, if their positions are previously secure.*

In speaking out more frequently on more issues than the segregationist leadership, the desegregationists are doing precisely what their side requires of them. For silence and inactivity favor the existing traditions, and bold public affirmations of the importance of social change are almost always re-

159

quired if that change is to come about. Strong support is given to this notion by the very illuminating remarks of the business man considered by many to be the most influential person in the community. This man is totally committed to segregation but he is also moderate in his activities in support of segregation. He said that he chose not to speak publicly because he believed that most matters were best settled through private channels in which one quietly exerted private influence. He felt no need for public exhortation.

The pattern emerges more clearly now. The educated and moderate, though committed, segregationists favor quiet but determined resistance, without public clamor. The educated and moderate, though committed, desegregationists, by contrast, favor vocal and frequent public talk. Both groups, then, seem to have sensed well the appropriate though competing strategies for leadership of their respective camps in the segregation issue.

Summing these last trends briefly, we note that local leaders are involved in a play of diverse forces, many of which are opposed to their personal predilections. They have to contend with and compromise the demands of (1) their parent oragnizations, (2) their clients, constituents, or customers; (3) their employees, (4) their immediate supervisors or trustees, and (5) the law. The play of these forces has compelled the desegregationists to accept less than they desire, and the segregationists more than they would like to see by way of desegregation. In this interplay, the desegregation leadership is appropriately vocal and public in their support of desegregation, and the segregation leadership appropriately quiet and personal in their fight to maintain segregation.[3]

---

[3] These segregationist leaders are noticeably different, in these regards, from other outstanding defenders of segregation in the South. Even in North Carolina, many of the leading prosegregationists are quite clamorous on behalf of their cause. But, as we later suggest, this is the segregationist camp on the defensive, forced into open and vocal activity by the Supreme Court ruling, which reverses the advantage normally enjoyed by the *status quo*. Moreover, our data suggest, if vocal and public argument is required to further the cause of desegregation when the segregationist leadership is relatively personal and silent in its actions, how much more activity and energy are required when the segregationists react, defensively, with their own spirited and public clamor?

The Quality and Role of Leaders

TACTICAL COMPROMISE. Opposing political camps sometimes join in support of the same proposal. They do so because each views the proposal from a different point of view and each sees the proposal serving different functions, corresponding to his own political interests. Such was the case in the sponsorship of the Pearsall Plan by some members of both camps. This was a plan designed to circumvent the Supreme Court ruling by providing that the State should pay those parents who did not wish to send their children to desegregated public schools. The State funds were to be used to send the children to private schools of their parents' choice.

The segregationists supported the measure, for they saw this as a way to evade the Supreme Court ruling and they thought the Plan would probably threaten the financial structure of the State enough to make the desegregationists hesitate before pushing any harder for implementation of the ruling.

Those desegregationists who supported the measure did so for quite different reasons. They felt that unless this much of a temporary appeasement was offered, the extremist and pro-violence elements in the segregationist camp could pose the situation as desperate, and rally additional support to the extreme point of view. The Pearsall Plan, they felt, would quiet down the fears about sudden and total reversal of a traditional way of life, and thus give more time in which to work back to a more moderate and acceptable method of implementing the Supreme Court ruling, without undue pressure for immediate and stark activity from the extremist elements in the pro-segregationist camp. In short, the moderates of both camps could move toward reducing their differences in a calmer and more sane climate of public opinion. But the desegregationists had no doubts regarding the unworkability and the impermanence of the Pearsall Plan. Nor did they hesitate to point out publicly that the Plan was almost certainly unconstitutional.

What appeared, then, to Northern observers, as a rank capitulation on the part of some Southern desegregationists,

---

And if the proponents of desegregation are already using every public opportunity to further their cause, then, perhaps, the extra voices and extra forces coming from outside the region are needed to aid their cause.

now emerges as a tactic calculated to serve the desegregation cause as best it could be served at that time. At least, this is the view which some of the desegregationists took. And there is no ground, at least not in our data, on which to doubt the sincerity of this view. However, it should also be noted that some of the desegregationists, notably the ministers and educators, openly opposed the Pearsall Plan. They did not share the view of its tactical advantages.

INFLUENCE OF THE LEADERS. On the question of influence the answers are unclear, partly because of the modesty of the panel and partly because the actual influence of leaders is so difficult to assess. The panel insisted that while they felt they had some influence and weight in the community, this might be simply illusory. In four cases, including one segregationist, the leaders felt that their stands on school-desegregation were already so well known that any further public iteration would mean very little. Prodding elicited some expression of greater confidence in the importance of their public pronouncements. The only general impression with which one was left, after questioning the panel on this matter, was that they probably felt they had had a good deal to do with the movement of events in their communities, but hesitated to claim credit for their actions.

THE ROLES OF CHANCE AND TIME. Whichever side of the desegregation question the leaders happen to take, the strategies of private and public action they adopt are likely to be based upon their sense for the chance of victory and the time required to win this victory.

In this regard, it is crucially important that all the panel, desegregationists and segregationists alike, considered desegregation of the public schools in their community as inevitable. They differed sharply on the rapidity with which this should transpire—ranging from an estimate of one year to one decade. But both the shortest- and longest-time estimates came from desegregationists. One ought, therefore, to expect considerable variations in the plans they advocate.

The differences in the time estimates arise in part from differences in opinion regarding the probable activities of different elements in both camps. Would the Patriots, the local

162

extremists, become increasingly more effective? Would local resistance be very moderate, because school desegregation would hardly change anything in view of the sharp residential segregation? How would the state legislature respond over the next two years? How active would the pressure for court tests become? How much counterreaction to such pressure from the courts would develop? How would the Governor and the Legislature respond to these movements of opinion?

Almost the entire panel saw the Governor, the Legislature, and further court trials as the most effective instruments of future change. It was reliably "rumored," for instance, that a number of communities in North Carolina were on the verge of desegregating their school systems until the Governor and the Legislature revised the statutes so that local communities were effectively, even if only implicitly, threatened with loss of State support if they desegregated their schools. No open threats were made, but the implied promise was there and a mechanism had been contrived to fulfill that promise. There was also considerable speculation that the Governor could have taken quite a different stand, on the side of the "law of the land" and could have found considerable support throughout the State for this view. But for a number of reasons, including, prominently, the domination of the legislature by a segregationist-minded rural contingent, the state officialdom had opposed the Supreme Court ruling by various strategems.

In ascribing so much importance to the acts of the official leaders, our own panel was testifying to their belief that the public was fluid and mixed, and that a majority support could have been had for obedience as well as defiance of the Court ruling. Courageous acts of acceptance of the "inevitable" by leaders would therefore have hastened the "inevitable." The leadership obviously exerted a decisive influence but apparently could have exerted the opposite influence just as successfully.

REACTION TO THE SUPREME COURT DECISION. "Leave us alone and we'll do the job by ourselves." This was the way in which even the staunchest desegregationists in the panel reacted to the Supreme Court ruling. But here there is apparent and real contradiction in the positions the desegregationists

163

take. For on the one hand they see the ruling as having worsened the situation, by helping intransigent counter-opposition to develop and by worsening personal relations between Negroes and Whites. Yet, in the same, and previous and subsequent breaths, they insist that it is through the courts and court rulings that the victory of desegregation will finally be won. They counsel moderation and urge that the pace of change be attuned to the local temper, yet they regret the Court ruling which specifically provides for such adjustment. They see themselves as requiring the assistance of larger social pressures, yet they deplore the edict which gave them just such a purchase. Standing for a basic change in long established traditions, and requiring therefore every available assistance for a most difficult job, they nevertheless wish that the Court had not "prematurely" and in "erroneous terms" provided this kind of assistance.

Why this apparent ambivalence on the part of the desegregation leadership? One can only guess that they genuinely felt they had the issue won; that the process of change was moving in their direction; and that they felt they understood the temper of their people and were providing the kind of leadership which would help move their community toward full acceptance of the Supreme Court order. But they also felt that unless this acceptance was seen by the local people as their own self-generated response to their own recognition of a need, they would refuse to go any further.

This implies that the commitment of the public to desegregation was as yet shallow and superimposed rather than arising from genuine internal conviction, a daring but tentative movement toward a new set of social forms. But if this is the case, surely any unpleasant incident—and there were bound to be many—which could be interpreted as a consequence of desegregation would also be enough to uproot the shallow and superimposed commitment, and to reverse the movement of opinion and social behavior back into its familiar and well-worn ruts.

If these guesses are right, the Southern desegregationists obviously need the kind of barrier against backward movement which the Supreme Court ruling sets up. In their conscious

The Quality and Role of Leaders

hearts, they are being truly representative of the range of feeling of their constituents, anxious to do the right thing, to obey the law, to be able to be proud of their behavior, to be able to hold up their heads in the national public and not simply to court favor in the hills. But they insist that it be *their* decision and action. Still, unconsciously, they appear to welcome the ruling, recognizing it for the kind of check against slip-back which it is, and for the kind of model of deportment which it suggests.

That some such unconscious welcome of the ruling is probably at work is seen in the responses of the panel to the question as to what they would do if the federal court in their district ordered an immediate implementation of the Supreme Court ruling. Not a single leader would publicly oppose the ruling. Ten of the fourteen desegregationists would speak out in its favor. Three of the nine segregationists would do the same. One of the desegregationists *would* not speak out and three said they *could* not. Three of the segregationists would not talk up; two say they could not; and one would not say what he would do.

In brief, the same pattern of speaking out on public issues *in general* now reasserts itself with regard to the possible federal court edict. Only, this time, the three segregationists who speak out would support the ruling. In short, the leadership of the community, on both sides, would use its private and public influence to support any court decision ordering desegregation of the public schools. No active resistance would be counselled by any of them. At worst, they would be silent.

The principal reason for support of such an edict is because "it is the law." Other reasons included: "the alternatives were exhausted . . . it is a highly desirable move anyway towards a better school system . . . it is the Christian point of view in favor of equality of persons. . . . I would not want to give the White Citizens Councils a chance to blow up. . . . We would not want the schools in this city to be shut. . . . Closing of the schools would be the worst calamity for us."

They would give uniform support, or silence, but no opposition. And this uniformity of action on top of a layer of diverse reasons, and diverse degrees of welcome to and desire for the edict.

Notice, above all, the way in which some of the desegregationists welcome the possible ruling as a force to forestall any moves by the extremist segregationist fringe. Surely, if this extremist-group action is what the desegregationists fear worst, and if they see the federal court implementation of the Supreme Court ruling as a blow against such action, then what can they mean by their expressed regret of the ruling itself? It is clear that however immersed they are in the tradition of local self determination, at bottom they welcome the impact of federal law and see it as a force for their side which they otherwise could not muster.

The Effects of Leadership

We can now answer at least some of the questions we raised at the outset of this chapter.

The leadership in this North Carolina city expressed, in its own attitudes, the range of sentiments of the majority of the people in the country. Included among them were all the major types of responses to the proposed school desegregation, except the willingness to close the schools and use violence if necessary in order to resist desegregation. Because they do not represent this end-portion of the segregationist continuum, one has to be wary about their ability to calculate the acts of these extreme segregationists. On the other hand, segregationists and desegregationists alike express concern about such people and are alerted to them.

The panel is moderate. They are aware of the larger issues at stake; they appreciate the complexities of the issues; they feel it important to help develop these perspectives regarding moderation and complexity among those whom they address.

They are all sensitive to the fact that desegregation implies and is involved with a host of other values, and that injudicious action may cost the community dearly. They seem anxious to develop more awareness of the possible costs to other values.

They are appreciative of the fact that the processes at work in their own community are local expressions of larger institutional arrangements, and that there are larger-than-local forces to which they must be attuned. At the same time, they press, in their responses, for more awareness by outsiders to the need for local self-determination, as they see it.

They see the desegregation issue as affecting diverse publics, not only White adults, but White children, and Negroes of all ages as well. They are to some degree concerned with the welfare of the Negroes. They recognize them as probably permanent and certainly valuable citizens of the community, when and if a proper mode of incorporating them into the community is worked out.

They know of the extent to which the outside world is concerned with the events in their area. They know it, and with one part, wish the outsiders were less concerned; with another part, they seem to welcome such intervention.

They are respecters of law and order. They see themselves as bound by the laws of the land. They hope to be able to impress others with the need to obey the laws. They feel that thereby they may prevent the extremist segregationist from coming into greater influence.

In summary, these leaders—almost without exception—have the kind of outlook, the type of perspective, the insistence on moderation, and the kind of respect for their nation as well as their region, which in the larger sample differentiate those most ready for desegregation from those less ready. This holds true even for some of those leaders who are nominally segregationist.[4]

Conclusions

As we turn to predict the likely course of events, and to assess the importance of various strategies in this context, a number of qualifications must be introduced which set cau-

[4] A crucial qualification must be introduced here. It is the fact that at least some of those who either favored rapid desegregation, or, at least, saw the likelihood of such action, whether they personally favored it or not, pointed to the fact that residential segregation would in large part annul the immediate impact of school desegregation. It is not possible from our data to say whether some of the desegregationists took their school desegregation stand because they felt it safe to do so, in view of residential segregation.

167

tions upon the extent to which one may generalize about the South from the materials presented here. They are as follows:

(a) North Carolina, the state in which this study was conducted, is not considered one of the hard-core states. The distribution of attitudes among leaders in more intransigent states may substantially differ from North Carolina.

(b) The county from which the larger panel was drawn, and the city from which the leadership panel was drawn, are among the most prosperous and industrialized political units in the State. The city is virtually a metropolis compared to other areas in the South. The attitudes of the leaders may therefore be deviant from those in other areas. It must especially be borne in mind that the city is one which is reported to have deliberately set its sights upon becoming a modern city.

(c) The leadership sample in this study consisted of men in positions of responsibility and legitimate power. They are the "best" the area has to offer. They do not contain in their ranks the most intransigent types of resisters found in the South. By virtue of their positions, they must have a larger-than-local perspective, which, it wlll be recalled, is an indispensable ingredient of readiness for desegregation.

With these reservations in mind, one can assert that: If the final outcome of the issue of desegregation is left to the play of competing opinions among these leaders and like-minded followers; and if they are allowed to pose their relative readinesses and resistances against each other within the scope of legitimate actions, then, *desegregation will not only surely triumph but will do so quickly and with relatively low intermediate costs.*

But it is equally apparent that:

1. The presence of a legal command to desegregate is a vital ingredient of this outcome. Such a command serves a number of functions:

    (a) It sets a model of proper behavior.

    (b) It reinforces the hand of those who are in positions of respected leadership and who possess legitimate power.

(c) It forces those leaders who are against the ruling to devise anti-legal strategems which undermine their claims to positions of legitimate power.

(d) It forces those who would preserve the segregated system to become active and alert, rather than rely on apathy, silence and the weight of habit. In short, there is a displacement of the advantage of the offensive, so that the habitual system is forced on the defensive, and thus loses some of the power ordinarily possessed by tradition.

2. Constant public speaking-out and keeping the public alert is equally vital to the successful achievement of the proposed new system. Though the traditional system is forced on to the defensive more than ever before by a legal mandate, continuous agitation for obedience and enforcement of the law is clearly required for its successful implementation.

3. Constant pressure from outside the region upon the local leadership is apparently important in keeping them active, even though they specifically disavow the need of such pressure, and even claim that it impedes their cause. Pressure from outside the region upon the local leadership serves for them much the same functions as pressure from them upon their constituents within the region.

4. It is eminently possible for leaders to speak out in support of apparently unpopular causes and still retain their positions of leadership. Indeed, depending on their official positions, their publics may exepct them to take sides with which the publics disagree.

5. The open posing of disagreements, i.e., the bringing of conflict out into the open, is positively functional for the side desiring social change and disfunctional for the side seeking to preserve the traditional way of life. Once the conflict is out in the open, the traditionalists are also forced into active conflict to preserve their power. In this fashion, the title of "trouble-maker" becomes equally applicable to both sides, and loses much of its power in public debate.

6. Leaders may be limited to apparently futile actions, such as moral denunciations of segregation and moral applause of

desegregation. But these are only apparently and not really futile. For such public stands by the respected and legitimate leadership:

(a) inform the public of where its leaders stand;

(b) attach moral sanction to one side;

(c) deprive the opposition of an appeal to morality;

(d) force the opposition to advocate anti-law and anti-morality action;

(e) set a model of decorous behavior toward which the majority leans, at least ambivalently;

(f) offer a viable and positive alternative to which the majority can respond when the situation is appropriate.

CHAPTER ELEVEN

TWO COLLECTIVE PORTRAITS: THE HARD CORE AND THOSE WHO ARE READY

WHO is ready and who is resistant to desegregation? This is the question we posed at the outset of this book, and now finally we may attempt a series of summary answers based on our findings of the foregoing ten chapters.

We cannot once again repeat the full and detailed complexity of the data as we have presented them in the body of the book. Instead we must now try to put together that kind of collective portrait of various groups in our sample, so that the configuration or the over-all patterning of our sample comes clear.

Throughout the volume we have taken a series of variables, such as education, income, and exposure to mass media, and divided our sample in terms of their different amounts of these factors. We then calculated the average scores on attitudes toward desegregation of such groups, and, on the basis of the differences in such scores, we made decisions as to which variables were more and which less significant.

Now we can reverse that procedure and divide our sample into groups based on their attitude scores. We can set off the high from the low resistants, and both of them from the intermediary groups, and ask what are the average life and background characteristics of each of these different attitude groups.

To do this, however, we must select out from among the five sets of attitude scores (the five scales) some simple measure which will, in some relevant senses, stand for the rest of the scores and, by itself, comment significantly on the orientation to Negro-White relations which is revealed.

Our decision is to work alone with the scores given by Scale V, which focuses specifically on resistance to School Desegregation.

We choose this one measure for a number of reasons. Almost without exception, every group (defined by age, or edu-

171

cation, or income, etc.) showed significantly lower segregationist tendencies on this scale than on any of the other scales.

This may seem as though we are picking a measure which puts the sample in the "best" possible light. But in fact this scale was constructed so that, of all the scales, it was most "loaded" in favor of eliciting the maximum possible *segregationist* sentiment. We say this because all the alternatives offered were on the pro-segregationist side of the dividing line. Any respondent who was either indifferent, neutral or actively opposed to segregation could express these sentiments only by disapproving the several alternatives. Moreover, the introductory statements preceding the choice of each alternative implied clearly that these alternatives had already been considered or used by others; that they had the weight of some community experience behind them; that, in short, they were not crackpot ideas at all.

Yet, even with all this loading of questions on the pro-segregationist side, the entire sample, and almost all of the subgroups we constructed, exhibited less segregationism (lower scores) here than any place else in the battery of scores.

For instance:

(a) The per cent of all responses which could be classified as pro-segregationist on Scale V was 50.3, compared to 51.8, 60.5, 67.4, and 67.8 per cent for the other four scales.

(b) The mean score for the whole sample on this set of questions was 2.06, which is 51.6 per cent of the distance between the two extremes of pro- and anti-segregationism, compared to 51.6, 60.0, 67.8 and 68.8 for the other four scales.

Why should this be so? Why should a set of questions loaded one way yield scores definitely tending the other way?

A number of reasons suggest themselves. First, of all the five sets of questions, the school set was most structured, concrete, and specific. The questions were tied to the real world, with known costs and consequences. These questions, more than any other, forced upon the respondents an awareness of the real context in which the issues at stake were being contested. This was in sharp contrast to the questions on Negro Image and General Ideology, where one could "have his cake and eat it too." For here one could entertain his private image of the Negro as an inferior creature, and of a world in which the White was completely dominant and apart, at points of his own choosing without having to consider the costs involved in translating this dream world into actual social relations.

On a second level, and therefore as a second reason for the lower per cent segregationism expressed on the school questions, the concreteness of the context seemed to help evoke an awareness of a world larger than a local, isolated region with traditional White dominance and separatism. It seemed, in short, to help remind the White respondents that they were more than residents of Twin Forks Culvert, more than residents on Greensboro Avenue; they were also citizens of Guilford County, of North Carolina, and ultimately of the United States. And each of these more-than-local regions is also a unit of membership and affiliation and of some degree of normative and ethical influence. The evocation of these larger contexts with their somewhat differing cultural themes seems to force upon the respondents a need to compromise their immediate personal preference-sets with what they know to be the permissible and tolerable limits of the larger units.

These are some of the reasons why the questions about the schools, though deliberately designed to make it easy for the respondents to express heavily pro-segregationist sentiment, actually resulted in the expression, on the average, of the least of this sentiment. Just as we found that exposure to the mass media decreases pro-segregationist sentiment, so, now, we find that *questions* which remind the individual that there are other places and persons and times, and that he has numerous values rather than one value system, and that his actions have consequences upon him as well as upon others—such questions perform much the same function as exposure to the mass media themselves. These questions carry messages just as do the news reports from other areas.

On the basis of the scoring tendencies just cited, we also feel confident that the responses on Scale V come as close or closer than those of any other scale to expressing about the amount of resistance which will be acted out in public. It is not that the school questions are better indicators of the total orientation of the White respondents. It is rather that they tend more than other scales, so far as we can judge, to indicate what our respondents would probably do when confronted with a live situation. The other questions, on Image, Ideology, Sentiment, and General Action Set are valid indicators—so far as we can tell—of different aspects of the orientation of the respondents. They do tell us how our respondents see the Negro, how they envision a desirable social world, how they feel, and how, in general, they might act. But our school questions seem to tell us better than any of these others how in particular our respondents probably would behave when faced with the necessity of acting.

A simple statistical test also reveals to us that there is a strong interrelationship among our various scales. For if we ask how close is this relationship, we find that at the maximum there are only two chances out of a hundred that persons scoring as they did on Scale I could have scored as they did on Scale V by chance alone. That is, one might expect two such sets of scores to come from the same set of respondents by chance alone only two times out of a hundred. And the probabilities for the other scales are even smaller. Statistical analysis shows that the scores on Scales II, III, and IV, as they relate to the scores on Scale V, could have occurred by chance alone only one time in a thousand. That is, only once out of a thousand times might one expect such close interlocking of scores from the same respondents to occur by chance alone.

In tabular form, the results of the statistical analysis are given below.

TABLE 54

Chi Square of Association Between Scale Scores on Attitudes Toward School Desegregation and Other Measures of Attitudes Toward Segregation

Scale	χ^2 with School Scale	p
Negro Image	6.0	.02
In General	15.4	.001
How Feel	63.1	.001
What Do	66.7	.001

The Hard Core and Those Who Are Ready

Further evidence of the relationship among these measures is revealed by an analysis of the significance of differences among the various school-attitude groups on their mean scores on the other scales previously described. Out of forty possible sets of differences, thirty-four were significant, and in the expected direction. The six non-significant differences occur between adjacent groups in middle-range scores.

These measures of relationship among the various sets of responses suggest considerable intercorrelation of the various components that each of these sets was designed to reveal. And, on grounds asserted earlier, it seems likely that the scale of questions on the issue of School Desegregation represents the readiness of the respondents, as they verbalize it, when they are forced most to take into account their memberships in larger-than-local communities and culture patterns, and are forced more than otherwise to consider costs and consequences.

So much, then, for the justification of our selection of the scores on the school questions as the basis on which to divide our respondents.

It will be remembered, from Chapter Two, that these questions constitute a scale whose coefficient of reproducibility is 95.65. This means that if we assign scores to various patterns of answers in certain specified ways, a knowledge of the scale score enables us to reproduce, with a high degree of accuracy, the pattern of scoring.

The scale consists of five points, ranging from extreme desegregationism, defined by a score of 0, to extreme pro-segregationism, defined by a score of 4. The intermediary scores of 1, 2, and 3 stand for intermediate sets of attitudes. Those who score 0, on the average, rejected all offered alternative ways in which to prevent school desegregation, and either would not oppose it or would positively work for it. Those who score 4, by contrast, accept all the alternatives offered, including the use of force if necessary. In between stand those who would try for a constitutional amendment, but nothing else; or, who would also be willing to withhold state funds; or, who would go on to closing the schools, if necessary.

175

The Hard Core and Those Who Are Ready

Table 55 gives the number and per cent of our respondents who fall into the five different score categories.

TABLE 55
Distribution of Scale Scores
(Questions on Schools)

Scale Score	Number	Per Cent
0	50	17.49
1	58	20.28
2	53	18.53
3	71	24.82
4	54	18.88
TOTAL	286	100.00

Now we can compare these five groups in terms of a set of characteristics whose significance for attitudes has been demonstrated.

It will be remembered that the most significant characteristics were education, exposure to mass media, occupation (blue- *vs.* white-collar), and income.

In Table 56 on p. 177 are the lineups of these five attitude groups on these most significant characteristics. Immediately following, we compare these groups, in Table 57, on certain characteristics whose influence on attitudes has been shown to be dubious.

The data in Table 56 give us almost total confirmation of our expectations. In every instance but two, the group with the greater readiness for desegregation is also higher on each measure of social position. The differences between adjacent groups are not always significant, but the trend of scores is completely persuasive. The more educated, the more exposed to mass media, the better the job and the higher the income, the greater is the readiness for desegregation.

Equally important is the fact that there tends to be a rather sharp break, on some of the measures of position, between Groups 4 and all others. Group 4, it will be recalled, contains those who would, they say, use force if necessary to prevent the schools from being desegregated. One cannot help but be

TABLE 56

Comparison of Different Attitude Groups on Certain Significant Social Characteristics

Scale Score Group	Mean Years of School Completed	Per Cent with Nine or more Years of School	Mean Exposure[a] to Mass Media	Per Cent in White-Collar Jobs	Per Cent Professionals	Mean Annual Income
(High Readiness)						
0	10.1	72.0	2.84	71.4	22.4	$6,194.
1	9.7	67.8	2.52	64.4	10.2	5,915.
2	9.3	62.3	2.69	64.2	9.4	4,940.
3	9.5	64.8	2.32	58.6	5.7	4,592.
4	8.0	40.7	2.06	35.8	1.8	3,500.
(High Resistance)						

[a] Maximum Exposure = 4.

TABLE 57

Comparison of Different Attitude Groups on Certain Social Characteristics of Dubious Significance

Scale Score Group	Mean Frequency[a] of Church Attendance	Per Cent Rural Residence	Per Cent Stable[b] Residence	Per Cent with Nine or more Years of School Whose Fathers Had Eight or Less Years	Per Cent White-Collar Respondents with Blue-Collar Fathers	Mean Age
(High Readiness)						
0	2.9	22.0	80.0	44.0	26.0	41.4
1	3.0	33.9	86.4	33.9	23.7	41.4
2	3.1	41.5	83.0	39.6	32.1	42.2
3	2.9	32.4	80.3	46.5	23.9	43.7
4	2.8	51.9	83.3	35.2	20.4	39.8
(High Resistance)						

[a] For calculating means: Never = 1; Less than 1 a month = 2; Less than 1 a week = 3; 1 a week or more = 4; Daily = 5.

[b] Stable = resident in given area five years or more.

struck by the fact that on such matters as mean years of school completed, per cent with nine or more years of school, per cent in white-collar jobs and mean annual income, the hard-core group, those in scale category 4, are significantly lower than those in 3. It is as though there were a graded range of positions for each of the first four attitude groups which then breaks off abruptly when one comes to those who would use force.

On the other end of the scale there is something of the same phenomenon, but more modestly expressed. The group that would not do anything to prevent desegregation, or would take positive means to help it along, also seems set off from the other attitude groups, at least on some of the measures. For instance, its mean annual income is significantly different from those of all groups from 2 on; its percentage of professionals is even more significantly different; and its mean exposure to mass media also differs markedly from the adjacent group 1.

In short, there is some tendency toward a bi-polarization, such that the most ready and the most resistant groups stand apart, at their respective extremes, from the intermediary groups. In some sense these two groups represent the deviants in the community—on the one hand those who deviate in their readiness and on the other those who deviate in their resistance. The large majority, those in Groups 1, 2, and 3, comprising some 64 per cent of the sample, are in the middle ground. The extreme groups together comprise 36 per cent of the population, and each contain almost the same number of respondents.

We can sum these findings briefly by noting that there are rather well delineated attitude groups in the sample, and the social characteristcs and positions of these attitude groups are also well delineated in the expected way.

When we turn to Table 57, where we have listed the distributions on certain characteristics which our analysis indicated were of dubious significance, we find our doubts are mostly sustained. Either the pattern of scores bears no relationship to our prior expectations, or it violates those expectations, or the differences between attitude groups are simply too slight to bear comment. The only striking figure is the 51.9 per cent in Group 4 who live in the rural areas. The nearest figure is 41.5 per cent for Group 2. But we have already seen how variable the meaning of rural-urban distinctions can get to be. This present finding does not merit further scrutiny.

If we now try to put together a collective portrait of Group 4, the most distinctive group, the one most set apart from all the others, the hard core who would use force, the summary sketch would read as follows:

The hard core is slightly younger than its neighbors.

It attends church about as frequently.

It is as stable in its residence patterns, but is somewhat more concentrated in the rural areas.

Its earning power is significantly lower than all of its neighbors.

There are many fewer white-collar workers in the group, and many fewer professionals, proportionately speaking.

All the other groups have significantly higher averages of number of years of school completed, though the actual differences are not very large.

Similarly, the hard core has a significantly smaller percentage of members who have achieved nine or more years of schooling. In this regard, it stands differentiated from all the other groups.

The hard core is not different from the other groups in the percentage of its members who have gone on in school beyond the grammar school level achieved by their fathers.

In the same vein, members of the hard-core group have moved as frequently as members of the other groups out of the manual work situations of their fathers into white-collar work of their own.

The mass society, through the agencies of the mass media, does not impinge upon the hard core to nearly the same extent as upon other groups.

This, then, is the group which is most resistant to desegregation. As one proceeds up the ladders of the various significant characteristics, one encounters changes in the patterns of significant variables, until one reaches the 0 group, those who would do nothing to prevent desegregation. Here one finds a group that outscores all others on crucial measures of position and life-chance, just as the hard-core group of resistants achieves less than all others on these measures.

The suggestion which these findings contain is that the hard core's position of "low-man-on-the-totem-pole" urges these respondents to an intransigent resistance to any improvement in the status of the Negro. The opposite social position of the most-ready group seems to make it easier for this group than for any other to accept the prospects of desegregation with some equanimity.

The split between the most-ready group and all others, while not sharp and decisive, is nevertheless very suggestive. The scores seem to imply that there is a cut-off point, defined by the average characteristics of this group, which must be reached before a solid reluctance to go against the law of the land becomes a reality. Only at the average high position occupied by this most-ready group does there seem to be cumulated enough of a stake in the society and enough of a perspective on time, person, place, and value to produce an *internal* discipline in its members, so that they restrain themselves from translating their evident prejudice into discriminatory action.

Three patterns, then, seem to emerge, with more or less clarity, from the analysis of the characteristics of the different attitude groups. The most distinct pattern is the separation of the hard-core group from all others. The second refers to the gradation of scores throughout all groups in the expected fashion. The final pattern—the least clear but most suggestive —is the separation of the most-ready group from all others.

If we put these three patterns together, one gets the very strong impression of a group of people who are graded into each other in many important social characteristics, and who therefore must be considered the same kinds of people, with the important reservation that their positions on the graded continua often are correlated with distinct differences in their attitudes. The hard core seems to be sufficiently far along toward the lower ends of the continua to form a distinct and distinguishable entity. So, too, but not quite so forcibly, the ready ones seem to be sufficiently far along toward the more advantageous ends of the continua to emerge as an entity distinguishable from the rest of the population.

We may think of the ways in which these two extreme groups are set off from the others in terms of different sets of norms and responsibility-reward systems into which they are integrated. The hard core seems to view the emergent and changing social system as one which does not contain enough by way of promised satisfaction in return for adherence to the new norms, and so seems to reject the emergent system in preference for the more traditional form of social organization. The ready group, by contrast, has good reason to see the emergent system as containing promises of even more of the relatively advantaged positions which they have come to enjoy, and hence they seem to welcome, or at least, to refuse to impede, the development of the new system.

One would ordinarily expect that groups who are objectively different from each other in the way shown for our attitude groups also would differ in their respective views of how well off they feel, how well they think they have done in life, and how they rate themselves against their contemporaries and other peers.

To tests out these notions, we asked our respondents first to compare their present jobs with the first jobs they held. In Table 58 are shown the per cent in each scale score group who said they feel better off now than they were in their first jobs.

TABLE 58
Comparison With Own First Job

Scale Score Groups	Per Cent Who Feel Better Off Now
0	87.5
1	89.3
2	73.5
3	80.0
4	85.7

We see little orderly patterning, at least little of the order we expect. Group 1 has the highest percentage of those who feel better off now. Group 4, the hard core, has more of those than Groups 2 or 3.

We then went on to ask our respondents to compare how well they felt in their present jobs relative to men with whom they started out in life. Table 59 gives these percentages.

TABLE 59
Comparison With Jobs of Former Peers

Scale Score Groups	Per Cent Who Feel Better Off
0	35.6
1	38.5
2	27.7
3	30.5
4	26.5

We see that in none of the groups do more than 38.5 per cent of the members feel better off than those with whom they started out in life, and no group has less than 25 per cent who feel this way. There is some rough ordering of the percentages in the expected direction, but there are significant deviations from expectations as well, and none of the differences is statistically significant.

If we focus on the same comparison with age-peers, but now ask how many feel as well off as the men with whom they started out in life, we get the results shown in Table 60.

TABLE 60
Comparison With Jobs of Former Peers

Scale Score Groups	Per Cent Who Feel The Same
0	46.7
1	48.1
2	55.3
3	45.8
4	59.2

We find here the thoroughly unexpected fact that the hard-core group clearly outscores all others in the per cent of its members who feel as well off as those with whom they started

183

out in life. The *array* of scores is also generally disorderly when judged by our expectations.

The next comparison we asked our respondents to make referred to how well off they felt relative to their fathers' job situations. Table 61 shows the percentages of those who felt better off and worse off than their fathers.

TABLE 61
Comparison With Father's Job

Scale Score Groups	Per Cent Who Feel Better Off	Per Cent Who Feel Worse Off
0	56.5	20.0
1	66.1	10.7
2	58.3	20.8
3	60.0	23.1
4	65.3	12.2

Once again our expectations are violently contradicted by the fact that the hard-core group of resistants feels virtually as well off as any other group, and, indeed, substantially out-scores the 0, or most-ready group. The same reversals of expectations are found in the per cent of those who feel worse off. And, once again, the patterning of the scores seems to bear little relation to the order expected.

A final comparison we tried was that between the respondents and their contemporaries who are presently in the same kind of job (i.e. all other carpenters, all other lawyers, etc.).

In Table 62 are shown the per cent in each of the scale score groups who said they feel better off than their contemporaries.

TABLE 62
Comparison With Contemporaries In Same Kinds of Jobs

Scale Score Groups	Per Cent Who Feel Better Off
0	36.4
1	32.1
2	27.1
3	19.0
4	16.7

The Hard Core and Those Who Are Ready

For the first time in all of these comparisons, our expected order of scores is fulfilled. The 0, or most-ready group, has the highest per cent of those who feel better off than their contemporaries, and each scale score down sees a decline in this percentage, till we reach the low of 16.7 per cent in the 4 group. In short, it is only when we ask our respondents to rate themselves next to their most easily perceivable peers, those who hold the same kinds of jobs, that they reveal relevant differences in how well off they feel.

We do not know whether our hard-core respondents are in fact relatively less well off than their fellow-workers in the same kinds of jobs. We only know that the hard core contains a higher percentage of persons in the lower-rated job categories. We cannot say therefore whether the subjective comparison corresponds with the objective facts. But we do know that major objective differences such as in occupation and income are not matched, in the subjective perceptions of our respondents, by any significant or orderly sense for a hierarchy of position.

Can it be, then, that our hard-core respondents do not feel very different about life in general from the rest of the sample? Can it be true that their views of life are about as reassuring to them, as the views of their fellow Southerners are to *them?* One ought not to expect this to be the case. And yet our data suggest that except when they compare themselves to their fellow workers in the same job categories, the hard-core respondents seem reasonably well set up in their own self-images.

To probe further into this, we have once again applied a test of "anomie" that is, a measure of the extent to which the individual feels well or poorly integrated into his society. Anomie is the antonym of integration.

Testing for anomie, it will be recalled, involves securing responses to a series of statements which constitute a scale and which therefore can be scored in the same general way as our other scales.

In Table 63 are shown the percentage of positive responses given to each of these items by the White sample.

TABLE 63
Per Cent Positive Responses To Anomie Questions[a]

Anomie Questions	Per Cent Positive Responses
Situation for average man getting better	76.57
Hardly fair to bring children into world	75.87
Must live pretty much for today	72.37
Little use in trying to influence public officials	56.64
A man doesn't know whom he can count on	47.90

[a] Coefficient of reproducibility = 90.32

In Table 64 shows the mean scores on the anomie scale for the five scoring groups on Scale V. In interpreting the results below, it should be noted that the higher the score on the anomie scale, the less is the anomie, whereas the higher the score on the desegregation scale, the greater is the resistance to desegregation.

TABLE 64
Mean Scores on Anomie Scale for Five Attitude Groups

Scale V Groups	Mean Anomie Scores
0	4.30
1	3.63
2	3.36
3	3.37
4	2.09

The results seen above are rather striking. There is a clear cut bi-polarity. The 0, or most-ready group, is clearly separated from all the rest by its low anomie, and the 4, or most-resistant group, is clearly separated at the other end by its high degree of anomie. Tests of significance show that the differences between the scores of the 0 group and each other group are significant far beyond chance, and so, too, are the differences between the 4 group and each other group. By contrast, the intermediary groups, 1, 2, and 3 do not differ significantly from each other.

186

The Hard Core and Those Who Are Ready

The direction of the differences throughout the five groups is relatively as expected, except for the virtually identical scores of groups 2 and 3.

Our results on this measure, then, tally well with the results on attitudes and with the differences in the objective facts such as education, occupation, and income. We get a picture of the most-ready group as one which is most thoroughly integrated into the society and of the most-resistant group as most alienated, with the intermediary groups falling about where they should according to our expectations.

Our picture of the factors which relate to attitudes toward desegregation now broadens, therefore, to include some minor sense of misfortune and underprivilege when our respondents compare themselves to their contemporary peers, and some general sense of alienation.

Before we make too much of these differences in anomie among the different school-attitude groups, we must take another set of findings into account. When we divide our respondents by their years of education, type of job, income level, etc., we find that there is no orderly pattern of anomie scores. In short, though our attitude groups differ on anomie; and though they differ in the same way on education, occupation, income, etc.: these types of differences do not hold up when we test directly for the relationship between education or occupation and anomie. Or, to put it in another way, though our educational and occupational groups differ on attitudes toward desegregation, they do not differ in the same way on anomie.

Only in certain selected aspects of their lives, then, is there an orderly correspondence of views of our respondents. The most persisting orderliness of relationship is between the objective measures of social position and exposure to mass society, on the one hand, and attitudes toward desegregation on the other. But the relationship between the objective measures and some subjective images of self and life is not nearly as persisting.

Could it be that the actors here are responding to the pressures of social institutions upon them in ways somewhat unknown to them, and unverbalizable by them, and hence not

187

as easily discernible as are the impacts of their differences in objective life situations?

It would seem that here we have examples of dissonant variations on the theme that what men define as real is real in its consequences. For the subjective views of life held by our respondents (as measured by their self-images and their anomie scores) do not tally nearly as expected with what in fact they appear to feel and are ready to do about desegregation. Indeed, the closest correspondences are between certain objective differences, relatively *unperceived* by the respondents, and their attitudes toward desegregation. It is this difference in correspondence which suggests that objective differences in position in the social order are more powerful variables than the subjective definitions of these positions.

Could it be, then, that if the inequalities in position and life chances between the hard core and the others were to be reduced over time, the differences between their attitudes toward the Negroes and desegregation would be correspondingly reduced, again in ways unknown to and unperceived by them, and perhaps in spite of their verbalizations to the contrary? Some such destratification and equalization seems to be strongly indicated by our findings.

CHAPTER TWELVE

TEN MAJOR FINDINGS AND
THEIR IMPLICATIONS

IN this last chapter we turn to underline some of the major themes which have dominated our findings, and to state some of their implications. First, however, a note about the quality of our evidence is needed.

An attitude is a rather complex affair. The name is simple, but the factors which produce attitudes, and the internal makeups of attitudes are complicated. Any analysis which tries to unravel and systematize the connections between the producing factors and the resulting attitudes inherits both sets of complexities, as well as a third set created by the assumption of relationships of cause and effect.

We are poorly equipped in the social sciences with the techniques, situations, and controls we need to produce decisive proof about cause and effect. The simple reason is that we cannot easily experiment with human relationships or the human psyche. We can and do try, however, to break through some of the barriers to understanding human behavior by using statistical analysis to test the best ideas we can muster about situations already in motion.

In the particular problem of this study, there is obviously a great deal more to the matter than what we have chosen to set aside for special attention. Obviously, also, our statements about the greater or lesser significance of certain factors, as they bear upon attitudes, are only as good as the data and the statistical analysis make possible. But when one deals with the interplay among six or more major variables, some considered as causes and some as effects, he must necessarily phrase his judgments about relationships in discursive terms that his numerical data do not themselves bespeak.

There are ways and ways to make such discursive statements. One can insist, on the one extreme, that the findings are incontrovertible. Or, on the other hand, one can lean over backwards to disclaim any strength and vigor for them. Each of these postures is to some extent awkward. We all stand to lose as much from the failure to recognize what is correct as from the insistence upon the correctness of that which is false or unproven. We all stand to gain much more from being both somewhat bold and somewhat modest. The boldness is proper in the form which one gives to one's judgments about relationships. The modesty is appropriate in the degree of finality one claims for his findings.

So we turn now to offer some summary judgments, phrased as though they had been demonstrated beyond doubt, but prefaced now with the strong reservation that these judgments are offered as tentative assessments rather than as claims to absolute truth. The proof we have offered for the existence of numerous relationships is unequal. Sometimes our case is much better made than at other junctures in the study. We have attempted to indicate these relative strengths and weaknesses as we went along.

The statements we are about to make, however, represent findings which have insistently protruded themselves upon us throughout the study. If the relationships of which they speak were unequally evident at different places, they were nevertheless persistently evident, and they almost always took about the same kind of form, even if the degree or intensity of relationship was variable. It is the persistence of form and direction of relationship which gives us the confidence to recite what we consider to be ten significant findings about readiness and resistance to desegregation among 287 members of the adult White labor force of Guilford County, North Carolina.

Finding 1. The sample is relatively homogeneous in its unfavorable Image of the Negro. No matter how we divide our respondents, whether by income, education, occupation, exposure to the mass media, or whatever, we find that the majority of them view the Negro as inferior to the White in certain essential regards—morality, intelligence, responsibility and ambition.

These images reflect the content of the "traditional Southern viewpoint." Probably this is an opinion held by many persons outside the South as well. It is in some senses a

190

set of judgment which has prevailed in our society for a long time. Corroded as it has become over the years, it nevertheless persists in sufficient intensity to constitute an important factor.

But we must qualify this finding by the fact that significant percentages of our respondents do not share this view. For instance, approximately 27 per cent consider the Negro to be equal or superior to the White in responsibility, 31 per cent in morality, 33 per cent in ambition, and 40 per cent in intelligence. In a region such as the South, where the ordinary assumption would be that there is total uniformity of belief on these issues, it is indeed a significant fact that so many do not entertain the traditional viewpoint.

It is not possible to say how large or small such percentages have been in the past. One guesses that these figures represent certain newer trends in belief and opinion about the Negro. To the extent that such Images are the rock-bottom elements in the prejudice against the Negro, against which countervailing forces must be posed, to that extent one can just as properly watch with hope the emergence of these modified views, as observe with despair the persistence of the traditional views.

Another perspective on the mixture of opinions which exists is given to us by the per cent who hold mixed Images. If we refer to Table 2 in Chapter Two, we see that some 16 per cent believe in the full equality of the Negro with the White in the four traits mentioned; some 6 per cent felt the Negro inferior only in responsibility; 13 per cent in responsibility and morality; 15 per cent in everything but intelligence; and some 50 per cent felt the Negro inferior in all four regards. Our respondents are therefore mixed in two regards. There are differences among them in the degree of unfavorable Image they hold; there are also differences in the aspects on which they consider the Negro inferior.

That these differences are consequential can be seen in two different ways. First, if we ask whether persons with different resistances to school desegregation also differ in their Images of the Negro, we get the results shown in Table 65.

TABLE 65

School Desegregation Scale Score	Mean Score on Image of Negro
0	2.16
1	2.59
2	2.79
3	2.84
4	3.31

We see that every increase in resistance to desegregation is accompanied by an increase in unfavorableness of Image. Tests for significance show that the 0 or most-ready group differs significantly from Groups 2, 3, and 4; and that the 4, or most-resistant group, differs significantly from all others. The differences among the intermediary groups are in the expected direction but are not statistically significant.

Next if we ask whether persons with different Images of the Negro differ in their attitudes to school desegregation, we get the results shown in Table 66.

TABLE 66

Negro Image Score Group	Mean Score on School Desegregation
0	1.62
1	1.53
2	2.00
3	1.65
4	2.43

The results shown above do not line up nearly as neatly as one would expect if one assumed that readiness or resistance to school desegregation would correspond closely with one's Image of the Negro. The score of the group which confesses to no unfavorable Images of the Negro is virtually identical with that of the group which believes the Negro inferior in all regards except intelligence. The group which has two out of four unfavorable Images has a greater resistance to desegregation than the group with three out of four unfavorable Images. The only finding which tallies with expectations is the decidedly greater resistance of the group with four unfavorable Images.

Since fifty per cent of the sample are in this fourth category, when we test for the relationship between the scoring on Image and the scoring on desegregation, we find that such correspondence between the two sets of scores could have occurred by chance alone very few times out of a hundred (Chi Sq. $= 6.026$: $p = .02$).

We surmise from these findings that these persons with mixed Images are mixed as well in their attitudes toward desegregation, and that they are not necessarily consistent in this regard. But we also discover that when the Image is totally unfavorable, as is manifested by being in Scale Group IV, the average resistance to desegregation is noticeably high.

Here then is evidence that while prejudice (Image) sometimes relates to discrimination (School Desegregation Scale), there is considerable variability and inconsistency. Surely there is no identity. Prejudice is significant, but not overwhelming, in its implications for discrimination. Our sample seems to be ready to do things with regard to desegregation which one would not have guessed from their scores on their Images of the Negro.

Finding 2. Every group in the sample (whether defined by education, or income, or occupation) and the sample taken as a whole had lower segregationist scores on their attitudes toward the schools than on their Image of the Negro. The variability between the scores on Image and those on the Schools, which we discussed above, showed us that discrimination does not necessarily follow close upon prejudice in the expected way. This second finding tells us that questions which call for a course of action evoke a smaller amount of segregationist sentiment than those which ask for the mental picture which the White has of the Negro. This holds true for the hard core of resistants as well as for the most ready group. It holds true for the college educated and the illiterate. And it holds for the sample taken as a whole.

However much the rank order of resistance on schools may vary from the rank order of resistance as implied by the Image responses, there is the persisting and invariable fact that the total average resistance on the former is less than that on the latter.

This finding permits us to say that if we know the level of resistance which is implied by Image scores, we can safely predict that the resistance, in terms of proposed courses of action, will almost surely be lower.

Since we are working with two sets of verbal responses—rather than one verbal response and one overt action pattern—we are informed, then, that the statements about courses of action are different indicators of probable action than are the statements about what the Negro is thought to be like. This would be untrue only if, when the sample came to take action, it acted more in accordance with its Image of the Negro than with its stated preferences for types of action. It is difficult to imagine when this would be true. Why, we ask, would our respondents be responding more frankly about their views of the Negro than about their willingness to act in a variety of ways? There is no good ground on which to assume that this differential in frankness is present.

Finding 3. The differences between various groups in the sample on their Image scores tend to be smaller and less significant than the differences in their scores on School Desegregation. This finding tells us that those factors which divide segments of the sample from each other in their attitudes, do not have as much *differentiating* influence on Image of the Negro as on attitudes toward desegregation of the schools.

Another way of saying this is that the sample is a more homogeneous cultural unit in its conception of what the Negro is like that in its judgments of what is the proper course of action to take with regard to relations with the Negroes.

This can be taken to mean that the traditions of the South, as they are ordinarily conceived, have greater endurance and resistance to change in the area of the mental image of the Negro than in the area of concrete social action and behavior. This tells us again that the South, like any other cultural unit, is unequally susceptible to change in different aspects of its traditional cultural pattern. This in turn suggests that though various elements of a cultural pattern tend to cohere and constitute an organic whole at one time in history, some of these elements can and do slip out of the organic unity and become dissonant in their emphases, relative to other elements which persist in greater consonance with times past. If the Image of the Negro represents what is in the hearts of men, and their attitudes toward school desegregation represents their probable behavior, we can say that behavior can be effectively modified without any prior commensurate modification of what is in men's hearts.

Finding 4. Among the major factors responsible for, or associated with, differences in attitudes between various segments of the sample are those which locate the individual on the ladders of property, power, and prestige. We are here considering our major variables of education and occupation with the implied levels of income and prestige. We are taking them in one of their major significances, namely, that of location in the social order, with special reference to the invidious rankings which these positions command, and the different life-chances which they make possible.

Put this way, the differences among our respondents which seem closely tied to differences in their attitudes are best thought of as matters relevant to the system of stratification. In short, these are class differences. Our respondents' attitudes seem to cleave along class lines. Their inequalities in social position correlate well with their inequalities in attitudes. The class structure of the sample is thus an important way in which to view the sample, so far as the distribution of attitudes is concerned. We shall consider, in a moment, some of the more subtle implications of these class differences, as they bear upon attitudes. But for this moment, the identification of these factors as *class* factors is an important sociological observation.

The way in which these class factors work is simple and expectable. Generally, the higher up on any of these ladders, the more favorable is the respondent's Image of the Negro and the more ready he is for school desegregation.

Expectably, too, respondents who are high on several of these ladders have more favorable attitudes toward the Negro than those respondents who are high on one, but low on another. A man with college education and high income tends to be more favorable to the Negro than one whose education is high but income low, or whose income is high but education low. There are exceptions to these generalizations throughout the analysis, but these are the most persisting patterns.

The single most important determinant of attitudes from among all the stratification or class variables is level of education. A repeated finding of our analysis shows that until the level of college education has been reached, the expected influence of class variables is not nearly so perceptible.

Finding 5. A crucial variable in addition to those which define class position is "exposure to mass media." Taken simply, and measured simply, such exposure appears to differentiate sharply our respondents in their attitudes to the Negro and to desegregation. The more exposure, the more favorable the Image and the greater the readiness for desegregation. The exposure to the media that brings news of the outside world, and inform the members of the region about the norms, customs and enforcement of the law of the larger society, seems to be significant when taken by itself, without any other variables controlled. When such other sources of difference as educational level are controlled, we find that the impact of the exposure is diminished if the class positions are low and is enhanced if the class positions are high. A high level of education seems required not only to make the person expose himself to the news of the larger society but also to be sensitive to its messages.

The single most striking cut-off point in the exposure scale is that between those who are exposed either to one or no medium as against all others. There is a definite leap in the scores of Images and readiness for desegregation of the schools at the point where the respondent is exposed fairly regularly to any two of the four media—radio news, TV news, daily newspapers, and national weekly magazines.

Finding 6. A significant difference among various groups in the sample concerns the way in which and the degree to which their scores change, as one goes from Image of the Negro, to the Ideology of Social Relations, To Sentiment

196

Structure, to General Action Set and finally to Specific Action Set. The most general pattern for the sample as a whole is the diminution in segregationist inclinations as one goes through these five measures, so that the sample average segregationism is highest on Image and lowest on Specific Action (School Desegregation).

When one studies subgroups in the sample, such as the different educational-level groups, the most general pattern is (1) the higher the educational level, the more quickly do the segregationist scores decline; (2) the higher the educational level, the greater the disparity between the score on Image and the score on School Desegregation.

By "quick decline" we refer to the fact that there is a marked break between the Image (Scale I) and Ideology (Scale II) scores of the college-educated group. But this noticeable difference in scores does not occur for the grammar school group until the questions on school desegregation are reached. In short, high education seems to reduce segregationism even in Social Ideology, whereas, such reduction does not noticeably and significantly occur for the low-education group until courses of action are called for. What the high-education group seems to be able to do by way of anticipatory modification of attitudes does not occur to the low-education group until it is confronted with a choice of actions. If such modification of segregationism can be equated with rationality and balance in viewpoint, then we may say that the high-education group exemplifies this rationality and balance more pervasively in its attitude structure and maintains it more consistently than the low-education group.

The greater disparity between scores on Scales I and V for the high-education group has a different implication. We take this difference to signify that the high-education groups do not allow their prejudicial feelings to enter into their choices of action nearly as much as do the low-education groups.

Or, one can say that the high-education groups have a larger number of considerations which they pose against their prejudicial feeling in deciding upon appropriate courses of action. We are back here at some notion of balance and rationality. The high-education groups are more balanced

197

and rational in their choices of action insofar as they seem to take a larger number of other factors more deeply into account.

Finding 7. Only the most ready group, that which sits high on the various ladders of stratification, and which is highly exposed to news of the outside world, reaches that dividing point at which we can talk in positive and absolute terms of favorable attitudes toward the Negro and some genuine readiness for desegregation. This most-ready group, as we have seen, contains respondents who have secured some college education; earn upwards of $6000 a year; are exposed to three or more mass media; have a relatively large percentage of professionals among them; and, have significantly more white-collar than blue-collar workers.

When this concatenation of high-status factors is achieved, then, the respondents seem to emerge into a positive orientation to desegregation and a positively favorable Image of the Negro. This combination of factors describes the condition of life which seems required before such a positive orientation becomes possible.

The medium-status groups also tend to have somewhat favorable attitudes to the Negro and desegregation. But one cannot properly speak of them as exhibiting a positive orientation in these matters. They are relatively more ready; and their Images of the Negro are relatively more favorable than low-status groups. But their absolute level of readiness is not one which would cause great enthusiasm among ardent advocates of desegregation.

The gradual emergence into a positive orientation by the most-ready group implies the gradual piling-up of changes in the attitudes of individuals. Then, it is as though some critical mass has been accumulated and the emergence from relatively less resistance to relatively more readiness takes place.

Social changes that would bring improvement in the social position for less advantaged segments of the population are thus likely to bring, in their wake, changes in their attitudes to desegregation.

Finding 8. The majority of the community are neither extreme segregationists nor extreme desegregationists. Between

Ten Major Findings and Their Implications

15–20 per cent of the population fall at each of the two poles. The remaining 60–70 per cent have intermediary sets of attitudes and responses. On any issue so sharply posed as segregation *vs.* desegregation, some polarization of the two opposing points of view is expectable. But the bulk of the community does not line up this way. Rather, only some members become, by the community's standards, ardent advocates or opponents of the proposed social change. Between these two sets of ardent partisans stand the majority of the population.

The implications here are critical. For, the majority, in its middle ground position, seems susceptible to being moved to support either of the two polar opposite viewpoints. It seems like a fluid majority. It is not rigid in its convictions; not so committed either way that it cannot be significantly modified by the trend of events.

The susceptibility of the majority to persuasion to adopt stronger points of view, either for or against the proposed social change, suggest that critical roles can be played by leaders of various kinds, by those who control formal and official power, and by external influences upon community opinion and action.

Finding 9. The principal advocacy of social change, as is implied in the term desegregation, comes from those who have the widest perspective on themselves and their communities, and the deepest sense of stake in the community-in-process. Perspective, as we have used that term, refers to the ability to recognize and care about the facts that: (1) there are long as well as short range consequences of one's actions; (2) that there are other communities besides one's own, and that there is also the larger society, where the norms of conduct are different from those in one's own province; (3) that there are other people besides oneself who will be affected by one's actions, and that the welfare of some of these people must be taken into account in deciding upon courses of action; (4) that one is himself a creature of many values and desires which simultaneously seek satisfaction and achievement, and what one does to satisfy any one of these many desires will affect one's ability to satisfy the others as well.

The development of this sense of perspective leads one to

199

be deliberate rather than impulsive; to be reflective rather than hasty; to be willing to bargain delayed gratification of several desires against immediate impulsive gratification of only one; to be concerned for the obligations of one's membership in the larger society along with the obligations of membership in one's local province; and, finally, to take into account, in deciding upon a course of action, some notion of responsibility to one's community and its organized patterns of life, as well as listening to the clamor of the inner voice which urges one to consider only himself when choices of action are at stake.

These are what we have termed countervailing perspectives. It is these which come to be mixed, by the more educated, better located, and more exposed group, with its traditional prejudice against the Negro, so that, when action is called for, decisions are made which indicate far greater readiness for desegregation.

Persons in whom these perspectives are well developed seem also to have the greatest sense of stake in the society as it is constituted and in the outlines of the new society into which it is developed. By contrast, persons in whom these perspectives are absent or relatively less well developed seem to be more integrated into the traditional norms of an older version of the society than into the emerging norms of the newer society. The group without perspective and without stake in the newer society appear to be threatened by the newer values.

Insofar as the proposed changes would imply a relative improvement in the position and power of the Negro, the resistance of the hard core to these changes is understandable. For, at least in the proximate future, these low men on the ladders of stratification would be most adversely effected by such relative improvement of the position of the Negro. Personal esteem and a sense of one's worth are based as much on how many people are below one of the ladders of worth, as these are symbolized and recognized by the society, as upon how many people are above one on these ladders. Viewed in these terms, the hard core, the lowest-ranking echelons of the White group, have little but the depreciated and devalued

200

position of the Negroes from which to derive any sense of their own relative worth.

By contrast, the most-ready group has least to fear, in the proximate future, from relative improvement of Negro standing. For the Negro would still, on the average, be considerably lower in his ranking and physically and socially distant from this high-status echelon of the White population.

Moreover, the most-ready group contains many of those persons whose interests in the economic growth and development of their area are being injured by the restrictive influences of the system of segregation. The changes they desire in economic institutions are impeded by the failure of talent and loss of manpower that result from segregation of Negroes.

The most-ready group can be said to be most ready, then, for three reasons: (1) In general, they are more balanced and rational, and more attuned to their responsibilities as citizens of the larger society; (2) they have less to fear in the proximate future from any improvement in Negro status; (3) they have much to lose, in their material concerns and in their social ideologies, from continued segregation and discrimination against the Negro population.

One ought to expect to be able to recruit advocates of desegregation, then, proportionate to the extent that this three-fold set of conditions can be more widely realized. One ought to expect continued resistance to desegregation from those to whom none of these reasons applies in any significant way. The movement of the majority of the population, standing in the middle on both their attitudes and in terms of their possession of these three sets of characteristics, will depend upon how much they can be persuaded to take the risks which are implied in the change, rather than those which are implied in the maintenance of the traditional system.

Students of desegregation processes must bear in mind the fact that the possible benefits of the changes implied in desegregation are somewhat more impersonal, more long run, more institutional and less easily perceivable, therefore, in terms of immediate and personal profit. By contrast, the personal and immediate *costs* of these changes are easy to conjure. Similarly, the costs of maintaining the traditional system of segregation are less personal and less immediate and hence of less concern than are the immediate and personal prices to be paid for the change.

It is extremely difficult therefore to envision a situation in the near future in which, without considerable persuasion and enlightenment, the majority of the community is likely to come by itself, voluntarily and willingly, to endorse and sponsor desegregation. Some external assistance to a new perspective seems required beyond any question.

Such external assistance, to be most effective, must take the form of clarifying and giving due weight to the costs which the community itself pays for its present system of segregation.

It must also encourage the local community to take into account, in its psychic bookkeeping, the cost to national welfare, (in terms both of domestic operation and international relations) of the continuation of the system of segregation.

It ought also to keep reminding the community of the importance of the maintenance of respect for law and basic constitutional principles, even though, in the given case, such respect may produce some immediate personal discomforts.

Most important of all, such external assistance ought to take the form of constant reminder to a given community that whatever prices it now pays for the privilege of segregation are likely to grow more severe, more intense, and more immediate in the future. If it would now take a great deal of time to produce a decent modus-vivendi under a system of desegregation, every delay in initiating such a system increases the difficulty, the cost, and the cumulated fears and bitterness which will go into the hopper.

Finding 10. Three types of leaders can and do play active roles in the determination of how resistant or ready to desegregate the community will be. These are (1) the legitimate and respected leaders who oppose desegregation; (2) the legitimate and respected leaders who either do not oppose or actively favor desegregation; and (3) the non-legitimate, ordinarily disrespected leaders who emerge into positions of prominence whenever the legitimate leadership fails to make its voice heard and fails to take action. In Guilford County, the respected leadership seems relatively evenly divided between those who oppose and those who in some way favor desegregation. Both the proponents and opponents of desegregation command respect in the community. They are men of prominence, some of whom occupy important official positions. They have been active and open in their concern for the issues and for a resolution of the problem in accord with some over-arching notion of community welfare and the welfare of the institutions of the nation. They appear to have given to the majority of the community a sense that the major points of view on the issue have been ably represented. In so doing, they have not left the majority with that sense of dissatisfaction which makes it amenable to the urgings and cajolings of the most extreme resistants. Nor have they permitted the creation of a vacuum of morality and power, so that an invitation is implicitly extended to the alienated ones to seize power and to create a new morality of violence.

To the contrary. Many of them have spoken out openly. They have forcefully reminded the community of the moral limits within which public debate and action can decently take place. They have forced those who advocate extreme measures of resistance to the defensive, both legally and morally.

In doing these things, the respected leadership, both for and against desegregation, have prevented the most alienated groups in the society from coming in to take over the instruments of power. They have also prevented the emergence of effective leadership and organization of this group of hard-core resistants. In these respects, Guilford County and its leaders stand in sharp contrast to Little Rock and its leaders.

Perhaps what Guilford County shows us most clearly is that when the respected and legitimate leaders, after much public debate, decide upon a course of action, the unity with which both the proponents and opponents move to implement the decision is very persuasive upon the majority.

The decision to desegregate schools in Greensboro was not met with loud clamors of approval and great public enthusiasm. But the exemplary conduct of the legitimate leaders on both sides of the issue encouraged the majority of the residents of that community to follow suit. That this majority might also have been encouraged to resist desegregation by every technique available is unquestionable. The community chose, instead, to follow the model set for them by their men of prominence, and to exhibit those qualities of character and conduct which insure peaceful change.

These models and these decisions have proven to be crucial factors in the developments since desegregation. For it seems reasonably sure that Greensboro will expand and implement its initial decisions in the future.

Nor is it at all unlikely that Greensboro will constitute a model for many of the other communities in the state that are presently debating the issues. Finally, it is quite possible that North Carolina will come to be looked upon, in years to come, as a state that set a model for desegregation which could be most easily followed by the most resistant states of the South.

APPENDICES

A. The Characteristics of the Sample and Some Comparisons with Other Populations 207
B. Sample Description 220
C. Coding and Scaling Procedures 224
D. Comparison of Scale Scores of Educational Groups with Other Factors Held Constant 239
E. Comparison of Scale Scores of Mass Media Exposure Groups with Other Factors Held Constant 244
F. Comparison of Scale Scores of Occupational Status Groups with Other Factors Held Constant 247
G. Comparison of Scale Scores of Mobility Groups with Other Factors Held Constant 250
H. Comparison of Scale Scores of Age Groups with Other Factors Held Constant 252
I. Comparison of Scale Scores of Religiosity Groups with Other Factors Held Constant 255
J. Comparison of Scale Scores of "Children" Groups with Other Factors Held Constant 260
K. Comparison of Scale Scores of Residence Groups with Other Factors Held Constant 266
L. Comparison of Scale Scores of Income Groups with Other Factors Held Constant 269

APPENDIX A

THE CHARACTERISTICS OF THE SAMPLE
AND SOME COMPARISONS WITH
OTHER POPULATIONS

In the following pages will be found a simple statistical description of the sample of 287 persons whom we interviewed. While some of the characteristics we tabulated proved to be irrelevant or insignificant for our analysis, the reader may nevertheless feel he has a better sense of just who are these 287 persons if he has these characteristics in front of him.

Once we present these tables, we then compare the sample in certain selected regards with the populations of Guilford County, North Carolina and the United States, and end with a summary statement of the regards in which our sample deviates from the other populations.

TABLE A-1
Age

Age Group	Number	Per Cent
18–24	20	6.96
25–34	79	27.53
35–44	76	26.49
45–54	66	23.00
55–64	33	11.50
65 or over	13	4.52
TOTALS	287	100.00

TABLE A-2
Residence

Residence Group	Number	Per Cent
Rural less than 5 years	11	3.83
Rural more than 5 years	93	32.40
Urban less than 5 years	39	13.59
Urban more than 5 years	144	50.18
TOTALS	287	100.00

Appendices

TABLE A-3
Education

Education Group	Number	Per Cent
No years	2	0.69
1–4 years	7	2.43
5–8 years	96	33.45
9–12 years	105	36.59
13 or more years	71	24.74
No information	6	2.10
TOTALS	287	100.00

Median education = 10.03 years.
Mean education = 10.17 years.
Standard Deviation = 4.04 years.

TABLE A-4
Occupation

Occupation Group	Number	Per Cent
Professional, technical, and kindred	14	4.87
Managers, officials, and proprietors (except farm)	39	13.59
Clerical and kindred	60	20.91
Sales workers	54	18.81
Craftsmen, foremen, and kindred	22	7.67
Farmers and farm managers	16	5.57
Protective service workers	15	5.23
Operatives and kindred workers	10	3.48
Farm laborers and farm foremen	6	2.09
Service workers (except protective and household)	9	3.14
Laborers (except farm and mine)	28	9.76
Looking for work	14	4.88
TOTALS	287	100.00

Appendices

TABLE A-5
Status

Status Group	Number	Per Cent
White-Collar	189	69.23
Blue-Collar	84	30.77
TOTALS	273	100.00

TABLE A-6
Industrial Exposure

Industrial-Exposure Group	Number	Per Cent
Wages and salaries, 51 or more employees, manufacturing	84	29.26
Wages and salaries, 51 or more employees, non-manufacturing	32	11.15
Wages and salaries, 31–50 employees, manufacturing	6	2.09
Wages and salaries, 31–50 employees, non-manufacturing	10	3.49
Wages and salaries, 1–30 employees, manufacturing	15	5.22
Wages and salaries, 1–30 employees, non-manufacturing	41	14.29
Self-employed, 51 or more employees, manufacturing	3	1.05
Self-employed, 51 or more employees, non-manufacturing	4	1.39
Self-employed, 31–50 employees, manufacturing	0	0
Self-employed, 31–50 employees, non-manufacturing	2	0.70
Self-employed, 1–30 employees, manufacturing	9	3.13
Self-employed, 1–30 employees, non-manufacturing	65	22.65
No information	16	5.58
TOTALS	287	100.00

Appendices

TABLE A-7
Annual Income

Income Group	Number	Per Cent	Cumulative Per Cent
$1–$999	9	3.14	3.14
$1000–$1999	14	4.87	8.01
$2000–$2999	39	13.59	21.60
$3000–$3999	60	20.91	42.51
$4000–$4999	54	18.81	61.32
$5000–$5999	22	7.67	68.99
$6000–$6999	16	5.57	74.56
$7000–$7999	15	5.23	79.79
$8000–$8999	10	3.48	83.27
$9000–$9999	6	2.09	85.36
$10,000 or more	28	9.76	95.12
No information	14	4.88	100.00
TOTALS	287	100.00	

Median Income = $4278.
Mean Income = $4943.
Standard Deviation = $3187.

TABLE A-8
Religious Membership

Religious Membership	Number	Per Cent
Catholic	3	1.04
Jewish	1	0.35
Other	3	1.04
None	23	8.02
Baptist	103	35.89
Methodist	79	27.52
Episcopalian	10	3.49
Quaker	3	1.04
Presbyterian	20	6.97
Other Protestant	39	13.60
No information	3	1.04
TOTALS	287	100.00

Appendices

TABLE A-9
Church Attendance

Church Attendance	Number	Per Cent
Never	36	12.54
Less than once a month	62	21.60
More than once a month, less than once a week	67	23.35
Once a week or more, but less than daily	115	40.07
Daily	2	0.69
No information	5	1.75
TOTALS	287	100.00

TABLE A-10
Number of Children

Number of Children	Number	Per Cent
0	51	17.9
1	65	22.8
2	89	31.3
3	45	15.7
4 or more	35	12.3
TOTALS	285	100.00

TABLE A-11
Mass Media[a] Exposure[b]

Number of Media Exposed To	Number	Per Cent
0	9	3.14
1	38	13.24
2	89	31.01
3	110	38.33
4	41	14.28
TOTALS	287	100.00

[a] Mass Media = Radio News, TV News, Daily Newspaper, National Magazines.

[b] Exposure = Listens to radio or TV news or reads Daily Newspaper "a couple of times a week or more," or, reads at least every other issue of a national weekly magazine.

Appendices

TABLE A-12
Frequency of Contact with Negroes

Frequency of Contact With Negroes[a]	*Number*	*Per Cent*
Frequent in one	27	9.40
Frequent in two	107	37.28
Frequent in three	114	39.73
No frequent contact	39	13.59
TOTALS	287	100.00

[a] Respondent has contact with Negroes several times a week or more in one or more of the following three situations:
1. As people who work for him at his place of work or business;
2. As customers in his store or clients in his profession; and
3. As people who work at the same place of work.

TABLE A-13

Occupational Status of Respondent Compared to Three Negroes Known Best		*Number*	*Per Cent*
Respondent high[a]	Negroes high	19	6.62
Respondent high	Negroes low[b]	139	48.43
Respondent low	Negroes high	8	2.78
Respondent low	Negroes low	89	31.02
No information		32	11.15
	TOTALS	287	100.00

[a] 19 white-collar.
[b] 19 blue-collar.

TABLE A-14
Political Party Affiliation

Party Affiliation	*Number*	*Per Cent*
Democratic	99	34.49
Republican	61	21.25
Eisenhower Democrat	45	15.68
Independent or no party	49	17.08
No information	33	11.50
TOTALS	287	100.00

212

Appendices

TABLE A-15
Number Who Voted

Did you vote?	*Number*	*Per Cent*
Yes	170	59.23
No	101	35.19
No information	16	5.58
TOTALS	287	100.00

TABLE A-16
For Whom Voted

For whom voted	*Number*	*Per Cent*
Democratic presidential candidate	63	21.95
Republican presidential candidate	99	34.49
Other	3	1.05
Didn't vote	100	34.85
No information	22	7.66
TOTALS	287	100.00

With these materials in front of us, we can make some selected comparisons between our sample and the populations of Guilford County and of North Carolina.

Table A-17 compares the age makeup of our sample with that of the county and the state. We can see that our sample contains a relatively much smaller portion of people in the 18–24 and 65-over age brackets. Our sample also has a significantly larger per cent of people in the 45–54 bracket. There are no clear-cut differences in the central tendencies of any of the three populations, relative to each other.

Appendices

TABLE A-17
Per Cent of White Males, 18 and Over in Various Age Groups

Age Group	Study Sample	Guilford[a] County	North[a] Carolina
18–24	6.96	17.43	19.93
25–34	27.53	26.87	25.69
35–44	26.49	22.56	21.04
45–54	23.00	16.35	14.75
55–64	11.50	9.43	9.97
65 or over	4.52	7.34	8.61
	(N = 287)	(N = 49,297)	(N = 927,372)

[a] Data taken from U.S. Census of Population, 1950, General Characteristics, North Carolina, P-B33.

In Table A-18 we compare the years of school completed by our sample with those of the populations of Guilford County, North Carolina and the United States.

TABLE A-18
Per Cent of Population Completing Different Years of School

Year of School Completed	Study Sample (White Males) Over 18	Guilford County[a] (All Males) Over 25	State of[a] North Carolina (All Males) Over 25	United States[b] (White Males) Over 25
0	0.69	2.6	4.3	2.09
1–4	2.43	13.3	19.9	7.36
5–8	33.45	35.3	38.7	37.14
9–12	36.59	31.3	25.1	35.53
13 or higher	24.74	16.3	10.0	14.84
No information	2.10	1.2	1.7	3.03
Median	10.03	8.8	7.6	9.3
	(N = 287)	(N = 49,015)	(N = 977,000)	(N = 38,683,835)

[a] Data taken from U.S. Census of Population, 1950, Detailed Characteristics, North Carolina, P-C33.

[b] Data taken from U.S. Census of Population, 1950, Detailed Characteristics, U.S. Summary, P-C1.

Appendices

Note that the data for our sample refer to white males 18 and over. For Guilford County and North Carolina, the data are for all males over 25. For the United States, the information refers to White males over 25. These differences must be kept in mind in considering how our sample varies from the other populations.

The first difference we may note is in the median years of school completed. Our sample is significantly higher in this regard. Much of this difference is due to our significantly smaller percentage of people without any formal education, and our significantly larger percentage of people with college education. These differences are doubtless due partly to the fact that our sample includes only Whites, while the Guilford County and North Carolina populations also include Negroes. It is also due partly to the fact that we include males from 18–24 who, relative to other portions of the age structure, are both more educated on the average, and specifically, contribute more to the population of those who have some college education.

On the other hand, it must be remembered (Table A-17), that in our sample there is a significantly smaller percentage of persons in the 18–24 age bracket, and that therefore their contribution to the high median educational achievement cannot be too great.

It seems clear that in general our sample simply happens to be better educated on the average than the county and state populations from which it was drawn. As we shall see later, this is a critical factor in the makeup of our sample population.

We may next compare the income distributions of different populations. In Table A-19 are seen the percentages of persons in different annual income brackets.

TABLE A-19
Per Cent of White Male Population in Different Income Groups

Income Group	Study Samples	Greensboro-High Point Metropolitan Area (Comprises Guilford County)[a]	State of North Carolina[a]
$1–$999	3.14	15.80	25.30
$1000–$1999	4.87	19.64	24.28
$2000–$2999	13.59	26.70	22.06
$3000–$3999	20.91	16.40	11.10
$4000–$4999	18.81	6.44	4.35
$5000–$5999	7.67	3.15	2.18
$6000–$6999	5.57	1.63	1.03
$7000–$9999	10.70	1.97	1.23
$10,000 or more	9.76	2.75	1.35
No information	4.88	5.47	7.07
	(N = 287)	(N = 46,980)	(N = 898,190)
MEDIAN INCOME	$4,278.00	$2,398.00	$1,872.00

[a] Data taken from U.S. Census of Population: 1950. Detailed Characteristics, North Carolina, P-C33.

Note that compared to Guilford County the median income of our sample is almost double, and compared with North Carolina, our sample median is more than 2.25 times as large.

Another interesting difference is in the per cent of each population earning under $3,000.00 a year. In our study sample this is less than 23 per cent; in Guilford County it is just over 62 per cent, or almost three times as great; and, in the State of North Carolina, it is almost 72 per cent.

If we look at the high-income earners, we see a comparable picture. In our study sample, over 25 per cent earn over $6,000.00 a year. In Guilford County, just over 6 per cent earn this much; and in the State, less than 4 per cent earn this much.

Our sample is clearly biased then in terms of its high education and high income averages.

The same type of bias ought to be found in the distributions of occupations. Here we can make two comparisons. The first, as seen in Table A-20, compares the population percentages in each of ten occupational categories. The second, as seen in Table A-21, condenses these ten categories into two.

216

Appendices

TABLE A-20
Per Cent of White Male Work Force in Different Occupational Categories

Occupation Group	Study Sample (Over 18)	Greensboro-High-Point[a] Metropolitan Area (Over 14)	State of[a] North Carolina (Over 14)
Professional, technical, and kindred	4.9	6.3	4.7
Managers, officials, and proprietors (except farm)	13.6	13.4	10.0
Clerical and kindred	20.9	6.8	4.4
Sales workers	18.8	10.2	6.9
Craftsmen, foremen, and kindred	7.7	21.3	16.8
Farmers and farm managers	5.6	6.0	19.6
Service workers	8.4	3.3	2.9
Operatives and kindred workers	3.5	26.8	22.3
Farm laborers and farm foremen	2.1	5.1	6.6
Laborers (except farm and mine)	9.8	3.2	4.4
No information	4.9	.6	1.2
	(N = 287)	(N = 44,255)	(N = 794,131)

[a] Data taken from U.S. Census of Population, 1950, Detailed Characteristics, North Carolina, P-C33.

Appendices

TABLE A-21
Per Cent of Employed White Males in White- and Blue-Collar Job Categories[a]

Job Category	Study Sample (Over 18)	Greensboro-High Point Metropolitan Area (Over 14)	North Carolina State (Over 14)
White-Collar	69.2	58.1	42.8
Blue-Collar	30.8	41.9	57.2
	(N = 287)	(N = 44,255)	(N = 794,131)

[a] White-Collar includes the following occupations:
Professional, technical and kindred
Managers, officials, and proprietors (except farm)
Clerical and kindred
Sales workers
Craftsmen, foremen, and kindred
Blue-Collar includes:
Farmers and farm managers
Protective service workers
Operatives and kindred workers
Farm laborers and farm foremen
Service workers, except protective and household
Laborers (except farm and mine)
Data calculated from Reports in U.S. Census of Population, 1950, P-C33.

From Table A-20, we see that while our sample has a much larger percentage of persons in some of the categories of occupations (clerical and sales) which ordinarily bring higher incomes and which usually command higher prestige, it is not nearly as disparate from the other populations in the two top-ranking occupations, namely, the professional and managerial classes. Moreover, our sample has a notably lower percentage in the craftsmen and foremen category. In short, the picture here is more mixed and differentiated than was true of the differences in education and income.

Still, when we combine categories, as is seen in Table A-21, so that the first five are considered the white-collar or high-status, and the bottom five form the blue-collar or low-status group, we find that our sample is over-represented in the white-collar categories somewhat by comparison with Guilford County and considerably by comparison with the State.

218

The general direction of difference, then, between the occupational characteristics of our sample and those of the other two populations is consonant with the differences in income and education.

Finally, by way of comparison, we note that Guilford County, from which our sample was drawn, has only 19.5 per cent non-White population compared to the 26.5 per cent of the State. Guilford also has 66 per cent urban residents, compared to the somewhat less than 30 per cent of such residents in the State at large. Since our own sample is all-White, no comparison on the percentage of non-White is possible. And since our own sample was drawn from Guilford County in proportion to the urban and rural distributions in the County, it is no accident that our sample contains almost 64 per cent urban residents.

In summary, then, our respondents may be characterized as predominantly urban, living in a county unit with a relatively lower than average percentage of non-Whites, relatively disproportionately located in white-collar occupations, enjoying higher average incomes than others in the State, and exposed far more than average to formal education.

APPENDIX B

SAMPLE DESCRIPTION

Woodrow Wilson Research Project

I. *Definition of Problem:*

To acquire a deeper understanding and appreciation of the South today. Part of this over-all problem is the attitude and opinion of the White male labor force toward working with the Negro.

II. *Definition of the Universe:*

White occupied dwelling units in Guilford County.

III. *Population:*

White males in the labor force 18 years old and older in Guilford County.

IV. *Sampling Unit:*

Cluster of 3 (expected) White households.

V. *Size of Sample:*

100 sampling units (expected 300 White households) in Guilford County.

VI. *Sample Design:*

(a) Measure of size: White occupied dwelling units as set forth in the 1950 U.S. Census of Housing.

(b) Stratification: 50 equal-sized strata (in terms of White households) within the county.

(c) Selection of Sampling Units: Two sampling units were selected at random within each stratum, with replacement.

The sample may be described as a stratified random sample wherein each sampling unit has an equal probability of selection in the sample.

Three copies of city and county maps showing the location of the 100 sampling units were prepared. One map was used in the field work, another for control of the field work, and a third copy was retained in the office file. Block sketches for city blocks were drawn to facilitate the within-block sampling.

220

Appendices

The allocation of the sample to urban and rural areas is shown in the following table.

SAMPLE ALLOCATION

UNIVERSE: White Occupied Dwelling Units in Guilford County

	White Occupied Dwelling Unit 1950 *Census*	*Number of Strata*	*Number of Sampling Units*
URBAN			
Greensboro	14,651	18	4,932
Urbanized Area			
(Around Greensboro)	2,210	2	548
High Point	9,050	11	3,014
West End	811	1	274
Total	26,722	32	8,768
RURAL			
Place			
Jamestown	256		87
Gibsonville	325		110
Open Country	13,983		4,735
Total	14,564	18	4,932
County Total	41,286	50	13,700

Sample Draw: 13,700 sampling units (su's) of approximately 3 HH's, 274 su's/stratum; 50 strata; approximately 825 HH's/stratum

Sampling Rate: 2 Sampling units/stratum = 2 Sampling units/274 = 1/137

VII. *Estimation and Reliability:*

    1. Totals for the county.

        (a) For the estimation of a *total* characteristic of the universe from the sample, the following estimate is used:

$$\hat{T} = \frac{N}{n} \sum_{i=1}^{K} \sum_{j=1}^{2} x_{ij} \qquad K = \text{Number of Strata}$$

where $\hat{T}$ is the estimate of the total, N is the total number of sampling units in the universe and x_{ij} is the characteristic measured in the jth sampling unit in the ith stratum ($j = 1, 2$ $i = 1, 2, \ldots , 50$ in the county).

221

Appendices

(b) The estimated variance of this estimator is

$$\hat{V}(\hat{T}) = N^2 \frac{s^2}{n}$$

where s^2 is the *pooled within strata mean square* computed by:

$$s^2 = \frac{\sum\limits_{i=1}^{K} \sum\limits_{j=1}^{2} (x_{ij} - \bar{x}_i)^2}{K} = \frac{\sum\limits_{i=1}^{K} (x_{i_1} - x_{i_2})^2}{2(K)}$$

where $\bar{x}_i$ is the mean of the characteristic for the ith stratum. (For computation, the right-hand formula can be used, where x_{i_1} and x_{i_2} are the characteristic totals for the two sampling units in the stratum.) The estimate of the relative sampling error of $\hat{T}$ is

$$R.\hat{S}.E.(\hat{T}) = \frac{\sqrt{\hat{V}(\hat{T})}}{T}$$

2. Averages:
   (a) For a ratio estimate, the following estimate is used:

$$\hat{z} = \frac{\sum\limits_{i=1}^{K} \sum\limits_{j=1}^{2} x_{ij}}{\sum\limits_{i=1}^{K} \sum\limits_{j=1}^{2} y_{ij}}$$

where $\hat{z}$ might be the average number of children per household, x_{ij} is the total number of children, and y_{ij} is the total number of households; in the jth sampling unit of the ith stratum.

   (b) The approximate estimated variance of this estimator is

$$\hat{V}(\hat{z}) = \hat{z}^2 \frac{\hat{V}(\hat{T}_1)}{\hat{T}_1{}^2} + \frac{\hat{V}(\hat{T}_2)}{\hat{T}_2{}^2} - \frac{2C\hat{o}v(\hat{T}_1\hat{T}_2)}{\hat{T}_1\hat{T}_2}$$

Where $\hat{T}_1$ is the estimate of the total number of children, $\hat{T}_2$ is the estimate of the total number of households in the county and the variances, $\hat{V}(\hat{T}_1)$ and $\hat{V}(\hat{T}_2)$ are obtained by the procedure indicated in 1a.

Appendices

The covariance, $C\hat{o}v(\hat{T}_1\hat{T}_2)$, is computed by:

$$C\hat{o}v(\hat{T}_1\hat{T}_2) = \frac{N^2}{n} \frac{\displaystyle\sum_{i=1}^{K}\sum_{j=1}^{2}(x_{ij}-x_i)(y_{ij}-y_i)}{K}$$

$$= \frac{N^2}{n} \frac{\displaystyle\sum_{i=1}^{K}(x_{i_1}-\bar{x}_{i_2})(y_{i_1}-\bar{y}_{i_2})}{2(K)}$$

The estimate of the relative sampling error is

$$R.\hat{S}.E.(\bar{z}) = \frac{\sqrt{\bar{z}(\bar{z})}}{z}$$

VIII. *Sample Results:*

The total number of eligible respondents (White males 18 years old and older in the labor force) in the sampling units was 341. Of these, 208 were located in the urban portion, 133 lived in the rural area.

Following the procedures outlined above, the estimate of the White male 18 years old and older labor force in Guilford County is:

$1 = (341)(137)$ where 341 is the sample total, 137 inverse of the sampling rate 1/137, or $\dfrac{N}{n}$

$= 46{,}717$

The *1950* Census estimate for the White male labor force 20 years old and over is *40,919*.

The relative sampling error of this estimate is 7.33 per cent.

The 95 per cent confidence limits on the estimate are:

$$46{,}717 \pm (2)(.0733)(46{,}717) = 39{,}868 - 53{,}566$$

A confidence statement on the sample results might read: "We are 95 per cent confident that the true number of White males 18 years old and over in the labor force in Guilford county lies between the interval 39,868–53,566."

APPENDIX C

CODING AND SCALING PROCEDURES

What should one ask to get the best indication of how a person will probably act when it is time for action? If we narrow this question to the field of segregation and desegregation, we can begin to suggest some answers.

It may even be that the answers which are specifically relevant to this particular field may also have some general relevance.

We reasoned that when any two groups, such as Negroes and Whites, are in contact with each other, and have to relate to one another, to mix with each other, to meet and serve and respond to each other's presences, there are a number of connected but separable aspects to this relationship.

First, each group has an image of what the other one is like. This image contains notions about the qualities and characteristics of the other group. What are its moral standards? How about its intelligence and capacities? Are the others trustworthy and dependable? Can they be relied upon to share the same ultimate values and desire the same kinds of things and the same way of life?

These questions are normally put in comparative terms. That is, group A will think of B's morality or capacity in terms of whether it is the same, superior, or inferior to its own. This tendency to make comparative evaluations is sometimes at a minimum, sometimes at a maximum. When two groups have historically been separated and kept at distances from each other, when, further, they are easily identified by some physical differences, and when the society at large emphasizes comparative ratings, then, the two groups' images of each other are likely to be heavily impregnated with invidious comparisons. Judgments of inferiority and superiority are likely to be the order of the day.

Other factors also help determine how invidious the distinctions are likely to be. If the groups are in some form of competition, whether it is economic, sexual, social, or whatever, they are not likely to be sparing with their invidious distinctions. In the case of Negro-White relations in the South, there is virtually every good reason to expect the White group to have a full set of images of the Negro, each of which is likely to contain heavy overtones of depreciation.

These depreciative images of the Negro are held not only by the Whites of the South but of the North as well. These are the stereotypes of the Negro which enjoy considerable currency. But there is a crucial difference. Some persons who see the Negro as inferior think that this is due to lack of opportunity and advantage, and that with the proper opportunity this inferiority in performance, standards, and the like, could be eliminated. By and large this is the notion on which those who most advocate equality for the Negro base their position.

Others, however, see the Negro as inferior by nature. They see the same biological factors at work in producing a dark skin and a lower intellectual capacity or a lower capacity for observing moral standards. They do not think that the differences between Whites and Negroes—whatever differences they think exist—can be eliminated by more opportunity for the Negro. Or, at least, they are dubious about how much of the difference can be eliminated.

It is obvious—or so it seemed to us—that if A thinks B is inferior, but that his inferiority is due to previous lack of opportunity, then he is likely to be more willing to provide more opportunity than someone else who thinks that B is inferior by nature. For if nature has set certain upper limits, there is not much point in providing opportunities from which this naturally inferior creature could hardly benefit.

With these considerations in mind, we constructed a measure of the Image which our White respondents held of the Negro. Out of the range of current stereotypes about Negroes, we selected four which seemed to us to be key factors with which any group would be concerned in determining how it ought to behave toward others. These were: intelligence, morality, ambition and responsibility. We recognize that these are terms with many connotations and many definitions. But they are sufficiently common so that we could be sure that everyone would have some ideas along these lines. And it would not make much sense to impose our own definitions of these terms, when it was the respondents' views about these matters in which we were interested.

There is a very specific reason why we select these four characteristics. The fact is that when Whites try to justify their resistance to proposals to allow the Negro to send his children to the schools of his own choice, they very frequently allege inferiority of the Negro on one or more of these four counts. One has only to think for a moment of the recent and present arguments against school integration. Most frequently one hears allegations of immorality, low intelligence, lack of ambition and irresponsibility of the Negro. Perhaps the first three are cited more often than the fourth. But all of them enjoy great popularity among those Whites most resistant to desegregation.

We therefore reasoned that the more of these four in which a White believed Negroes to be inferior by nature, the more resistant would he be to any plan to desegregate the schools.

Now we make a simple translation and we say that those Whites who believe the Negro to be by nature inferior on all of these counts have the greatest amount of prejudice. By contrast, those on the opposite end, who believe the Negro inferior only in one or in none of these, and who think the inferiority is man-made rather than biologically natural, are least prejudiced. In short, we translate our measure of Image into a measure of prejudice.

Some readers may object to this terminological equation. They will say: But that isn't prejudice at all. Prejudice, they will insist, literally means prejudgment. And saying the Negro is inferior by nature on these four counts is not prejudgment, but factual observation.

The only answer to this assertion is that it is simply not true. At least, there is no decent scientific research which will bear out this contention. To grant the most that the facts will allow, we would have to say that no case has been established either for Negro inferiority "by nature" or for Negro superiority or for Negro equality. At best, it is a moot issue. And we are hardly ever likely to resolve this issue if we keep using such terms as Negroes and Whites. For, by now, these have come to refer to groups of persons who overlap with each other in many characteristics and who get called what they are by social convention rather than by clear-cut physical and biological distinctions.

Therefore, to claim strongly that the case for Negro inferiority has been proven is to prejudge. Literally, then, such claims are prejudiced. An instrument that measures how many such claims are made, and how strongly they are made, is a measure of prejudice.

That we all are bearers of some prejudices about some groups is probably true. This does not make any of our prejudices less worthy of the name. We use the term here not to point a finger of scorn or to impute bad motives. We use it simply because it is the term which most closely, in its literal and shared meanings, describes the beliefs as they are held.

Actually, we are not so much concerned with whether these are truly prejudgments. We are more concerned with who believes these things to be true of the Negro and what if anything can one expect from persons who differ in these beliefs. We want to know whether and in what why Whites who have different Images of the Negro also differ in their willingness to open the schools to Negro children.

I. IMAGE. Each of our respondents was asked:

So far as intelligence is concerned, would you say that, compared to Whites, Negroes are by nature:

1. Superior to Whites
2. The same as Whites
3. Inferior to Whites

On each of these items, once the respondent had indicated where he thought the Negro ranked relative to the White, we asked the following: Does this apply to all Negroes, some or none? Will this always be the case? If not, under what conditions will it change?

We used these follow up questions to make as sure as we could that the respondent was saying that the Negro was inferior by nature or that he was not. We listed as pro-segregationist responses only those cases where all the doubt, which could be eliminated by these brief probes, had been eliminated. In this way, we strained toward reducing the number of responses which would be called prejudiced or pro-segregation.

By contrast, we balanced this strain with the opposing strain simply by counting as prejudiced cases all those where the person said he did not know or where his answer was unclear, in addition, of course, to those where he definitely said the Negro was inferior. Non-prejudiced answers, then, or favorable Images of the Negro were recorded only where the respondent said the Negro was the same as the White or superior to the White. All other responses were classed as unfavorable images of the Negro.

We then repeated this procedure for the other characteristics of morality, ambition, and responsibility.

We thus end with four categories of response:

1. The Negro is superior to the White.
2. The Negro is the same as the White.
3. The Negro is inferior to the White.
4. The respondent does not know or cannot say how the Negro rates.

It should be remembered that we put in this fourth category all those answers which were unclear, and that this fourth category was then counted as on the side of the unfavorable Image scoring, along with category 3.

The number and per cent of the respondents who were classified in each of the four scoring categories on each of the four characteristics is seen below:

CHARACTERISTIC

Scoring Category	Responsibility No.	Per Cent	Morality No.	Per Cent	Ambition No.	Per Cent	Intelligence No.	Per Cent
1. Negro superior	3	1.04	5	1.74	16	5.57	7	2.43
2. Negro same	75	26.13	84	29.26	80	27.87	110	38.32
3. Negro inferior	186	64.80	168	58.53	175	60.97	158	55.05
4. Don't know, can't say, no answer, etc.	23	8.01	30	10.45	16	5.57	12	4.18
TOTALS	287	99.98	287	99.98	287	99.98	287	99.98

In the text we report the per cent giving segregationist answers. These we secure by adding the per cents in categories 3 and 4, so that we end with the following percentages: 72.8, 69.0, 66.5, and 59.2.

Are we sure that this is an accurate measure of the per cent of the respondents who are prejudiced against the Negro in the stated regards? Yes, to the best of our judgment, if prejudiced persons are those who give responses which indicate they believe the Negro to be inferior by nature.

II. IDEOLOGY. Ideology refers to the type of social relations between Negroes and Whites which the respondent says he would like to see put into effect. We tried to get ideological versions of eight different commonplace situations of contact: restaurants, buses, churches, co-residence on block, co-work, schools, susupervisor-employee situations at work, and social visiting.

The actual questions asked were open-ended and code categories were developed on the basis of the actual responses. The general form of question for each of the eight situations is seen in the sequence presented below, which is reproduced verbatim from the schedule.

I would like to ask you a few questions about different kinds of situations in which you might find yourself, and ask you how you feel about these things. For instance:

Appendices

1. Suppose you were eating in a restaurant (cafe, bar, soda shop) here in (whatever town is appropriate). Suppose then a Negro comes in and sits down and wants to be served. Suppose the proprietor serves him. How would you feel about this?
2. What would you do? (EXPLORE IF HE WOULD LEAVE, FORCE NEGRO TO LEAVE, ETC.)
3. Does it matter at all what kind of Negro it happened to be? (EXPLORE CLASS FACTOR HERE.)
4. Would it make a difference if it were a number of Negroes instead of one?
5. Suppose all this happened not here in _____ town but in Greensboro. What would you do, then, if this occurred in Greensboro? (FOR GREENSBORO PEOPLE, USE DURHAM, OR RALEIGH.) (EXPLORE THE "WHY" IF HE WOULD DO DIFFERENTLY.)
6. Suppose all this happened in New York City while you were there on a visit. Then what would you do? (EXPLORE THE "WHY" IF HE WOULD DO DIFFERENTLY.)
7. In general, how do you feel about Negroes eating with Whites? What do you think should be the way in which facilities are set up in public places? (GET HIS PICTURE OF HOW HE WOULD LIKE TO SEE THE PARTICULAR RELATIONSHIP HANDLED IN GENERAL, IF HE COULD MAKE IT WHATEVER HE WANTED IT TO BE.)

These seven questions were then repeated for each of the other situations, with, of course, the necessary adaptations of wording in questions 1 and 7 for the different situations. Thus, on the question of residing on the same block with a Negro, question 1 read:

"All right: let's look at another kind of situation. Suppose some way or another a Negro buys a house on your block or in your neighborhood. How would you feel about this?"

And question 7 read:

"In general, how do you feel about Negroes living near or next to Whites? How should housing be arranged?"

The follow up on question 7 always stressed the fact that we wanted the respondent to tell us just how he would set up these relations if he could set them up any way he wanted to.

The code categories for Ideology were then developed out of the responses to question 7.

Appendices

287 respondents naturally gave us 287 different answers. But equally naturally, there were broad patterns or types of answers within which the 287 individual responses could be classified.

Since we were interested in securing categories of answers which could be distinguished from each other by their segregationist or desegregationist implications, we coded as follows:

1. As is, separate (with no mention that it is OK because it is equal now).
2. Separate but equal (whether now or in the future).
3. Separate but unequal.
4. Desegregation with internal segregation (e.g. let Negroes ride on same buses, but make them sit in separate section).
5. Graduated desegregation.
6. Desegregation without restriction.
7. No plan given except to cite locus of authority, e.g., let the state handle it.
8. Don't know, no idea, can't say.
9. No answer, no information, answer unclear.
0. Up to the individual to decide for himself.

Certain situations seemed to need other categories. Thus, for instance, with regard to riding on buses, we needed a category in which could be placed those responses which said, in effect, "Make the relations even more separate than they are now." For the schools we needed another category which pulled together responses which implied: "It is all right to mix Negroes and Whites, but keep the sexes apart." For the co-work and supervisory situations, we required a category which expressed the frequent response: "I'll mix with Negroes if the boss forces me," or "if that's company policy," or, "if that's what I have to do."

We then went on to analyze the responses to the questions of ideological preferences in terms of whether the response was qualified or unqualified, and, if qualified, what was the character of the qualification.

The qualifications were coded as follows:

1. If no agitation, coercion, or force.
2. In the absence of separate facilities for Negroes.
3. Asserts inevitability, unavoidability, impotence in face of law or trends.
4. So long as present status relations are unaltered.
5. Qualified by some aspect of Negro character, ability, aptitude, performance, status, etc.

6. So long as situationally limited, i.e., with no further implications for any social relations other than those under consideration.
7. Defers by time or place.
8. Qualified by reference to occupational context, e.g., all right for doctors to mix, etc.
9. Qualified by appeal to group consensus, or group customs, e.g., if everyone does it, it is OK with me.
0. If no threat to person, property, or position (job).
X. Limits it to contact of White Males with Negro Males and Females, but specifically excluding White Females.
Y. Qualified by reference to number of Negroes.

We next went on to content-analyze the responses in terms of the reasons that some respondents gave for their answers. The codes were as follows:

1. Children not mature enough to handle the situation.
2. Negroes are better off by themselves.
3. Negroes themselves want segregation.
4. Respondent just plain believes in segregation.
5. Present situation is believed to be adequate.
6. Desegregation won't work.
7. Believes in desegregation, that Negroes have equal rights, or that segregation is immoral, un-Christian, etc.
8. Fears downgrading of present standards.
9. To keep peace, avoid conflict, keep harmony.
0. To avoid further consequences, e.g., intermarriage.
X. Negroes are equal to Whites.

Again, some of the situations required added coding. Thus, for the question of segregation of the schools, we coded for two possible reasons offered for the answers, and included, in addition to the code categories just listed, the following:

1. Economic cost of segregation, of separate facilities, of the taxes Whites will have to pay, etc.
2. Negroes are not yet ready for it.

With the scoring on these categories recorded, we now had to make a decision as to which responses we would call segregationist and which desegregationist. For this decision, we worked principally with the first set of categories which summarized the answers in terms of whether some form of segregation or desegregation was being advocated.

Appendices

The following responses were considered segregationist:

1. As is, separate.
2. Separate but equal, whether now or in the future.
3. Separate but unequal.
4. Desegregation with internal segregation.
X. Even more separate than now.
Y. Desegregation with internal segregation by sex.
X. (For co-work). If I am forced to, if that's company policy, etc.

In addition all the don't knows, unsures, can't says, etc., were coded as segregationists.

Only responses 5 and 6, i.e., advocacy of graduated desegregation, or of desegregation without restriction were coded as desegregationist responses.

The per cent of respondents who, by this system of scoring, gave segregationist responses in each situation was then tabulated. As we have noted in the text, the responses on the co-residence and co-visiting patterns were above the 80 per cent cut-off point accepted as a scaling convention. In fact, as the text tabulations show, the segregationist responses to the restaurant situation also slightly exceeded the 80 per cent line, but we deviated here, and included these anyway.

We were able to develop considerable confidence about our locating a response as either segregationist or desegregationist by using the extra material on the qualifications offered and the reasons given for the answers. These materials enabled us to minimize the number of responses that we might otherwise have had to classify as unclear.

III. SENTIMENT STRUCTURE. The codes for this dimension of attitudes were developed from the responses to question 1, "How would you feel."

The following codes were used:

1. Would dislike strongly, strongly opposed (anything which is a direct expression of a strong negative sentiment or from which this type of sentiment may unambiguously be inferred).

    e.g. "Wouldn't like it at all"
    "Quit"
    "Would not under any circumstances work for Negro."

232

2. Would dislike, opposed, feel funny, feel bad, doesn't approve, hope it doesn't happen, hate to see it (anything which is a direct expression of a moderately negative sentiment, or from which this type of sentiment may unambiguously be inferred).

> e.g. "Wouldn't like it"
> "Wouldn't feel good"
> "Opposed"
> "Not too good"
> "Wouldn't cause trouble, just leave"
> "Unhappy"
> "Would not approve"
> "Hope it doesn't happen"
> "Feel funny, no joke about it, not used to it."

3. Wouldn't mind too much, wouldn't mind, wouldn't be bothered (gruding acceptance leaning toward opposition).

> e.g. "Tolerate it, might not like it"
> "Have to be mighty good friend for me to stay"
> "Wouldn't get mad at either friend or Negro"
> "Wouldn't be bothered, but doesn't approve."

4. It's ok, would accept, would tolerate it (gruding acceptance, leaning toward acceptance).

> e.g. "Would have to be tolerated if Negro had ability"
> "Wouldn't leave"
> "When in Rome, do as the Romans do"
> "If fit man so that he got to that job, I guess I would take him"
> "ok if capable"

5. For (definite ungrudging affirmation).
6. Don't know.
7. Gives no sentiment, i.e., doesn't express whether he is for or against.

> e.g. "Most people would resent it a little"
> "Wouldn't happen"

8. No answer

Categories 1, 2, 6, 7, and 8 were considered segregationist, categories 3, 4, and 5 were classified as desegregationist. Again;

the don't knows, can't says, etc., were counted as segregationist responses.

Here, too, we probed the responses for patterns of qualifications attached to the answers, or amplifications of the responses which would be useful in making firmer decisions how to classify them. These qualifications were coded as follows:

1. Predicts trouble or bad outcome, or further implications in other areas which he rejects.

    "Really mess things up"
    "Cause cross-breeding"

2. Denies possibility

    "Bus companies wouldn't allow it"
    "Never happen here"

3. Predicts inevitability; or unavoidability; or expects it.

    "Nothing you could do if accepted company practice"
    "Hope it doesn't happen"

4. Rejects personal relevance

    "Children out of school"

5. Qualified level of Negro's performance, ability, character, attitude, behavior, status:

    "Depend on how much he knew"
    "If fit man so that he got to that job I guess I would take them"
    "Weigh the situation, see what kind of guy he was"
    "OK if capable"
    "If he was there and worked his way up—then his place to have job"
    "According to who he was and a whole lot of things"

6. Legalism (would have to obey law)
7. Qualifies time, place or situation (e.g., in 20 years, OK in college) depends on amount of personal acquaintance.
8. Qualified by opposite or opposing ideology.

    "I know different, but wouldn't feel good"

9. Qualified by appeal to community acceptance or rejection, or number of others who do it.
0. Immediate personal threat to status, property or person.

Appendices

X. Reference to female-male difference, e.g., OK for white male but not female.

Y. Reference to number of Negroes.

IV. GENERAL ACTION SET. The responses to question 2, "What would you do" were the material used to construct this dimension of attitudes. The code we developed utilized the following categories.

1. Take action to prevent the situation or get rid of Negro.
2. Take action by leaving situation, or refraining from participating in it.
3. Take action by objecting, protesting, etc.
4. Put up with situation at the moment, but avoid any future participation.
5. Tolerate the situation.
6. Would do nothing.
7. Would actively facilitate or cooperate.
8. Don't know, undecided, can't say.
9. Answer is evasive, or put in terms of the reactions of others.
0. No answer, response unclear.

Categories 1, 2, 3, 4, 8, 9, and 0 were classified as segregationist. Categories 3, 4, and 5 were defined as desegregationist responses. Once again we sought for qualifications and amplifications and coded them as follows:

1. If no agitation, coercion, or force.
2. In absence of separate facilities for Negroes.
3. Asserts unavoidability, inevitability, impotence in face of law or trends.
4. So long as present status relations are unaltered.
5. Qualified by some aspect of Negro character, ability, aptitude, performance, status, etc.
6. So long as situationally limited, i.e., with no further implications for any social relations than the ones under consideration, so long as temporary.
7. Defers by time, place.
8. Qualified by reference to occupational context, e.g., all right for doctors to do this.
9. Qualified by appeal to group consensus, or group customs, e.g., everyone does it.
0. If no threat to person, property, or position (job).
X. Limits it to contact of male and Negro, excluding White females.
Y. Qualified by reference to number of Negroes.

235

Appendices

V. SPECIFIC ACTION SET. This final set of questions was focussed on the issue of desegregation of the public schools. Although questions referring to the schools had been included in the three sets of questions dealing with situations of hypothetical contact, we felt much more could be learned about this most topical issue if we concentrated upon it specifically. Accordingly, each respondent was asked the following four questions:

1. Some people have suggested that the Supreme Court Decision ordering desegregation was wrong and that the States ought to be permitted to decide for themselves on this question. The proposal is to go through the process of getting an amendment to the United States Constitution to take power away from the Supreme Court.

   How do you feel about this kind of proposal to try to amend the U.S. Constitution?

   1. strongly approve
   2. approve
   3. undecided
   4. disapprove
   5. strongly disapprove

2. In Texas, the Governor has threatened to withhold State school funds from any school district which desegregates the schools, i.e., which permits Negro children to attend the same schools as White children. How do you feel about withholding State money from school districts here in North Carolina—if and when any of these districts start letting Negro children go to school together?

   1. strongly approve
   2. approve
   3. undecided
   4. disapprove
   5. strongly disapprove

3. Some people have suggested that if need be, the public schools ought to be closed altogether rather than have Negro and White children go to school together. How do you feel about this?

   1. strongly approve
   2. approve
   3. undecided
   4. disapprove
   5. strongly disapprove

236

4. Once in a while you hear it said, too, that if need be, people ought to get together and resist, with force if need be, any attempts to mix Negro and White children in the same schools. How do you feel about this?

    1. strongly approve
    2. approve
    3. undecided
    4. disapprove
    5. strongly disapprove

The first three responses (strong approval, approval, and undecided) were classified as segregationist, and disapproval and a strong disapproval were categorized as desegregationist.

We checked on each respondent by studying the responses he had previously given to the question of schools when this was considered as one of several possible situations of contact about which we had previously asked, "How would you feel," "What would you do?," and, "In general, how do you think these relations ought to be set up?"

This completes the details of the operations we performed to arrive at a tabulation of the number and per cent of respondents who gave either segregationist or desegregationist responses to the various questions. From these tabulations, we developed the scales and the scale scores which are reported and analyzed in the text.

One other set of scale scores, called "anomie," was developed as follows.

Every respondent was interviewed with the following items, reproduced verbatim from the schedule.

Now, Mr._____, there are just a few more statements I want to read to you and get your feelings about. These are statements you hear from time to time—expressing how people, how some people that is, feel about life in general these days. And I'd like to get your reactions to these.
The first is:

____1. There's little use in trying to influence public officials these days, because often they aren't interested in the problems of the average man. GET ANSWER FOR ALL KINDS OF OFFICIALS, LOCAL, ETC. (If man wants to distinguish between national and local level, write down his ideas.)

1. Agree
2. Undecided
3. Disagree

____2. Nowadays a person has to live pretty much for today and let tomorrow take care of itself.

1. Agree
2. Undecided
3. Disagree

____3. In spite of what some people say, the situation for the average man is getting better all the time.

1. Agree
2. Undecided
3. Disagree

____4. It's hardly fair to bring children into the world today, with the way things look for the future.

1. Agree
2. Undecided
3. Disagree

____5. These days a person really doesn't know whom he can count on.

1. Agree
2. Undecided
3. Disagree

It will be noticed that statement 3 differs from the other four statements, once agreement with the statement implies a sense of optimism. Agreement with the other four items, by contrast, implies a certain type of disaffection with the society and its norms. With proper adjustments for this difference, we classified any agreement or indecision as anomic or disaffected, and scored as positive or integrated only the disagreements.

We have least confidence in the scale which we developed out of the responses to these items, since the percentage distributions hardly satisfy the minimum requirements of scaling conventions. The principal failure lies in the closeness of the percentages on items 2, 3, and 4, respectively, 72.37 per cent, 76.57 per cent, and 75.87 per cent disaffected responses.

Because of the doubt one may properly entertain about this scale we make relatively little use of it in our analysis.

APPENDIX D

COMPARISON OF SCALE SCORES
OF EDUCATIONAL GROUPS WITH OTHER
FACTORS HELD CONSTANT

TABLE D-1
Mean Scores on Scale I and Scale V for Three Educational Groups
Holding Occupational Status Constant

	Blue-Collar (N = 117)			White-Collar (N = 167)		
	Grammar School (N = 73)	High School (N = 40)	College (N = 4)	Grammar School (N = 35)	High School (N = 63)	College (N = 69)
Scale I Image	2.84	2.85	3.25	2.91	2.73	2.48
Scale V School Desegre-gation	2.37	2.45	2.75	2.31	1.92	1.49

TABLE D-2
Mean Scores on Scale I and Scale V for Three Educational Groups
Holding Income Constant

	Under $5000 per year (N = 176)			Over $5000 per year (N = 97)		
	Grammar School (N = 90)	High School (N = 70)	College (N = 16)	Grammar School (N = 12)	High School (N = 31)	College (N = 54)
Scale I Image	2.81	2.81	2.56	3.25	2.64	2.50
Scale V School Desegre-gation	2.39	2.37	2.06	2.00	1.61	1.33

Appendices

TABLE D-3
Mean Scores on Scale I and Scale V for Three Educational Groups
Holding Residence Constant

	Urban (N = 183)			Rural (N = 104)		
	Grammar School (N = 64)	*High School* (N = 61)	*College* (N = 58)	*Grammar School* (N = 45)	*High School* (N = 42)	*College* (N = 17)
Scale I Image	2.86	2.84	2.53	2.89	2.69	2.59
Scale V School Desegregation	2.14	2.08	1.46	2.69	2.19	1.88

TABLE D-4

Means Scores on Scale I and Scale V for Three Educational Groups Holding Religiosity Constant

	Low Religiosity (N = 98)			Medium Religiosity (N = 67)			High Religiosity (N = 117)		
	Grammar School (N = 49)	High School (N = 31)	College (N = 18)	Grammar School (N = 23)	High School (N = 29)	College (N = 15)	Grammar School (N = 34)	High School (N = 43)	College (N = 40)
Scale I Image	2.96	2.68	3.00	2.48	3.31	2.80	3.00	2.49	2.20
Scale V School Desegregation	2.24	2.68	2.39	2.26	2.24	1.53	2.53	2.12	1.48

Appendices

TABLE D-5
Mean Scores on Scale I and Scale V for Three Educational Group Holding Mass Media Exposure Constant

	High Exposure (N = 151)			Low Exposure (N = 136)		
	Grammar School (N = 34)	High School (N = 61)	College (N = 56)	Grammar School (N = 75)	High School (N = 42)	College (N = 19)
Scale I						
Image	2.94	2.64	2.62	2.84	2.98	2.32
Scale V						
School						
Desegre-						
gation	2.24	1.80	1.46	2.43	2.60	1.84

TABLE D-6
Mean Scores on Scale I and Scale V for Three Educational Groups Holding Number of Children Constant

	No Children (N = 51)			1–3 Children (N = 196)			4 or More Children (N = 35)		
	Grammar School (N = 15)	*High School* (N = 25)	*College* (N = 11)	*Grammar School* (N = 64)	*High School* (N = 74)	*College* (N = 58)	*Grammar School* (N = 23)	*High School* (N = 9)	*College* (N = 3)
Scale I Image	3.07	2.80	2.64	2.94	2.82	2.48	2.52	2.22	2.67
Scale V School Desegregation	2.13	2.44	2.27	2.30	2.00	1.41	2.74	2.00	2.33

APPENDIX E

COMPARISON OF SCALE SCORES
OF MASS MEDIA EXPOSURE GROUPS WITH OTHER
FACTORS HELD CONSTANT

TABLE E-1
Mean Scores on Two Scales for Low and High Exposure Groups,
Holding Education Constant

	Grammar School		High School		College	
	Low Exposure (N = 75)	High Exposure (N = 34)	Low Exposure (N = 42)	High Exposure (N = 61)	Low Exposure (N = 19)	High Exposure (N = 56)
Scale I Image	2.84	2.94	2.98	2.64	2.32	2.62
Scale V School Desegre- gation	2.43	2.24	2.60	1.80	1.84	1.46

TABLE E-2
Mean Scores on Two Scales for Low and High Exposure Groups
Holding Number of Children Constant

	0 Children		1–3 Children		4 + Children	
	Low Exposure (N = 24)	High Exposure (N = 27)	Low Exposure (N = 93)	High Exposure (N = 106)	Low Exposure (N = 19)	High Exposure (N = 16)
Scale I Image	2.88	2.81	2.88	2.68	2.37	2.56
Scale V School Desegre- gation	2.29	2.33	2.10	1.52	2.53	2.50

Appendices

TABLE E-3
Mean Scores on Two Scales for Low and High Exposure Groups, Holding Religiosity Constant

| | Low Religiosity | | Medium Religiosity | | High Religiosity | |
	Low Exposure (N = 58)	High Exposure (N = 40)	Low Exposure (N = 27)	High Exposure (N = 40)	Low Exposure (N = 48)	High Exposure (N = 69)
Scale I Image	3.02	2.68	2.70	3.05	2.58	2.51
Scale V School Desegregation	2.46	1.55	2.52	1.80	2.17	1.91

TABLE E-4
Mean Scores on Two Scales for Low and High Exposure Groups Holding Residence Constant

| | Rural | | Urban | |
	Low Exposure (N = 60)	High Exposure (N = 76)	Low Exposure (N = 44)	High Exposure (N = 107)
Scale I Image	2.92	2.72	2.54	2.77
Scale V School Desegregation	2.65	2.20	1.95	1.70

TABLE E-5
Mean Scores on Two Scales for Low and High Exposure Groups, Holding Income Constant

| | Under $5000 | | Over $5000 | |
	Low Exposure (N = 96)	High Exposure (N = 80)	Low Exposure (N = 30)	High Exposure (N = 67)
Scale I Image	2.82	2.75	2.77	2.58
Scale V School Desegregation	2.47	2.21	2.10	1.24

245

Appendices

TABLE E-6
Mean Scores on Two Scales for Low and High Exposure Groups, Holding Status Constant

| | Low Status | | High Status | |
	Low Exposure (N = 75)	High Exposure (N = 42)	Low Exposure (N = 59)	High Exposure (N = 108)
Scale I				
Image	2.83	2.90	2.74	2.62
Scale V				
School Desegregation	2.55	2.17	2.17	1.64

APPENDIX F

COMPARISON OF SCALE SCORES
OF OCCUPATIONAL STATUS GROUPS WITH OTHER
FACTORS HELD CONSTANT

TABLE F-1

Mean Scores on Scales I and V for Two Occupational Status Groups
Holding Education Constant

| | Grammar School (N = 108) | | High School (N = 103) | | College (N = 73) | |
	Blue-Collar (N = 73)	White-Collar (N = 35)	Blue-Collar (N = 40)	White-Collar (N = 63)	Blue-Collar (N = 4)	White-Collar (N = 69)
Scale I Image	2.84	2.91	2.85	2.73	3.25	2.48
Scale V School Desegregation	2.37	2.31	2.45	1.92	2.75	1.49

TABLE F-2

Mean Scores on Scales I and V for Two Occupational Status Groups
Holding Number of Children Constant

| | 0 Children (N = 51) | | 1–3 Children (N = 196) | | 4+ Children (N = 34) | |
	Blue-Collar (N = 18)	White-Collar (N = 33)	Blue-Collar (N = 72)	White-Collar (N = 124)	Blue-Collar (N = 22)	White-Collar (N = 12)
Scale I Image	3.06	2.73	2.93	2.66	2.50	2.58
Scale V School Desegregation	2.39	2.27	2.33	1.68	2.77	2.17

Appendices

TABLE F-3
Mean Scores on Scales I and V for Two Occupational Status Groups
Holding Religiosity Constant

	Low (N = 98)		Medium (N = 67)		High (N = 117)	
	Blue-Collar (N = 46)	White-Collar (N = 52)	Blue-Collar (N = 30)	White-Collar (N = 37)	Blue-Collar (N = 41)	White-Collar (N = 76)
Scale I Image	2.89	2.86	2.67	3.11	2.95	2.32
Scale V School Desegregation	2.50	1.73	2.30	1.92	2.39	1.82

TABLE F-4
Mean Scores on Scales I and V for Two Occupational Status Groups
Holding Residence Constant

	Rural (N = 104)		Urban (N = 180)	
	Blue-Collar (N = 54)	White-Collar (N = 50)	Blue-Collar (N = 63)	White-Collar (N = 117)
Scale I Image	2.70	2.82	2.98	2.60
Scale V School Desegregation	2.48	2.22	2.33	1.66

TABLE F-5
Mean Scores on Scales I and V for Two Occupational Status Groups
Holding Income Constant

	Under $5,000 (N = 175)		Over $5,000 (N = 95)	
	Blue-Collar (N = 101)	White-Collar (N = 74)	Blue-Collar (N = 11)	White-Collar (N = 84)
Scale I Image	2.77	2.80	3.64	2.49
Scale V School Desegregation	2.42	2.23	2.09	1.43

Appendices

TABLE F-6
Mean Scores on Scales I and V for Two Occupational Status Groups Holding Mass Media Constant

	Low Exposure (N = 134)		High Exposure (N = 150)	
	Blue-Collar (N = 75)	White-Collar (N = 59)	Blue-Collar (N = 42)	White-Collar (N = 108)
Scale I				
Image	2.83	2.74	2.90	2.62
Scale V				
School Desegregation	2.55	2.17	2.17	1.64

APPENDIX G

COMPARISON OF SCALE SCORES OF MOBILITY GROUPS, WITH OTHER FACTORS HELD CONSTANT

TABLE G-1
Mean Scores on Scales I and V for Two Mobility Groups
Holding Education Constant

| | Grammar School (N = 102) | | High School (N = 100) | | College (N = 73) | |
	Mobile (N = 36)	Non-Mobile (N = 66)	Mobile (N = 40)	Non-Mobile (N = 60)	Mobile (N = 23)	Non-Mobile (N = 50)
Scale I Image	2.53	3.04	3.10	2.57	2.52	2.52
Scale V School Desegregation	2.22	2.45	2.28	1.98	1.70	1.50

TABLE G-2
Mean Scores on Scales I and V for Two Mobility Groups
Holding Mass Media Exposure Constant

| | Low Exposure (N = 130) | | High Exposure (N = 148) | |
	Mobile (N = 42)	Non-Mobile (N = 88)	Mobile (N = 58)	Non-Mobile (N = 90)
Scale I Image	2.62	2.88	2.86	2.62
Scale V School Desegregation	2.45	2.35	2.07	1.73

250

Appendices

TABLE G-3
Mean Scores on Scales I and V for Two Mobility Groups
Holding Residence Constant

	Rural (N = 99)		*Urban* (N = 179)	
	Mobile (N = 36)	*Non-Mobile* (N = 63)	*Mobile* (N = 64)	*Non-Mobile* (N = 115)
Scale I				
Image	2.92	2.71	2.67	2.61
Scale V				
School Desegregation	2.30	2.40	1.98	1.84

TABLE G-4
Mean Scores on Scales I and V for Two Mobility Groups
Holding Children Constant

	0 Children (N = 49)		*1–3 Children* (N = 194)		*4+ Children* (N = 33)	
	Mobile (N = 22)	*Non-Mobile* (N = 27)	*Mobile* (N = 67)	*Non-Mobile* (N = 127)	*Mobile* (N = 9)	*Non-Mobile* (N = 24)
Scale I						
Image	2.82	2.92	2.82	2.75	2.00	2.54
Scale V						
School Desegregation	2.54	2.11	1.96	1.90	2.11	2.71

TABLE G-5
Mean Scores on Scales I and V for Two Mobility Groups
Holding Age Constant

	Under 35 (N = 104)		*Over* 35 (N = 182)	
	Mobile (N = 35)	*Non-Mobile* (N = 69)	*Mobile* (N = 65)	*Non-Mobile* (N = 117)
Scale I				
Image	2.86	2.65	2.71	2.83
Scale V				
School Desegregation	2.63	1.93	1.82	2.14

APPENDIX H

COMPARISON OF SCALE SCORES OF AGE GROUPS WITH OTHER FACTORS HELD CONSTANT

TABLE H-1
Mean Scores on Scales I and V for Two Age Groups
Holding Education Constant

	Grammar School (N = 108)		High School (N = 103)		College (N = 73)	
	Under 35 (N = 27)	Over 35 (N = 81)	Under 35 (N = 48)	Over 35 (N = 55)	Under 35 (N = 23)	Over 35 (N = 50)
Scale I Image	2.67	2.92	2.85	2.71	2.39	2.58
Scale V School Desegregation	2.59	2.27	2.25	2.02	1.39	1.64

TABLE H-2
Mean Scores on Scales I and V for Two Age Groups
Holding Status Constant

	Blue-Collar (N = 117)		White-Collar (N = 167)	
	Under 35 (N = 39)	Over 35 (N = 78)	Under 35 (N = 59)	Over 35 (N = 108)
Scale I Image	2.77	2.90	2.64	2.68
Scale V School Desegregation	2.46	2.38	1.93	1.77

Appendices

TABLE H-3
Mean Scores on Scales I and V for Two Age Groups
Holding Mass Media Constant

	Low Exposure (N = 136)		High Exposure (N = 151)	
	Under 35 (N = 46)	Over 35 (N = 90)	Under 35 (N = 53)	Over 35 (N = 98)
Scale I				
Image	2.85	2.79	2.58	2.76
Scale V				
School Desegregation	2.56	2.79	1.81	1.76

TABLE H-4
Mean Scores on Scales I and V for Two Age Groups
Holding Income Constant

	Under $5,000 (N = 176)		Over $5,000 (N = 97)	
	Under 35 (N = 71)	Over 35 (N = 105)	Under 35 (N = 25)	Over 35 (N = 72)
Scale I				
Image	2.68	2.87	2.64	2.64
Scale V				
School Desegregation	2.39	2.32	1.36	1.56

TABLE H-5
Mean Scores on Scales I and V for Two Age Groups
Holding Religiosity Constant

	Low (N = 98)		Medium (N = 67)		High (N = 117)	
	Under 35 (N = 31)	Over 35 (N = 67)	Under 35 (N = 26)	Over 35 (N = 41)	Under 35 (N = 40)	Over 35 (N = 77)
Scale I						
Image	2.71	2.96	2.81	2.98	2.62	2.49
Scale V						
School Desegregation	1.97	2.15	2.15	2.05	2.22	1.91

Appendices

TABLE H-6
Mean Scores on Scales I and V for Two Age Groups
Holding Residence Constant

	Rural (N = 104)		Urban (N = 183)	
	Under 35 (N = 35)	Over 35 (N = 69)	Under 35 (N = 64)	Over 35 (N = 119)
Scale I				
Image	2.80	2.74	2.66	2.80
Scale V				
School Desegregation	2.28	2.39	2.09	1.81

TABLE H-7
Mean Scores on Scales I and V for Two Age Groups
Holding Number of Children Constant

	0 Children (N = 51)		1–3 Children (N = 199)		4+ Children (N = 35)	
	Under 35 (N = 22)	Over 35 (N = 29)	Under 35 (N = 76)	Over 35 (N = 123)	Under 35 (N = 6)	Over 35 (N = 29)
Scale I						
Image	2.82	2.86	2.60	2.88	3.17	2.31
Scale V						
School Desegregation	2.50	2.17	2.03	1.87	2.17	2.59

TABLE H-8
Mean Scores on Scales I and V for Two Age Groups
Holding Mobility Constant

	Mobile (N = 100)		Non-Mobile (N = 186)	
	Under 35 (N = 35)	Over 35 (N = 65)	Under 35 (N = 69)	Over 35 (N = 117)
Scale I				
Image	2.86	2.71	2.65	2.83
Scale V				
School Desegregation	2.63	1.82	1.93	2.14

APPENDIX I

COMPARISON OF SCALE SCORES OF
RELIGIOSITY GROUPS, WITH
OTHER FACTORS HELD CONSTANT

TABLE I-1
Mean Scores on Scales I and V for Three Religious Groups Holding Education Constant

| | Grammar School (N = 106) | | | High School (N = 103) | | | College (N = 91) | | |
	Low Rel. (N = 49)	Med. Rel. (N = 23)	High Rel. (N = 34)	Low Rel. (N = 31)	Med. Rel. (N = 29)	High Rel. (N = 43)	Low Rel. (N = 36)	Med. Rel. (N = 15)	High Rel. (N = 40)
Scale I Image	2.96	2.48	3.00	2.68	3.31	2.49	3.00	2.80	2.20
Scale V School Desegregation	2.24	2.26	2.53	2.68	2.24	2.12	2.39	1.53	1.48

Appendices

TABLE I-2
Mean Scores on Scales I and V for Three Religious Groups with Occupational Status Held Constant

	Blue-Collar (N = 117)			White-Collar (N = 165)		
	Low (N = 46)	Med. (N = 30)	High (N = 41)	Low (N = 52)	Med. (N = 37)	High (N = 76)
Scale I Image	2.89	2.67	2.95	2.86	3.11	2.32
Scale V School Desegregation	2.50	2.30	2.39	1.73	1.92	1.82

TABLE I-3
Mean Scores on Scales I and V for Three Religious Groups Holding Mass Media Constant

	Low Exposure (N = 133)			High Exposure (N = 149)		
	Low (N = 58)	Med. (N = 27)	High (N = 48)	Low (N = 40)	Med. (N = 40)	High (N = 69)
Scale I Image	3.02	2.70	2.58	2.68	3.05	2.51
Scale V School Desegregation	2.46	2.52	2.17	1.55	1.80	1.91

TABLE I-4
Mean Scores on Scales I and V for Three Religious Groups Holding Residence Constant

	Rural (N = 103)			Urban (N = 179)		
	Low (N = 29)	Med. (N = 25)	High (N = 49)	Low (N = 69)	Med. (N = 42)	High (N = 68)
Scale I Image	2.83	2.60	2.82	2.90	3.10	2.34
Scale V School Desegregation	2.28	2.32	2.39	2.01	1.95	1.75

TABLE I-5

Mean Scores on Scales I and V for Three Religious Groups with Number of Children Held Constant

	0 Children (N = 50)			1–3 Children (N = 196)			4+ Children (N = 34)		
	Low (N = 17)	*Med.* (N = 13)	*High* (N = 20)	*Low* (N = 65)	*Med.* (N = 47)	*High* (N = 84)	*Low* (N = 15)	*Med.* (N = 7)	*High* (N = 12)
Scale I Image	2.88	3.62	2.35	2.97	2.72	2.62	2.47	2.86	2.17
Scale V School Desegregation	2.12	2.31	2.40	2.00	1.89	1.88	2.60	3.00	2.17

Appendices

TABLE I-6
Mean Scores on Scales I and V for Three Religious Groups
Holding Age Constant

	Under 35 (N = 97)			Over 35 (N = 185)		
	Low (N = 31)	Med. (N = 26)	High (N = 40)	Low (N = 67)	Med. (N = 41)	High (N = 77)
Scale I Image	2.71	2.81	2.62	2.96	2.98	2.49
Scale V School Desegregation	1.97	2.15	2.22	2.15	2.05	1.91

259

APPENDIX J

COMPARISON OF SCALE SCORES OF
"CHILDREN" GROUPS, WITH
OTHER FACTORS HELD CONSTANT

TABLE J-1
Mean Scores on Scales I and V for Three "Children" Groups Holding Education Constant

	Grammar School (N = 102)			High School (N = 108)			College (N = 72)		
	0 (N = 15)	1–3 (N = 64)	4+ (N = 23)	0 (N = 25)	1–3 (N = 74)	4+ (N = 9)	0 (N = 11)	1–3 (N = 58)	4+ (N = 3)
Scale I Image	3.07	2.94	2.52	2.80	2.82	2.22	2.64	2.48	2.67
Scale V School Desegregation	2.13	2.30	2.74	2.44	2.00	2.00	2.27	1.41	2.33

Appendices

Mean Scores on Scales I and V for Three "Children" Groups
Holding Status Constant

| | Blue-Collar (N = 112) Number of Children | | | White-Collar (N = 169) Number of Children | | |
	0 (N = 18)	1–3 (N = 72)	4+ (N = 22)	0 (N = 33)	1–3 (N = 124)	4+ (N = 12)
Scale I Image	3.06	2.93	2.50	2.73	2.66	2.58
Scale V School Desegre- gation	2.39	2.33	2.77	2.27	1.68	2.17

TABLE J-3
Mean Scores on Scales I and V for Three "Children" Groups
Holding Mass Media Constant

| | Low Exposure (N = 136) Number of Children | | | High Exposure (N = 149) Number of Children | | |
	0	1–3	4+	0	1–3	4+
Scale I Image	2.88	2.88	2.37	2.81	2.68	2.56
Scale V School Desegregation	2.29	2.10	2.53	2.33	1.52	2.50

Appendices

TABLE J-4
Mean Scores on Scales I and V for Three "Children" Groups
Holding Residence Constant

	Rural (N = 103) Number of Children			Urban (N = 182) Number of Children		
	0 (N = 15)	1–3 (N = 73)	4+ (N = 15)	0 (N = 36)	1–3 (N = 126)	4+ (N = 20)
Scale I Image	2.87	2.71	2.80	2.83	2.81	2.20
Scale V School Desegre-gation	2.53	2.18	2.93	2.22	1.78	2.20

TABLE J-5

Mean Scores on Scales I and V for Three "Children" Groups Holding Religiosity Constant

	Low (N = 97) Number of Children			*Medium* (N = 67) Number of Children			*High* (N = 116) Number of Children		
	0 (N = 17)	1–3 (N = 65)	4+ (N = 15)	0 (N = 13)	1–3 (N = 47)	4+ (N = 7)	0 (N = 20)	1–3 (N = 84)	4+ (N = 12)
Scale I Image	2.88	2.97	2.47	3.62	2.72	2.86	2.35	2.62	2.17
Scale V School Desegregation	2.12	2.00	2.60	2.31	1.89	3.00	2.40	1.88	2.17

Appendices

TABLE J-6
Mean Scores on Scales I and V for Three "Children" Groups
Holding Mobility Constant

	Mobile (N = 98) Number of Children			Non-Mobile (N = 178) Number of Children		
	0 (N = 22)	1–3 (N = 67)	4+ (N = 9)	0 (N = 27)	1–3 (N = 127)	4+ (N = 24)
Scale I Image	2.82	2.82	2.00	2.92	2.75	2.54
Scale V School Desegregation	2.54	1.96	2.11	2.11	1.90	2.71

TABLE J-7
Mean Scores on Scales I and V for Three "Children" Groups
Holding Age Constant

	Under 35 (N = 104) Number of Children			Over 35 (N = 181) Number of Children		
	0 (N = 22)	1–3 (N = 76)	4+ (N = 6)	0 (N = 29)	1–3 (N = 123)	4+ (N = 29)
Scale I Image	2.82	2.60	3.17	2.86	2.88	2.31
Scale V School Desegregation	2.50	2.03	2.17	2.17	1.87	2.59

APPENDIX K

COMPARISON OF SCALE SCORES OF RESIDENCE GROUPS, WITH OTHER FACTORS HELD CONSTANT

TABLE K-1
Mean Scores on Scales I and V for Two Residence Groups
Holding Age Constant

| | Under 35 (N = 99) | | Over 35 (N = 188) | |
	Rural (N = 35)	Urban (N = 64)	Rural (N = 69)	Urban (N = 119)
Scale I				
Image	2.80	2.66	2.74	2.80
Scale V				
School Desegregation	2.28	2.09	2.39	1.81

TABLE K-2
Mean Scores on Scales I and V for Two Residence Groups
Holding Education Constant

| | Grammar School (N = 109) | | High School (N = 103) | | College (N = 75) | |
	Urban (N = 64)	Rural (N = 45)	Urban (N = 61)	Rural (N = 42)	Urban (N = 58)	Rural (N = 17)
Scale I						
Image	2.86	2.89	2.84	2.69	2.53	2.59
Scale V						
School Desegre- gation	2.14	2.69	2.08	2.19	1.46	1.88

Appendices

TABLE K-3
Mean Scores on Scales I and V for Two Residence Groups
Holding Status Constant

| | Blue-Collar (N = 117) | | White-Collar (N = 167) | |
	Rural (N = 54)	Urban (N = 63)	Rural (N = 50)	Urban (N = 117)
Scale I				
Image	2.70	2.98	2.82	2.60
Scale V				
School Desegregation	2.48	2.33	2.22	1.66

TABLE K-4
Mean Scores on Scales I and V for Two Residence Groups
Holding Mass Media Constant

| | Low Exposure (N = 104) | | High Exposure (N = 183) | |
	Rural (N = 60)	Urban (N = 44)	Rural (N = 76)	Urban (N = 107)
Scale I				
Image	2.92	2.54	2.72	2.77
Scale V				
School Desegregation	2.65	1.95	2.20	1.70

TABLE K-5
Mean Scores on Scales I and V for Two Residence Groups
Holding Religiosity Constant

| | Low (N = 98) | | Medium (N = 67) | | High (N = 117) | |
	Rural (N = 29)	Urban (N = 69)	Rural (N = 25)	Urban (N = 42)	Rural (N = 49)	Urban (N = 68)
Scale I						
Image	2.83	2.90	2.60	3.10	2.82	2.34
Scale V						
School Desegre- gation	2.28	2.01	2.32	1.95	2.39	1.75

Appendices

TABLE K-6
Mean Scores on Scales I and V for Two Residence Groups Holding
Number of Children Constant

	0 *Children* (N = 51)		1–3 *Children* (N = 199)		4 + *Children* (N = 35)	
	Rural (N = 15)	*Urban* (N = 36)	*Rural* (N = 73)	*Urban* (N = 126)	*Rural* (N = 15)	*Urban* (N = 20)
Scale I Image	2.87	2.83	2.71	2.81	2.80	2.20
Scale V School Desegre-gation	2.53	2.22	2.18	1.78	2.93	2.20

TABLE K-7
Mean Scores on Scales I and V for Two Residence Groups
Holding Mobility Constant

	Mobile (N = 100)		*Non-Mobile* (N = 178)	
	Rural (N = 36)	*Urban* (N = 64)	*Rural* (N = 63)	*Urban* (N = 115)
Scale I Image	2.92	2.67	2.71	2.61
Scale V School Desegregation	2.30	1.98	2.40	1.84

APPENDIX L

COMPARISON OF SCALE SCORES OF INCOME GROUPS WITH OTHER FACTORS HELD CONSTANT[1]

TABLE L-1

Mean Scores on Scales I and V for Two Income Groups
Holding Education Constant

	Grammar School (N = 102)		High School (N = 101)		College (N = 70)	
	Under $5,000 (N = 90)	Over $5,000 (N = 12)	Under $5,000 (N = 70)	Over $5,000 (N = 31)	Under $5,000 (N = 16)	Over $5,000 (N = 54)
Scale I Image	2.81	3.25	2.81	2.64	2.56	2.50
Scale V School Desegregation	2.39	2.00	2.37	1.61	2.06	1.33

TABLE L-2

Mean Scores on Scales I and V for Two Income Groups
Holding Status Constant

	High Status (N = 158)		Low Status (N = 112)	
	Under $5,000 (N = 74)	Over $5,000 (N = 84)	Under $5,000 (N = 101)	Over $5,000 (N = 11)
Scale I Image	2.80	2.49	2.77	3.64
Scale V School Desegregation	2.23	1.43	2.42	2.09

[1] Because of certain discrepancies in tallies on the group which earns over $5000 a year, four of cross-tabulations originally scheduled to appear in this appendix have been omitted.

Appendices

TABLE L-3
Mean Scores on Scales I and V for Two Income Groups
Holding Mass Media Constant

	Low Exposure (N = 126)		*High Exposure* (N = 147)	
	Under $5,000 (N = 96)	*Over* $5,000 (N = 30)	*Under* $5,000 (N = 80)	*Over* $5,000 (N = 67)
Scale I				
Image	2.82	2.77	2.75	2.58
Scale				
School Desegregation	2.47	2.10	2.21	1.24

TABLE L-4
Mean Scores on Scales I and V for Two Income Groups
Holding Age Constant

	Under 35 (N = 96)		*Over* 35 (N = 177)	
	Under $5,000 (N = 71)	*Over* $5,000 (N = 25)	*Under* $5,000 (N = 105)	*Over* $5,000 (N = 72)
Scale I				
Image	2.68	2.64	2.87	2.64
Scale V				
School Desegregation	2.39	1.36	2.32	1.56

Date Due